DISSERTATIONS
IN AMERICAN LITERATURE
1891-1966

JAMES WOODRESS

DISSERTATIONS
IN AMERICAN LITERATURE
1891-1966

newly revised and enlarged
with the assistance of
Marian Koritz

Duke University Press

Durham, N. C.

1968

FOR ROBERTA

FOREWORD

Since the first edition of this compilation appeared in 1957, the number of dissertations in American literature has almost doubled. The original work listed some 2,500 titles; the present volume lists close to 4700. The original list spanned the years from 1891, when the first dissertation was produced at Cornell, to 1955. The second edition added the years from 1956 through 1961 and contained more than 800 additional titles. The third edition brings the compilation down through 1966 and includes another 1,300 dissertations.

A rough calculation suggests that the rate of scholarly production continues to increase. The first 65 years of the study of American literature at the doctoral level produced 2,500 titles, but only 402 dissertations were written during the first 43 years. From 1933 to 1948 another 1,142 titles were added, and between 1948 and 1956 an additional 936. Between 1956 and 1961 the interest in American literature remained steady, increasing slightly to an annual rate of about 135 dissertations per year, but since 1961 graduate schools throughout the world have been granting the doctorate to students of American literature at the rate of about 260 per year, or double the rate in the fifties.

One will note in using this compilation that the interest in American literature in Germany, which began early and always has been strong, continues at an accelerated pace. French interest, while never so strong as the German, also continues and increases slightly. The most significant growth in interest is recorded in the rather sizable number of Ph.D.'s granted by British universities. This development has taken place almost entirely within the past decade. Of equal interest perhaps, though statistically insignificant, is the fact that this volume lists for the first time dissertations undertaken in India and New Zealand.

The third edition, as were the first two issues, is the work of many hands. The first edition built on the earlier compilations made by Ernest Leisy, Jay B. Hubbell, and Lewis Leary, which were published in *American Literature* in 1933 and 1948, plus such printed sources as were then available. These included the annual compilations of the Library of Congress and the Wilson Company, Richard Mummendey's *Die Sprache und Literatur des Angelsachsen im Spiegel der Deutschen Universitätsschriften, 1885-1950* (Bonn, 1954), and the quarterly "Research in Progress" published in *American Literature. Dissertation Abstracts,* which has become increasingly inclusive and useful and now includes more than 140 institutions, appeared in time to be used in compiling the second edition of this book. The present edition uses all these sources plus others: The annual bibliographical issue of *The American Quarterly, Index to Theses Accepted for Higher Degrees in the Universities of Great Britain and Ireland, Jahrbuch für Amerikastudien, Mitteilungsblatt der Deutschen Gesellschaft für Amerikastudien, Eine Bibliographie der Aufnahme Amerikanischer Literatur in Deutschen Zeitschriften, 1945-1960,* Gerhard H. W. Zuther, ed. (Munich, 1965), and the bulletin of the Harvard University Graduate School of Arts and Sciences.

I am indebted to many individuals who answered queries and contributed lists during the process of getting this volume ready for the press. Specifically I wish to thank Roger Asselineau of the University of Paris, Olov Fryckstedt of the University of Uppsala, and Klaus Lubbers of the University of Mainz. For help in preparing and typing copy and proofreading the manuscript I am grateful to Nancy Anderson, Ginny Johnson, and Roberta Woodress. For monumental assistance in collecting data, checking sources, and preparing the index I am indebted to Marian Koritz, whose labors I have acknowledged on the title page.

JAMES WOODRESS

University of California at Davis
June, 1967

TABLE OF CONTENTS

NOTES ON FORM, SYMBOLS, ABBREVIATIONS, AND PRINCIPLES OF ORGANIZATION AND SELECTION

The titles in this compilation have been arranged alphabetically by subject, first by individual authors, then by general topics. Within each subject classification the dissertations are alphabetized by writer. The titles have been shortened wherever possible by using a symbol for the subject author, as "HA" for Henry Adams. The name of the degree-granting institution has been abbreviated as much as seemed practical: "Columbia" for Columbia University, "NYU" for New York University, "Boston" for Boston University, "Geo Wash" for George Washington University, etc. State Universities are indicated by standard state abbreviations: "Pa" for Pennsylvania, "Mich" for Michigan, etc. Washington University at St. Louis is "Wash (St. Louis)"; the University of Southern California is "So Cal," and when there is more than one institution with the same name it is represented thus: "Loyola (Chicago)." The various branches of the University of California are represented as follows: "UCB" for Berkeley, "UCSB" for Santa Barbara, "UCD" for Davis, etc. Various branches of the State University of New York have been indicated thus: "SUNY (Buffalo)." To identify the two universities in Berlin the symbol (H) or (F) has been placed after titles begun or completed after 1945 to indicate Humboldt Universität or Freie Universität. Finally, "Ohio" is Ohio University at Athens, which should not be confused with "Ohio State" at Columbus.

The two digits which follow the name of the institution indicate the year in which the dissertation was completed, and if there is no date given, the omission means that the dissertation was still in progress at the time this list went to press. Sometimes the completion dates for foreign dissertations are only approximate, and in some instances dissertations listed as in progress may have been dropped. This edition relists titles reported as in progress in the second edition unless they are known to have been dropped. On occasion, when the information was readily available, the abbreviation "publ" follows the date of a foreign title to indicate that the work has been published. If a dissertation was *not* written in a department of English, the following symbols have been used to record the various disciplines involved:

A	American Civilization or Studies	LS	Library Science
		M	Medicine
CL	Comparative Literature	Mu	Music
D	Drama	P	Philosophy
Econ	Economics	R	Religion
FA	Fine Arts	RL	Romance Languages
H	History	S	Speech
J	Journalism	Soc	Sociology
L	Linguistics	T	Theater

The classification of items under the general-topic headings often proved difficult, and to compensate for occasional arbitrary decisions frequent cross-references have been used. Cross-references also have been used freely to draw attention to topics that cut across two or more subjects. Items under

General Topics are classified in the smallest or most specific unit possible. For example, items dealing with Indians or the Negro have been put in categories with those subject headings rather than under "Literary History" or perhaps in the several fictional categories where they also could have been placed. One sometimes needs to look in more than one section, however, despite the frequent use of cross-references. In general the principle has been followed to put the title in the place one might first look for it, but this principle is sometimes hard to apply.

This edition of the dissertation list also breaks up large categories such as "Fiction," "Novel," "Poetry," "Foreign Relations," etc. into many more subdivisions than were used before. For example, there are now nine subdivisions for "Drama," though the drama section does not try to list all possible theater topics and omits dissertations dealing with technical theater or acting. Writers who are tangential to the study of American literature are not covered exhaustively. Dissertations on figures like Jefferson, Lincoln, Santayana, etc. are included only if the title seemed to have some interest for students of literature.

It should be noted that the number of dissertations listed in this compilation slightly exceeds the number assigned to the last title in this book. Dissertations reported after the numbers had been assigned in the manuscript have been inserted with A-numbers. It also should be pointed out that in a few cases numbers have been deleted to avoid duplicate entries resulting from changes made in dissertation titles between the time they were reported in progress and completed.

DISSERTATIONS
IN AMERICAN LITERATURE
1891-1966

INDIVIDUAL AUTHORS

ADAMIC, LOUIS

1 Christian, Henry A. One Immigrant's America: A Study of the Work and Life of LA. Rutgers.

ADAMS, C. F.

2 Auten, Arthur H. CFA., Jr., Historian: An Appraisal. Western Reserve H 65.

ADAMS, HENRY

3 Altenbernd, A. Lynn. The Influence of European Travel on the Political and Social Outlook of HA, William Dean Howells, and Mark Twain. Ohio State 54.
4 Baym, Max I. The French Education of HA. Columbia H 51.
5 Brunner, John C. HA: His Decline and Fall. UCLA 56.
6 Bunker, Robert M. The Idea of Failure in HA, Charles Sanders Peirce, and Mark Twain. NM A 55.
7 Cater, Harold D. HA and His Friends: A Collection of His Unpublished Letters. Columbia H 47.
8 Chalfant, Edward. HA and History. Pa 54.
9 Crumley, Moreene. The Reputation of HA. Chicago 54.
10 Donovan, Timothy P. HA and Brooks Adams: The Search for a Law. Okla H 60.
11 Harbert, Earl. The Influence of Family Tradition upon Selected Works of HA. Wis 65.
12 Healy, Sister Mary Aquinas. A Study of Non-Rational Elements in the Works of HA as Centralized in His Attitude toward Women. Wis 56.
13 Hochfield, George. The Mind of HA. UCB 57.
14 Hume, Robert A. *The Education of HA:* A Critical Estimate. Cornell 40.
15 Hunner, Wesley L. Art and Esthetics in the Life of HA. Wash 51.
16 Jordy, William H. HA: Science and Power in History: A Study in the Historical Temperament. Yale A 48.
17 Joyce, James L. HA: Etude sur la formation de ses idées et de son oeuvre (1858-1890). Paris 51.
18 Kauffman, Herbert L. Form and Meaning in HA's *History.* Stanford 60.
19 Levenson, Jacob C. HA: The Historian as Artist. Harvard A51.
20 Lyon, Melvin E. Symbol and Idea in the Major Works of HA. Wis 60.
21 Meyer, Andrew G. HA, Historian. NYU H 48.
22 Miller, Richard F. HA as a Reformer, with an HA Bibliography. Wash 47.
23 Page, Evelyn. HA, Aristarch. Pa H 52.
24 Preuschen, Karl A. Das Problem der "Unity" und "Multiplicity" in seiner literarischen Gestaltung bei HA. Frankfort 54 publ.
25 Rule, Henry B. Irony in the Works of HA. Colo 60.
26 Samuels, Ernest. The Early Career of HA. Chicago 42.
27 Sandelin, Clarence K. The Educational Philosophy of HA: A Brahmin Contribution to Critical Realism. Wis 56.
28 Vandersee, Charles A. The Political Attitudes of HA. UCLA 64.
29 Vitzthum, Richard C. The Art of Paraphrasing: A Study of HA's Use of the Paraphrastic Technique in the *History of the United States of America.* Stanford 63.
30 Wasser, Henry. HA, Lay Philosopher of Science. Columbia 51.
See also 367, 392, 1755, 4167a.

ADAMS, JOHN

31 Little, John E. JA and American Foreign Affairs, 1755-1780. Princeton H 66.

ADAMS, J. Q.

32 Banninga, Jerald L.   JQA: A Critic in the Golden Age of American Oratory. Ind S 63.

33 Goodfellow, Donald.   The Literary Life of JQA.   Harvard 45.

34 Morris, Walter J.   JQA: Germanophile.   Pa State 63.

ADAMS, SAMUEL

35 Somerville, James K.   Patriot Moralist: An Intellectual Portrait of SA.   Western Reserve H 65.

36 Townsend, Charles B.   The Thoughts of SA.   Wis.

ADE, GEORGE

37 Coyle, Leo P.   GA: Playwright.   Western Reserve 59.

38 Nordhus, Philip B.   GA: A Critical Study.   Iowa 57.

AGEE, JAMES

39 Behar, Jack.   JA: The World of His Work.   Ohio State 63.

40 Ohlin, Peter.   JA: A Critical Study.   NM 64.

AIKEN, CONRAD

41 Chapin, Henry B.   The Poetry of CA.   NM 65.

42 Francisco, Richard L.   The Conative Search: The Critical Writings of CA, 1910-1952. Yale 61.

43 Martin, Jay H.   CA: A Life of His Art.   Ohio State 60.

44 Robillard, Douglas J.   The Poetry of CA: A Critical Study.   Wayne 65.

45 Rountree, Mary M.   The Fiction of CA.   Pittsburgh 65.
See also 2331a.

ALBEE, EDWARD

46 Rule, Margaret.   EA in Germany.   Ark.
See also 2046.

ALCOTT, A. B.

47 Haefner, George E.   A Critical Estimate of the Educational Theories and Practices of ABA.   Columbia E 37.

48 Herrnstadt, Richard L.   The Letters of ABA.   Md 60.

49 McCuskey, Dorothy A.   ABA, Educator.   Yale E 36.

50 Nowicki, Lawrence P.   ABA and Fruitlands: A Study in Transcendental Idealism.   NYU.

ALDRICH, T. B.

51 Koch, Warren J.   TBA: Anticipator of New Trends in American Literature.   St. John's (Brooklyn) 55.

52 Mangam, Charles.   A Critical Biography of TBA.   Cornell 50.

53 Tuttle, Donald R.   TBA's Editorship of the *Atlantic Monthly.*   Western Reserve 39.
See also 4019.

ALGREN, NELSON

54 Laukaitis, William E.   NA: The Literary Achievement.   Md.

55 Veler, Richard P.   *The Man with the Golden Arm:* A Genetic Study.   Ohio State 64.

ALLEN, HERVEY

56 Culver, Montgomery M., Jr.   HA, Historical Novelist.   Ill 59.

ALLSTON, WASHINGTON

57 Bartlett, Mabel R.   WA as Critic.   Boston FA 60.

58 Goethals, Martha G.   A Comparative Study of the Theory and Work of WA, Thomas
    Cole, and Horatio Greenough.   Harvard R 66.
59 Winston, George P.   WA as a Man of Letters.   Syracuse 55.

AMES, FISHER

60 Bernhard, Winfred E.   FA, Spokesman of Federalism.   Columbia H 61.
    See also 413.

ANDERSON, MAXWELL

61 Bailey, Mabel D.   MA: The Playwright as Prophet.   Iowa 55.
62 Blanchard, Fred C.   The Place of MA in the American Theater.   NYU S 39.
63 Buchanan, Randall J.   MA's Dramatic Theories and Rules of Playwriting and Their
    Application to His Plays.   La 64.
64 Cox, Martha H.   MA and His Critics.   Ark 55.
65 Foote, Ronald C.   The Verse Dramas of MA in the Modern Theatre.   Tulane 56.
66 Lauterbach, Charles.   Imagery in the Plays of MA.   Mich State.
67 Lee, Henry G.   The Use of History in the Historical Plays of MA.   Tulane.
68 Mitchell, Albert O.   A Study of Irony in the Plays of MA.   Wis 39.
69 Weimann, Richard J.   The "Core of Belief" of MA and the Structure of His
    Tragedies.   Ind 65.

ANDERSON, SHERWOOD

70 Anderson, David D.   SA and the Meaning of the American Experience.   Mich
    State 60.
71 Carlson, G. Bert, Jr.   The Political Thought and Activities of SA.   Md.
72 Christ, Robert L.   SA's *Dark Laughter:*   Sources, Composition, Reputation.
    Chicago 65.
73 Cole, Janice E.   *Many Marriages:*   SA's Controversial Novel.   Mich 65.
74 Ferres, John H.   The Right Place and the Right People: SA's Search for
    Salvation.   La 59.
75 Hilton, Earl R.   The Purpose and Method of SA.   Minn 50.
76 Love, Glen A.   SA's American Pastoral.   Wash 64.
77 Phillips, William L.   SA's *Winesburg, Ohio:*   Its Origins, Composition, Technique,
    and Reception.   Chicago 50.
78 Sutton, William A.   SA's Formative Years (1876-1913).   Ohio State 43.
79 Taylor, Welford D.   SA's "Buck Fever":   A Critical Edition.   Md.
80 Thurston, Jarvis A.   SA: A Critical Study.   Iowa 46.
81 White, Ray L.   SA: Virginia Newspaper Editor.   Ark.
    See also 1718, 3360, 4388, 4628.

ARTHUR, T. S.

82 French, Warren G.   TSA Views His Times.   Tex H 54.
83 Koch, Donald A.   The Life and Times of TSA.   Western Reserve 54.

ATKINSON, BROOKS

84 McNeely, Jerry C.   The Criticism and Reviewing of BA.   Wis S 56.

AUSTIN, M. H.

85 McClanahan, Muriel H.   Aspects of Southwestern Regionalism in the Prose Works of
    MHA.   Pittsburgh 40.
86 Wynn, Dudley T.   A Critical Study of the Writings of MHA, 1868-1934.   NYU 40.

BABBITT, IRVING

87 Bode, Adolf.   Die amerikanische Zivilisation im Urteil von IBs Humanismus.
    Berlin 42.

88 Hansen, Erik A. IB and His View of Tradition. Yale.
89 McKean, Keith. Ethical Judgments in the Criticism of IB, Paul Elmer More, and Yvor Winters. Mich 50.
90 Ruland, Richard E. A Usable American Past in the Criticism of IB, More, Sherman, and Mencken. Mich 60.
91 Schorsch, Robert S. IB and Rousseauism. Notre Dame P 40.
92 Warren, Howard B. IB and Paul Elmer More: A Comparison. Drew R 40.
    See also 2897.

BACHELLER, IRVING

93 Samuels, Charles E. IB: A Critical Biography. Syracuse 53.

BAGBY, G. W.

94 King, J. L. Dr. GWB: A Study in Virginian Literature, 1850-1880. Columbia 27.

BAKER, G. P.

95 Hinkel, Cecil E. An Analysis and Evaluation of the 47 Workshop of GPB. (Volumes I and II). Ohio State 60.
96 Kinne, Wisner P. GPB: Scholar, Teacher, Dramatist. Harvard 52.

BAKER, R. S.

97 Bannister, Robert C. The Mind and Thought of RSB: 1890-1919. Yale.
98 Levy, David W. The Life of RSB. Wis.
99 Semonche, John E. Progressive Journalist: RSB, 1870-1914. Northwestern H 62.

BALDWIN, JAMES
See 3414.

BALDWIN, J. G.

100 Stewart, S. Boyd. JGB. Vanderbilt 41.
     See also 1743.

BALLOU, ADIN

101 Padelford, Philip S. AB and the Hopedale Community. Yale H 42.

BANCROFT, GEORGE

102 Duley, Eleanor I. GB, Diplomat. Radcliffe H 39.
103 Levin, David. Literary and Moral Attitudes in GB, Prescott, Motley, and Parkman. Harvard A 55.
104 Nye, Russel B. The Mind and Art of GB. Wis 40.
105 Oard, Ronald J. GB and Hildreth: A Critical Evaluation. St. Louis H 61.

BARKER, J. N.

106 Musser, Paul H. JNB (1784-1858), with a Reprint of His Comedy *Tears and Smiles.* Pa 28.

BARLOW, JOEL

107 Cantor, Milton. The Life of JB. Columbia H 54.
108 Dietrich, Rosalia K. American Literature in Poland: A Preliminary Check List, 1790-1940, with a Critical Introduction Concerning the Reputation of JB, Franklin, and Irving. Columbia 65.
109 Zinser, Hans. Studien zu JBs *Columbiad.* Giessen 44.
110 Zunder, Theodore A. JB: His Life and Works up to 1790. Yale 27.
     See also 990.

BARRY, PHILIP

111 Boston, Leslie P. An Analytical Study of Structure, Characterization, and Language in Selected Comedies of PB. So Cal S 66.
112 Hamm, Gerald C. The Dramas of PB. Pa A 46.
113 Johnson, Robert E. The Comic Universe of PB in Relation to the Construction of His Plays. Ind.
114 Mays, David D. The Theme of Responsibility in the Plays of PB. Tulane S 63.
115 Osborne, C. Eugene. A Critical Analysis of the Plays of PB. Denver 54.

BARTRAM, JOHN

116 Earnest, Ernest P. The Two Bartrams: A Chapter in the Cultural History of America. Princeton 36.

BARTRAM, WILLIAM

117 Fagin, N. Bryllion. WB: Interpreter of the American Landscape. Johns Hopkins 31.
See also 116.

BEECHER, LYMAN

118 Wood, Raymond L. LB, 1775-1863: A Biographical Study. Yale R 61.

BEHRMAN, S. N.

119 Heniford, Lewis W. SNB as a Social Dramatist. Stanford S 64.
120 Levin, Milton I. SNB: The Operation and Dilemmas of the Comic Spirit. Mich 58.

BELASCO, DAVID

121 Batcheller, Joseph D. DB. Minn S 42.
122 Forde, Gladys I. DB: An Evaluation of the Man and His Contributions to American Theatrical History. Western Reserve S 55.
123 Kleinfield, H. L. The Theatrical Career of DB. Harvard A 56.
124 Modisett, Noah F. A Historical Study of the Stage Directing Theory and Practice of DB. So Cal D 63.

BELLAMY, EDWARD

125 Bowman, Sylvia E. Le Développement des idées d'EB. Paris 52.
126 MacNair, Everett H. Soft Spoken Prophet: EB and the Nationalist Movement. Columbia P 53.
127 Schiffman, Joseph. EB: Literary Aspects of an Original Mind. NYU A 51.

BELLOW, SAUL

128 Dutton, Robert R. The Subangelic Vision of SB: A Study of His First Six Novels, 1944-1964. Univ. of Pacific 66.
129 Markos, Donald. The Humanism of SB. Ill.
130 Opdahl, Keith M. "The Crab and the Butterfly": The Themes of SB. Ill 61.
See also 2566, 3414, 4285.

BENCHLEY, ROBERT

131 Redding, R. W. RB and the Drama. NM.

BENET, S. V.

132 Donner-Esch, Jane. Amerika im Spiegel von SVBs John Brown's Body. Berlin 40 publ.
133 Lewis, Mary D. SVB: His Major Work, His Preparation for It, and a Bibliography of His Writings. Ill 53.

134 Maddocks, Gladys L. SVB: A Modern Interpreter of American Tradition. Tex 49.
135 Richardson, Robert D., Jr. Epic on an American Theme: A Study of *John Brown's Body*. Harvard 61.

BEVERIDGE, A. J.

136 Ross, Herold T. The Oratorical Career of AJB. Iowa S 32.

BIERCE, AMBROSE

137 Behrens, Robert H. AB (1842-1914). Tübingen 51.
138 Berkove, Lawrence I. AB's Concern with Mind and Man. Pa 62.
139 Flinn, Eugene C. AB and the Journalization of the American Short Story.
     St. John's (Brooklyn) 54.
140 Grenander, Mary E. The Critical Theories of AB. Chicago 49.
141 Sheller, H. Lynn. The Satire of AB, Its Objects, Forms, Devices, and Origins.
     So Cal 45.
142 Woodruff, Stuart C. The Short Stories of AB: A Critical Study. Conn 62.

BIRD, R. M.

143 Foust, Clement E. The Life and Dramatic Works of RMB. Pa 17.

BISHOP, J. P.

144 Bier, Jesse. A Critical Biography of JPB. Princeton 56.
145 Moore, Stephen C. Variations on a Theme: The Poetry and Criticism of JPB.
     Mich 63.

BLACK, H. M.

146 Closs, Frederic T. Symbol Cast in Steel: The Verse of HMB. Pa 64.

BLACKMUR, R. P.

147 Eikhoff, Michael E. Methodik und Sensibilität in der Dichtungskritik RPBs.
     Munich 59.

BLITZSTEIN, MARC

148 Talley, Paul M. Social Criticism in the Original Theatre Librettos of MB. Wis S 65.

BODENHEIM, MAXWELL

149 DeVoe, Edward T. "A Soul in Gaudy Tatters": A Critical Biography of MB.
     Pa State 57.

BOKER, G. H.

150 Bradley, E. Sculley. GHB: Poet and Patriot. Pa 25.

BOUCICAULT, DION

151 Andersen, Jesse M. DB: Man of the Theatre. Chicago 26.
152 Clay, Jack. The Theatre of DB. Northwestern S.
153 Folland, Harold. The Plays of DB. Harvard 40.
154 Orr, Lynn E. DB and the Nineteenth-Century Theater. La S 53.
155 Rohrig, Gladys M. An Analysis of Certain Acting Editions and Promptbooks of
     Plays by DB. Ohio State 56.
156 Tolson, Julius H. DB. Pa 51.

BOURNE, RANDOLPH

157 Filler, Louis. RB. Columbia H 44.
158 Harris, Mark. RB: A Study in Immiscibility. Minn 56.
159 Moreau, John A. RB, a Biography. Va H 64.
160 Tomkins, Mary E. RB: Majority of One. Utah 64.

161 True, Michael D. The Social and Literary Criticism of RB: A Study of His Development as a Writer. Duke 64.

BOYD, JAMES

162 Whisnant, David. JB, 1888-1944: A Literary Biography. Duke 65.
See also 3440.

BOYESEN, H. H.

163 Eckstein, Neil T. The Marginal Man as Novelist: The Norwegian-American Writers, HHB and O.E. Rølvaag, as Critics of American Institutions. Pa 65.
164 Glasrud, Clarence A. HHB: A Biographical and Critical Study. Harvard 53.
165 Ratner, Marc L. HHB: Critic of Literature and Society. NYU 59.

BOYLE, KAY

166 Gado, Frank. KB: From the Aesthetics of Exile to the Politics of Return. Duke.
167 Jackson, Byron K. The Achievement of KB. Fla 64.

BRACKENRIDGE, H. H.

168 Hendrickson, John R. The Influence of *Don Quixote* on *Modern Chivalry.* Fla State 59.
169 Marder, Daniel. The Best of HHB. Pittsburgh 62.
170 Newlin, Claude M. The Life and Writings of HHB. Harvard 29.
171 Seeger, Wendy M. A Critical Analysis of HHB's *Modern Chivalry.* UCD.

BRADFORD, ANDREW

172 DeArmond, Anna J. AB. Pa 47.

BRADFORD, GAMALIEL

173 Capon, Reginald L. GB as Literary Critic, with Particular Reference to Elizabethan Drama. Boston 55.
174 Maikoski, Matthew J. GB: Psychographer. Pittsburgh 54.
175 Murphy, Irene. The Plays of GB in Relation to Some of His Other Work. Kan 53.

BRADSTREET, ANNE

176 Rowlette, Edith J. The Works of AB. Boston 64.
177 White, Ann Stanford. The Poetry of AB. UCLA 62.

BRANN, W. C.

177a Randolph, John W. The Apostle of the Devil: A Biography of WCB. Vanderbilt 38.

BROMFIELD, LOUIS

178 Brown, Morrison. LB: A Critical Biography. Pa State 55.
179 Zipser, Gerda. Die Schilderung der Frau in den Romanen von LB. Vienna 51.

BROOKS, CLEANTH

180 Hart, Sister Mary J. CB and the Formalist Approach to Metaphysical and Moral Values in Literature. So Cal 63.
181 Tassin, Rev. Anthony G. The Phoenix and the Urn: The Literary Theory and Criticism of CB. La 66.
182 Tegethoff, Inge. Die Methode der Literaturkritik bei CB. Munich.
See also 2882.

BROOKS, NOAH

183 Temple, Wayne C. NB, 1830-1903. Ill H 56.

BROOKS, V. W.

184 Dowell, Peter W. VWB and the Mind of His Generation. Minn 65.
185 Roberts, Susanne. The Early Critical Thinking of VWB. Pa.
186 Steinlein, Leo J. The Critical Theories of VWB. NYU E 48.

BROUGHAM, JOHN

187 Hawes, David S. JB as American Playwright and Man of the Theatre. Stanford 54.

BROWN, C. B.

188 Bernard, Kenneth. The Novels of CBB: Studies in Meaning. Columbia 62.
189 Berthoff, Warner B. The Literary Career of CBB. Harvard A 54.
190 Clark, David L. CBB. Columbia 23.
191 Coyle, James J. The Problem of Evil in the Major Novels of CBB. Mich 61.
192 Craft, Harvey M. The Opposition of Mechanistic and Organic Thought in the Major Novels of CBB. Tulane 64.
193 Flanders, Jane Townsend. CBB and William Godwin: Parallels and Divergences. Wis 65.
194 Fricke, Max. CBBs Leben und Werke. Kiel 11 publ.
195 Hayne, Barrie S. The Divided Self: The Alter Ego as Theme and Device in CBB, Hawthorne, and James. Harvard 64.
196 Just, Walter. Die romantische Bewegung in der amerikanischen Literatur: CBB, Poe, Hawthorne: Ein Beitrag zur Geschichte der Romantik. Münster 10 publ.
196a Kimball, Arthur G. Rational Fictions: A Study of CBB. Claremont 65.
197 Shapiro, Morton. Sentimentalism in the Novels of CBB. Ala 66.
198 Witherington, Paul. Narrative Technique in the Novels of CBB. Tex 64.
      See also 413, 3423.

BROWNE, C. F.

199 Reed, John. Artemus Ward: A Critical Study. Iowa 55.

BROWNELL, H. H.

200 Brown, G. Victor. The Poems of HHB, Selected and Annotated with a Biographical and Critical Introduction. NYU 26.

BROWNELL, W. C.

201 Allen, Glen O. WCB, Critic. Cornell 51.
202 Campbell, Harry M. A Criticism of the Works of WCB. Vanderbilt 42.
202a Fletcher, Frank. The Critical Values of WCB. Mich 51.
203 Tang, Me-tsung K. WCB, Literary Adviser: A Monograph. Pa 46.

BROWNSON, O. A.

204 Campbell, Jefferson H. OAB's Doctrine of Communion. Duke R 63.
205 Conroy, Paul R. OAB: American Political Philosopher. St. Louis H 37.
206 Corrigan, Sister M. Felicia. Some Social Principles of OAB. Catholic Soc 39.
207 Daley, Brother John E. OAB and Transcendentalism. Fordham P 55.
208 Farrell, Rev. Bertin B. OAB and the Existence of God. Catholic R 50.
209 Gilhooley, Brother Leonard. OAB and the American Idea, 1838-1860. Fordham 61.
210 Haggerty, William J., Jr. Realism in the Philosophy of OAB. Boston P 60.
211 Hollis, Charles C. The Literary Criticism of OAB. Mich 54.
212 McCarthy, Rev. Charles R., C.S.P. The Political Philosophy of OAB. Toronto P 62.
212a McCarthy, Rev. Leonard J., S.J. Rhetoric in the Works of OAB. Fordham 61.
213 McGrath, James W. The Catholicism of OAB. NM H 61.
214 Marshall, Rev. Hugh, M.S.SS.T. OAB and the American Civil War. Catholic H 62.
215 Michel, Virgil G. The Critical Principles of OAB. Catholic 18.
216 Roemer, Lawrence. The Political Philosophy of OAB. Loyola (Chicago) PS 47.

217 Whalen, Sister Mary R. G.   Some Aspects of the Influence of OAB on His
    Contemporaries.   Notre Dame 34.
    See also 4548.

BRYANT, W. C.

218 Bryant, William C., II.   WCB: The Middle Years: A Study in Cultural Fellowship.
    Columbia 54.
219 Christensen, Norman F.   The Imagery of WCB.   Wis 60.
220 Jelliffe, Rebecca R.   The Poetry of WCB: Theory and Practice.   UCB 64.
221 McDowell, Tremaine.   WCB.   Yale 27.
222 Otto, Walter.   WCBs poetische Werke und Übersetzungen.   Leipzig 02.
223 Ringe, Donald A.   Poetry and the Cosmos: WCB.   Harvard 54.
224 Silber, Robert B.   WCB's "Lectures on Mythology."   Iowa S 62.
    See also 2914, 4434.

BUCK, PEARL

225 Kreuchel, Elfriede.   Die Stellung der Frau in PBs China-Romanen.   Vienna 50.
225a Ly, Rev. Doan C.   The Image of the Chinese Family in PB's Novels.   St. John's
    (Brooklyn) 65.
226 Magnus, Ilse.   Die Frau in China in den Werken PBs.   Kiel 54.

BUCKMINSTER, J. S.

227 Minnis, Jack H.   JSB: A Critical Study.   Pa 63.
228 Simpson, Lewis P.   The Era of JSB: Life and Letters in the Boston-Cambridge
    Community, 1800-1815.   Tex 48.

BURGESS, GELETT

229 Backus, Joseph M.   GB: A Biography of the Man Who Wrote "The Purple Cow."
    UCB 61.

BURGOYNE, GEN. JOHN

230 Orr, Guss.   General JB as an Author.   La S 41.

BURKE, KENNETH

231 Holland, Laura V.   Aristotelianism in the Rhetorical Theory of KB.   Ill S 54.
232 Kirk, John W.   Dramatism and the Theatre: An Application of KB's Critical
    Methods to the Analysis of Two Plays.   Fla D 62.
233 Knox, George A.   KB as a Literary Theorist and Critic.   Wash 54.
234 Macksoud, Saleem J.   The Literary Theories of KB and the Discovery of Meanings
    in Oral Interpretation.   UCLA 64.
235 Rueckert, William H.   The Rhetoric of Rebirth: A Study of the Literary Theory
    and Critical Practice of KB.   Mich 56.
    See also 2264.

BURROUGHS, E. R.

236 Pickett, Roy.   ERB: American Mirror.   NM.

BURROUGHS, JOHN

237 Garrison, Joseph M., Jr.   JB as a Literary Critic: A Study Emphasizing His
    Treatment of Emerson, Whitman, Thoreau, Carlyle, and Arnold.   Duke 62.
238 Pelfrey, Charles J.   Elements of Mysticism in the Writings of JB and John Muir:
    A Study of Post-Transcendental Concepts of Nature.   Ky 58.

BURTON, WARREN

239 Buck, Whitney W.   WB: Classmate of Emerson and Kindly Reformer-at-Large.
    Mich 64.

BUSHNELL, HORACE

240 Baird, Robert D. Religion is Life: An Inquiry into the Dominating Motif in the Theology of HB. Iowa R 64.
241 Crosby, Donald A. HB's Theory of Language: A Historical and Philosophical Study. Columbia R 63.
242 Cross, Barbara M. HB, 1802-1876. Radcliffe A 56.
243 Faber, Warren H. A Critical Rhetorical Study of the Effect of HB's Theory of Language upon His Theory of Homiletics and His Practice of Preaching. Northwestern S 62.
244 Henderlite, Rachel. The Theological Basis of HB's *Christian Nurture.* Yale R 47.
245 Howell, John E. A Study of the Theological Method of HB and Its Application to His Cardinal Doctrines. Duke R 63.
See also 633, 4565.

BYRD, WILLIAM

246 Beatty, Richmond C. WB of Westover. Vanderbilt 32.

CABELL, J. B.

246a Arons, Peter L. The Romanticism of JBC. Yale 64.
247 Bellamy, John E. JBC: A Critical Study of His Reputation. Ill 54.
247a Canary, Robert H. The Cabellian Landscape: A Study of the Novels of JBC. Chicago 64.
248 Gibson, Lary H. The Disenchanted Garden: A Study of the Major Fiction of JBC's *The Biography of the Life of Manuel.* Ore 65.
249 Rothman, Julius L. A Glossarial Index to the *Biography of the Life of Manuel.* Columbia 54.
250 Smith, Nelson J. Jesting Pilate: A Critical Study of the Fictional World of JBC. Ind 65.
251 Wells, Arvin R. Jesting Moses: A Study in Cabellian Comedy. Mich 59.
See also 3317.

CABLE, G. W.

252 Butcher, Philip. GWC as a Social Critic. Columbia 56.
253 Ekström, Kjell. GWC: A Study of His Early Life and Work. Uppsala 50.
254 King, James K. GWC and Thomas Nelson Page: Two Literary Approaches to the New South. Wis 64.
255 Pugh, Griffith T. GWC: A Critical Biography. Vanderbilt 44.
256 Walston, Rosa L. GWC: A Critical Study. Duke 31.
See also 1062, 1619.

CAHAN, ABRAHAM

257 Pollock, Theodore M. The Solitary Clarinetist: A Critical Biography of AC, 1860-1917. Columbia 59.

CALDWELL, ERSKINE

258 Bubloz, Eric. The Themes of EC's Short Stories. Neuchâtel.
259 Cater, Althea C. Social Attitudes in Five Contemporary Southern Novelists: EC, William Faulkner, Ellen Glasgow, Caroline Gordon, and T. S. Stribling. Mich 46.
260 Cross, Carlyle. EC as a Southern Writer. Ga 63.
261 Golle, Günter. Sprache und Stil bei EC. Jena 61 publ.
262 Rosenthal, Gisela. EC: Wesen und Grenzen seiner Kunst. Berlin (H) 52.
263 Scheffel, Werner. Die Darstellung der weissen Anteilpächter in den Romanen und Kurzgeschichten ECs. Jena 62 publ.
See also 4481.

CALDWELL, J. H.

264 Hostetler, Paul S. JHC: New Orleans Theatrical Manager. La State 64.

CALVERT, G. H.

265 Everson, Ida G. GHC, American Literary Pioneer. Columbia 43.

CANBY, H. S.

266 Harvey, LeRoy. HSC and American Culture. Mich.

CAREY, MATHEW

267 Bradsher, Earl L. MC: Editor, Author, and Publisher: A Study in American Literary Development. Columbia 12.
268 Rowe, Kenneth W. MC: A Study in American Economic Development. Johns Hopkins 33.

CARITAT, HOCQUET

269 Raddin, George Y., Jr. HC: Enlightenment and Cosmopolitanism in Federal New York. Columbia 50.

CARTWRIGHT, PETER

270 Agnew, Theodore L. PC and His Times: The First Fifty Years, 1785-1835. Harvard H 53.

CARUTHERS, W. A.

271 Davis, Curtis C. Chronicler of the Cavaliers: The Career and Opinions of WAC, M.D. (1802-1846). Duke 47.
See also 1636.

CATHER, WILLA

272 Adams, Theodore S. Six Novels of WC: A Thematic Study. Ohio State 61.
273 Baker, Bruce. Image and Symbol in Selected Writings of WC. Tex Christian.
274 Bash, James R. WC: A Study in Primitivism. Ill 54.
275 Charles, Sister Peter D., O. P. Love and Death in the Novels of WC. Notre Dame 65.
276 Curtin, William M. The Relation of Ideas and Structure in the Novels of WC. Wis 59.
277 Finestone, Harry. WC's Apprenticeship. Chicago 54.
278 Fox, Clyde M. Revelation of Character in Five WC Novels. Colo 63.
279 Gerber, Philip L. WC: Novelist of Ideas. Iowa 52.
280 Giannone, Richard J. Music in WC's Fiction. Notre Dame 64.
281 Green, George W. Elements of Form in the Novels of WC. Harvard 56.
282 Hancock, Wanda J. Theme and Form in the Novels of WC. Stanford.
283 Handy, Yvonne. L'Oeuvre de WC. Rennes 47 publ.
284 Lambert, Maude E. Theme and Craftsmanship in WC's Novels. NC 65.
285 Lewison, Nora V. The Achievement of WC. Iowa 44.
286 Nestlbichler, Paul. WC als Darstellerin nordamerikanischen Pionierlebens. Vienna 44.
287 Randall, John H., III. WC's Search for Value: A Critical and Historical Study of Her Fiction. Minn 57.
288 Reisch, Ingeborg. Das Pionierideal in der Darstellung der amerikanischen Gesellschaft bei WC und Sinclair Lewis. Berlin (F) 58.
289 Ross, Janet. WC and the Realistic Movement in American Fiction. Iowa 60.
290 Schmittlein, Albert E. WC's Novels: An Evolving Art. Pittsburgh 62.
291 Schroeter, James M. WC's Literary Reputation. Chicago 59.
292 Thorberg, Raymond. WC: A Critical Interpretation. Cornell 54.
293 Throckmorton, Jean L. WC: Artistic Theory and Practice. Kan 54.
294 Toler, Sister Colette, S. C. Man as Creator of Art and Civilization in the Works of WC. Notre Dame 65.

295　White, Harold N.　WC's Apprenticeship:　A Collection of Her Writings in the *Nebraska State Journal,* 1891-1895.　Tex 55.
　　　See also 2617, 4465.

CATHERWOOD, M. H.

296　Price, Robert.　A Critical Biography of Mrs. MHC:　A Study of Middle Western Regional Authorship, 1847-1902.　Ohio State 43.

CHANDLER, RAYMOND

297　Wodarz, Ingeborg.　Die Kritik an der modernen Welt im Erzählwerk RCs.　Mainz.

CHANNING, E. T.

298　Anderson, Dorothy I.　ETC's Philosophy and Teaching of Rhetoric.　Iowa S 44.

CHANNING, W. E., THE ELDER

299　Brown, Arthur W.　Always Young for Liberty:　A Critical Biography of Dr. WEC.　Syracuse 50.
300　Downs, Lenthiel H.　Emerson and Dr. WEC.　Iowa 40.
301　Edgell, David P.　WEC:　A Chapter in American Intellectual History.　Brown 50.
302　Hochmuth, Marie K.　WEC, D.D.:　A Study in Public Address.　Wis S 46.
303　McGeehon, Carl W.　The Controversial Writings of WEC.　Iowa R 40.
304　Schober, Franz.　WEC Gedankengut:　Eine Untersuchung seiner weltanschaulichen Grundideen.　Erlangen 56.

CHANNING, W. E., THE YOUNGER

305　Hudspeth, Robert N.　The Life and Work of WEC, the Younger.　Syracuse.

CHAPMAN, J. J.

306　Bernstein, Melvin H.　The Mind of JJC.　NYU 51.
307　Hovey, Richard B.　JJC:　The Early Years.　Harvard 50.
308　Stocking, David M.　The Ideas of JJC.　Mich 49.

CHASE, M. E.

309　Dodge, Evelyn C.　A Critical Study of the Writings of MEC.　Boston 63.

CHAUNCY, CHARLES

310　Griffin, Edward M.　A Biography of CC (1705-1787).　Stanford.
311　Jones, Barney L.　CC and the Great Awakening in New England.　Duke R 58.

CHAYEFSKY, PADDY

312　Blasingame, D. Michael.　A Study of the Plays for Stage, Television, and Cinema by PC.　Mich State.

CHEETHAM, JAMES

313　Lasher, Lawrence M.　JC:　Journalist and Muckraker.　Md 65.

CHESNUTT, C. W.

314　Lyons-Render, Silvia.　Eagle with Clipped Wings:　Form and Feeling in the Fiction of CWC.　Peabody 62.

CHILD, F. J.

315　Reppert, James D.　FJC and the Ballad.　Harvard 53.

CHILD, L. M.

316　Lamberton, Bernice G.　A Biography of LMC.　Md 53.

317 Taylor, Lloyd C., Jr. To Make Men Free: An Interpretative Study of LMC. Lehigh H 56.

CHIVERS, T. H.

318 Watts, Charles H., II. THC: His Literary Career and His Poetry. Brown 53.

CHOPIN, KATE

319 Rankin, Daniel S. KC and Her Creole Stories. Pa 32.

CHURCHILL, WINSTON

320 Irvin, Frederic B. The Didacticism of WC (1871-1947). Pittsburgh 47.
321 Killat, Johannes. Das Amerikabild des Schriftsstellers WC. Berlin 40.
322 Titus, Warren I. WC, American: A Critical Biography. NYU A 57.

CLARKE, J. F.

323 Colville, Derek K. JFC. Wash (St. Louis) 53.
324 Thomas, John W. JFC, Apostle of German Culture to America. Pa State G 42.

CLEMENS, S. L.

325 Andrews, Kenneth R. MT's Hartford. Ill 48.
326 Aspiz, Harold. MT's Reading: A Critical Study. UCLA 50.
327 Asselineau, Roger M. The Literary Reputation of MT, 1910-1950. Paris 53 publ.
328 Baender, Paul E. MT's Transcendent Figure. UCB 56.
329 Baetzhold, Howard. MT's Attitudes toward England. Wis 53.
330 Bailey, Mary M. MT and the Fine Arts. Pittsburgh 38.
331 Bates, Allan C. MT and the Mississippi River. Chicago.
332 Bellamy, Gladys C. MT as a Literary Artist. Okla 47.
333 Benson, Ivan. The Western Development of MT. So Cal 37.
334 Bicknese, Günther. MT und die Tradition der Alten Welt. Marburg 53.
335 Branch, Edgar M. The Literary Development of MT, 1852-1865. Iowa 41.
335a Brashear, Minnie M. Formative Influences in the Mind and Writing of MT. NC 30.
336 Bredeson, Robert C. MT's Landscapes: A Study in Changing Literary Conventions. Minn 63.
337 Burhans, Clinton S. MT on the Inconsistencies in American Democracy. Wis.
338 Burnam, Thomas B. MT and the Machine. Wash 50.
339 Carter, Paul J., Jr. The Social and Political Ideas of MT. Cincinnati 39.
340 Coleman, Philip Y. MT's Desperate Naturalism. Ill 64.
341 Covici, Pascal, Jr. Humor as Form: A Study of Structure in MT's Works. Harvard 57.
342 Cox, James M. MT: A Study in Nostalgia. Ind 55.
343 Crossman, Lester G. SLC in Search of MT: A Study of SLC's Changing Conception of His Role as Writer. Wash 57.
344 Cummings, Sherwood P. MT and Science Wis 51.
345 da Ponte, Durant. American Periodical Criticism of MT, 1869-1917. Md 53.
346 Davidson, W. E. MT and Conscience. Mo 40.
347 Dickinson, Leon T. MT's *Innocents Abroad:* Its Origin, Composition, and Popularity. Chicago 45.
348 Donner, Stanley T. The Speaking and Reading of MT. Northwestern S 47.
349 Duke, Keith E. A Contribution to the History of Transcontinental Travel in the Middle of the Nineteenth Century: MT's *Roughing It.* Bordeaux 50.
350 Durrigl, Karl. Die Abweichungen von Standard English in *The Adventures of Tom Sawyer* von MT. Vienna 23.
351 Emberson, Frances G. The Vocabulary of SLC from 1852 to 1884. Mo 32.
352 Ensor, Allison R., Jr. MT and the Bible. Ind 65.
353 Ervin, Jean C. MT, Speechmaker. Mo S 50.
354 Feinstein, George W. MT's Literary Opinions. Iowa 45.

355   Feinstein, Herbert. MT's Lawsuits. UCB.

356   Fenger, Gerald J. The Short Stories of MT. Tex Christian.

357   Flowers, Frank C. MT's Theories of Morality. La 41.

358   Frantz, Ray, Jr. The Place of Folklore in the Creative Art of MT. Ill 54.

359   French, Bryant M. A Critical Study of MT's *The Gilded Age.* So Cal 61.

360   Fried, Martin B. The Sources, Composition, and Popularity of MT's *Roughing It.* Chicago 51.

361   Gaudek, Ida. Personliches Erleben in den Werken MTs. Vienna 38.

362   Gibson, William M. MT and William Dean Howells: Anti-Imperialists. Chicago 40.

363   Gilkey, Robert. MT voyageur et son image de l'Europe. Paris 51.

364   Gold, Charles H. MT and Subscription Publishing. Wash (St. Louis).

365   Goldman, Robert L. MT's Unpublished Plays. Duke.

366   Goold, Edgar H., Jr. MT's Literary Theories and Opinions. NC 50.

367   Gordon, Joseph. MT and Henry Adams in Politics and Government. Pa State.

368   Greenagel, Frank L. The Irony of MT: An Analysis of a Rhetorical Strategy. Minn S 65.

369   Grimm, Clyde L. MT: The Unreconstructed Temperament. Ill 63.

370   Havens, Charles B. MT's Use of Native American Humor in His Principal Literary Works. Vanderbilt 54.

371   Hays, John Q. The Serious Elements in the Writings of MT. UCB 42.

372   Hemminghaus, Edgar H. MT in Germany. Columbia G 39.

373   Hill, Hamlin L., Jr. The American Publishing Company and the Writings of MT, 1867-1880. Chicago 59.

374   Hiner, James H. The Boatman and the Boat: MT's Relation to the Technology of His Age. Minn.

375   Jones, Alexander E. MT and Religion. Minn 50.

376   Jurich, Joseph. MT's *Joan of Arc:* Origins, Purposes, and Accomplishment. Ill 62.

377   Klaus, Rosemarie. MT, der Kritiker seiner Zeit. Berlin (H) 55.

378   Kunst, Arthur E. Twenty-Four Versions of *Huckleberry Finn:* Studies in Translation. Ind 61.

379   Lennon, Edward J., Jr. MT: The Speaker. Wis S 52.

380   Lowenherz, Robert J. MT and W. D. Howells: A Literary Relationship. NYU 54.

381   McNamara, Eugene J. MT's Theory and Practice of Fiction: *The Adventures of Tom Sawyer, Adventures of Huckleberry Finn, The Tragedy of Pudd'nhead Wilson.* Northwestern 64.

382   Möhle, Günter. Das Europabild MTs: Grundlagen und Bildungselemente: Irving, Hawthorne, MT. Bonn 40 publ.

383   Moore, William E. MT's Techniques of Humor. Peabody 47.

384   Pfeiffer, Benjamin. Religious, Moral, and Social Ideas in the Works of MT. Nev 64.

385   Poli, Bernard. MT, écrivain de l'Ouest. Paris 65   publ.

386   Rees, Robert A. MT and the Bible: Characters Who Use the Bible and Biblical Characters. Wis 66.

387   Regan, Robert C. The Unpromising Hero in the Writings of MT. UCB 65.

388   Rodney, Robert M. MT in England: A Study of the English Criticism of and Attitude toward MT, 1867-1940. Wis 46.

389   Rogers, Franklin R. The Role of Literary Burlesque in the Development of MT's Structural Patterns, 1855-1885. UCB 58.

390   Rowlette, Robert. MT's *Pudd'nhead Wilson.* Duke.

391   Salomon, Roger B. MT's Conceptions of History. UCB 57.

392   Schieber, Alois J. Autobiographies of American Novelists: MT, Howells, James, Adams, and Garland. Wis 57.

393   Schmidt, Paul S. SLC's Use of the English and Italian Past. Minn 52.

394   Scholtz, Ulrike. MT and *The Mysterious Stranger.* Frankfurt.

395   Scott, Arthur L. MT as a Critic of Europe. Mich 48.

396 Scott, Harold P. MT's Theory of Humor: An Analysis of the Laughable in Literature. Mich 17.

397 Shane, Marion L. Spiritual Poverty in Selected Works of Four American Novelists: MT, Crane, Fitzgerald, Dreiser. Syracuse 53.

398 Smith, J. Harold. The Expressed Opinions of MT on Heredity and Environment. Wis 55.

399 Spengemann, William C. The Meaning of Innocence in the Works of SLC. Stanford 61.

400 Stevenson, Dwight W. SLC as a Literary Artist: A Study of His Use of the Novella Form. Mich 65.

401 Stone, Albert E., Jr. MT's Children: A Literary, Social, and Biographical Study in the Beginnings of a Genre. Yale A 58.

402 Strong, Leah. Joseph Hopkins Twichell: A Biography of MT's Pastor. Syracuse 53.

403 Tuckey, John S. MT as a Satirist. Notre Dame 53.

404 Vogelback, Arthur L. The Literary Reputation of MT in America, 1869-1885. Chicago 38.

405 Wager, Willis J. A Critical Edition of the Morgan Manuscript of MT's *Life on the Mississippi.* NYU 42.

406 Wagner, Gerard. MT, Political Orator. Ind S.

407 Wallace, Robert D. An Analytical-Historical Study of the Factors Contributing to the Success of MT as an Oral Interpreter. So Cal S 62.

408 Wiggins, Robert A. MT's Novels: Principles and Practice of Realism. UCB 53.

409 Williams, James D. The Genesis, Composition, Publication, and Reception of MT's *A Connecticut Yankee.* NYU 61.
See also 3, 6, 1062, 1184, 1246, 1343, 1351, 1374, 1908, 2150, 3357, 3988, 4535.

CLIFFTON, WILLIAM

410 Bressler, Leo A. WC: Philadelphia Poet, 1772-1799: A Critical and Biographical Essay and a Collection of His Writings. Pa A 52.

COBBETT, WILLIAM

411 Clark, Mary E. Peter Porcupine in America, Being the Career of WC, Editor and Publisher, Pamphleteer and Bookseller, 1792-1800. Pa 37.

COFFIN, R. P. T.

412 Pendexter, Hugh, III. A Critical Study of the Poetry of RPTC. Pa 54.

COLDEN, CADWALLADER

413 Martin, John S. Social and Intellectual Patterns in the Thought of CC, Benjamin Thompson (Count Rumford), Thomas Cooper, Fisher Ames, Timothy Dwight, David Humphreys, Benjamin Silliman, and Charles Brockden Brown. Wis 65.

CONWAY, M. D.

414 Burtis, Mary E. MDC. Columbia 48.

COOKE, J. E.

415 Beaty, John O. JEC, Virginian. Columbia 22.

416 Walker, William E. JEC: A Critical Biography. Vanderbilt 57.

COOKE, P. P.

417 Allen, John D. PPC: A Critical and Biographical Study. Vanderbilt 39.

COOKE, R. T.

418 Downey, Jean. A Biographical and Critical Study of RTC, 1827-1892. Ottawa 57.
See also 4475a.

COOPER, J. F.

419 Abcarian, Richard. The Literary Reputation of JFC in America 1820-1955. UCB 61.

420 Ball, Lee H., Jr. JFC's Artistry in the Characterization of Leather-Stocking. Wis 58.

421 Beard, James F., Jr. JFC: Craftsman of Democratic Fiction. Princeton 49.

422 Bleasby, George. The Frontier in JFC's Leatherstocking Tales. Pittsburgh 52.

423 Bosset, Georgette. JFC et le roman d'aventure en France vers 1830. Lausanne 28.

424 Clagett, John H. JFC and the Sea: Naval Life and Naval History in the Writings of JFC. Yale 54.

425 Clark, Harold E. JFC's Leather Stocking Tales: A Study in Race. Ind 55.

426 Clavel, Marcel. JFC and His Critics: American, British, and French Criticism of His Work. Paris 38 publ.

427 Clavel, Marcel. JFC: Sa vie et son oeuvre, la jeunesse (1789-1826). Paris 38 publ.

428 Clees, James C. JFC's *The Monikins:* Social Criticism, Satire, and Allegory. Columbia 65.

429 Collins, Frank. JFC's Religious and Ethical Ideas. Wis 53.

430 Cunningham, Richard E. JFC and the New England Mind. Ill 65.

431 Diemer, James S. The European Novels of JFC: A Study in the Evolution of JFC's Social Criticism, 1820-1833. Northwestern 50.

432 Döring, Walter. Mensch und Natur bei JFC. Cologne 55.

433 Fischer, Lillian. Social Criticism in JFC's *Leatherstocking Tales:* The Meaning of the Forest. Yale A 57.

434 Gibb, Margaret M. Le Roman de Bas-de-Cuir: Etude sur JFC et son influence en France. Paris 27.

435 Gill, Katharine Tracy. Frontier Concepts and Characters in the Fiction of JFC. Ill 56.

436 Hall, Edwin M. JFC and the Navy. (Parts I and II.) Pa State 59.

437 Hartung, George W. JFC's Attitude toward England. Wis 57.

438 House, Kay S. JFC's American Characters. Stanford 63.

439 Johnson, Manly. The Visual and the Visionary in the Work of JFC. Minn 58.

440 Kuiper, Kenneth W. JFC's *The Oak Openings, or The Bee-Hunter:* An Interpretation and Evaluation. Mich 63.

441 Lanier, Sterling. The Moral, Social, and Political Theories of JFC. Harvard A 55.

442 Morris, George D. JFC et Edgar Poe d'àpres la critique française du dixneuvième siècle. Paris 12 publ.

443 Müller, Willi. *The Monikins* von JFC in ihrem Verhältnis zu *Gulliver's Travels* von J. Swift. Rostock 99 publ.

444 O'Donnell, Charles R. The Mind of the Artist: JFC, Thoreau, Hawthorne, Melville. Syracuse 57.

445 Outland, Ethel R. The "Effingham" Libels on JFC: A Documentary History of the Libel Suits of JFC Centering around the Three Mile Point Controversy and the Novel *Home as Found,* 1837-1845. Wis 29.

446 Paine, Gregory L. JFC as an Interpreter and Critic of America. Chicago 24.

447 Philbrick, Thomas L. JFC and the Development of American Sea Fiction. Harvard 59.

448 Pickering, James H. JFC and the History of New York. Northwestern 64.

449 Ross, John F. A Study of JFC's Social Criticism. UCB 29.

450 Ross, Morton L. The Rhetoric of Manners: The Art of JFC's Social Criticism. Iowa 6

451 Sandy, Alan Francis, Jr. The Sublime, the Beautiful, and the Picturesque in the Natural Description of JFC. UCB 65.

452 Schauble, Roman J. JFC's Use of and Attitude toward Time Schemes, History, and Tradition in His European, Pre-Revolutionary, and Leatherstocking Novels. Wis 66.

453 Schneider, Konrad. Die Naturschilderung bei JFC (Dargestellt an Hand seiner Lederstrumpfgeschichten). Vienna 40.

454 Shulenberger, Arvid. JFC's Theory of Fiction: His Prefaces and Their Relation to His Novels. Chicago 51.
455 Stein, Paul. The Mask and the Face: Aspects of Reality in the Novels of JFC. Western Reserve.
456 Stockton, Edwin L., Jr. The Influence of the Moravians upon the Leather-Stocking Tales. Fla State 60.
457 Walker, George W. The Personal and Literary Relationships of Sir Walter Scott and JFC. NC 50.
457a Walker, Warren S. Folk Elements in the Novels of JFC. Cornell 51.
458 Waples, Dorothy. The American Reputation of JFC, 1821-1841. Yale 32.
458a Wehmeyer, William A. The European Novels of JFC: A Critical Study. Notre Dame 62.
459 Zoellner, Robert H. JFC's Sea Novels: His Social Theories as Expressed Symbolically through the Gentleman-Leader of the Microcosmic Ship on the Sea-Frontier. Vols. I and II. Wis 62.
See also 2914, 3338, 4128, 4434.

COOPER, THOMAS
See 413.

COTTON, JOHN

460 Come, Donald R. JC, Guide of the Chosen People. Princeton H 49.
461 Laird, James H. The Influence of JC in the Massachusetts Bay Colony. Boston H 47.
462 Poole, Harry A. The Unsettled Mr. JC. Ill H 56.
463 Rosenmeier, Jesper. The Image of Christ: The Typology of JC. Harvard A 66.
464 Warren, Alice F. JC: The Father of Boston. Wis H 29.
465 Ziff, Larzer. JC: Congregationalist, Theocrat, Puritan. Chicago 55.

COZZENS, J. G.

466 Galligan, Edward L. Within Limits: The Novels of JGC. Pa 58.
467 Mooney, Harry J., Jr. JGC: Novelist of Intellect. Pittsburgh 62.
468 Parrish, James. JGC: A Critical Analysis. Fla State 55.
469 Wiegand, William G. JGC and the Professional Man in American Fiction. Stanford 60.
See also 2588.

CRADDOCK, C. E.

470 Parks, Edd W. CEC: A Study of Local Color in the South. Vanderbilt 32.
471 Reichert, Alfred. CEC und die amerikanische Short-Story. Leipzig 12.

CRANCH, C. P.

472 Miller, F. DeWolfe. CPC: Transcendentalist. Va 42.

CRANE, HART

473 Dembo, Lawrence S. The Poetry of HC. Cornell 55.
474 Dickie, Margaret. HC: A Critical Study. Brown A.
475 Foster, Margaret. Arthur Rimbaud and HC: An Essay in Influence and Parallels. Ohio State 40.
476 Guiguet, Jean. L'univers poétique de HC. Paris 62 partly publ.
477 Ickstadt, Heinz. Die Bildersprache HCs. Berlin.
478 McMahon, William E. The Rationale of HC. Chicago 64.
479 Marchl, Herbert. Rimbaud und HC. Munich.
480 Newman, Arnold E. The Romantic Image in the Poetry of HC. Wis 65.
481 Quinn, Vincent G. Transcendence in the Poems of HC. Columbia 59.
482 Trisolini, Anthony G. An Analysis of the Structure of HC's *The Bridge*. Northwestern S 59.

483 Uroff, Margaret D. HC's *White Buildings.* Brown 65.
483a Vogler, Thomas A. Preludes to Vision: The Epic Venture in Blake, Wordsworth, Keats, and HC. Yale 64.
     See also 668, 2222a.

CRANE, STEPHEN

484 Bushman, John C. The Fiction of SC and Its Critics. Ill 44.
485 Colvert, James B. SC: The Development of His Art. La 53.
486 Elconin, Victor A. Studies in the Fiction of SC. Ohio State 47.
488 Gibson, Donald B. The Fiction of SC. Brown 62.
489 Gullason, Thomas. Some Aspects of the Mind and Art of SC. Wis 53.
490 Haack, Dietmar. Die Erzähltechnik SCs: Theoretische Prinzipien und dichterisches Werk. Berlin (F).
491 Hart, Andrew W. SC's Social Outlook as Revealed in His Writings. Mich State 55.
492 Hoffman, Daniel G. The Poetry of SC. Columbia 56.
493 Holton, William M. The Cylinder of Vision: The Sketches, Stories, and Novels of SC. Yale 66.
494 Hurd, Carol E. The Meaning of Anti-Realistic Devices in the Fiction of SC, Norris, London, and Dreiser. Geo Wash.
495 Hyde, Frederic G. American Literature and the Spanish-American War: A Study of the Work of SC, Norris, Fox, and R. H. Davis. Pa 63.
496 Jumper, Will C. Tragic Irony as Form: Structural Problems in the Prose of SC. Stanford 58.
497 LaFrance, Marston. The Role of Illusion in the Work of SC. Wis 65.
498 Lowe, Mervin R. SC's *The Red Badge of Courage:* A Study of a Novel. Pa 51.
499 Mazzorana, Sister Mary P., O. S. F. The Problem of Determinism in the Short Fiction of SC. Catholic 65.
500 O'Donnell, Bernard. An Analysis of Prose Style to Determine Authorship: *The O'Ruddy,* A Novel by SC and Robert Barr. Harvard 63.
501 Peck, Richard E. Method and Meaning in the Poetry of SC. Wis 65.
502 Petersen, Hans. Der künstlerische Werdegang SCs. Greifswald 59.
503 Toerne, Richard A. The Establishment of SC: A Study of the Emergence of a Classic American Author, 1893-1948. Northwestern 61.
504 Wertheim, Stanley C. SC's *The Red Badge of Courage:* A Study of Its Sources, Reputation, Imagery, and Structure. NYU 63.
505 Westbrook, Max R. SC and the Revolt-Search Motif. Tex 60.
506 Whitehead, Jean V. The Art of SC. Cornell 44.
     See also 397, 3381.

CRAWFORD, F. M.

507 Phillips, Raymond C., Jr. FMC's Fiction: A Critical Study. Pa.
508 Pilkington, John, Jr. The Life of FMC. Harvard 52.
509 Saltus, Charles N. FMC. Wis 29.
     See also 1124.

CRÈVECOEUR, ST. JEAN DE

510 Adams, Percy G. SJC's *Voyage dans la haute Pennsylvanie et dans l'état de New York.* Tex RL 47.
511 Armstrong, Harold C. The Significance of SJC's *Letters from an American Farmer* and *Sketches of Eighteenth Century America* in the Pastoral Literary Tradition and in the Literary Polemic of Revolutionary America. Wash 53.
512 Mitchell, Julia P. SJC. Columbia 16.

CROCKETT, DAVID

513 Shackford, James A. An Annotated Autobiography of DC. Vanderbilt 48.

CROTHERS, RACHEL

514   Abrahamson, Irving.   The Career of RC in the American Drama.   Chicago 56.

CUMMINGS, E. E.

515   Beloof, Robert L.   EEC: The Prosodic Shape of His Poems.   Northwestern 54.
516   Dougherty, James P.   EEC's *The Enormous Room* and its Relation to His Poetry.   Pa 62.
517   Maurer, Robert E.   EEC: A Critical Study.   Wis 55.
518   Rus, Louis C.   Structural Ambiguity in the Poetry of EEC.   Mich 55.
519   Wegner, Robert E.   The Prose and Poetry of EEC: A Study in Appreciation.
       Western Reserve 59.

CURTIS, G. W.

520   Chadbourne, Charles C., Jr.,   GWC: A Critical Biography.   Syracuse 51.
521   Dora, Lucile.   GWC: littérateur américain.   Montpellier 22 publ.
522   Milne, William G.   GWC and the Genteel Tradition: A Revaluation.   Harvard 51.

DALY, AUGUSTIN

523   Cutler, Jean V.   AD's Realism in Productions of Contemporary Plays.   Ill 62.
524   Felheim, Marvin.   The Career of AD.   Harvard 48.
525   Michalak, Marion V.   The Management of AD's Stock Company, 1869-1899.   Ind D 61.

DANA, R. H., JR.

526   Hart, James D.   RHD, JR.   Harvard 36.
527   Lucid, Robert F.   The Composition, Reception, Reputation, and Influence of *Two Years
       Before the Mast.*   Chicago 58.

DANA, R. H., SR.

528   Weimar, G. M.   RHD, the Elder, as Critic.   NYU 20.

DAVIES, SAMUEL

529   Pilcher, George W.   Preacher of the New Light: SD, 1724-1761.   Ill H 63.

DAVIS, H. L.

530   Jenkins, Eli S.   HLD: A Critical Study.   So Cal 60.

DAVIS, M. E. M.

531   Wilkinson, Clyde W.   The Broadening Stream: The Life and Literary Career of MEMD.
       Ill 47.

DAVIS, REBECCA H.

532   Grayburn, William F.   The Major Fiction of RHD.   Pa State 65.
533   Sheaffer, Helen W.   RHD, Pioneer Realist.   Pa 48.

DAVIS, R. H.

534   Osborn, Scott.   RHD: The Development of a Journalist.   Ky 53.
       See also 495.

DAY, H. F.

535   Houpt, William P.   Maine Long Logging and Its Reflection in the Works of HFD.
       Pa 64.

DE BOW, J. D. B.

536   Skipper, O. C.   A Life of JDBD.   Harvard H 42.

DE FOREST, J. W.

537   Croushore, James H.   JWD: A Biographical and Critical Study to the Year 1868.
       Yale 44.

538 Davidson, James. JWD and His Contemporaries: The Birth of American Realism. NYU 58.
539 Ford, Philip H. The Techniques of JWD, Transitional Novelist. Ohio State 54.
540 Gargano, James W. JWD: A Critical Study of His Novels. Cornell 55.
541 Geffen, Arthur. *Miss Ravenel's Conversion from Secession to Loyalty:* Its Sources, Composition, Publication, Reputation, and Influence. Chicago.
542 Hagemann, E. R. JWD and the American Scene: An Analysis of His Life and Novels. Ind 54.
543 Nall, Kline A. A Critical Evaluation of JWD. Tex 52.
544 Sullivan, Philip Edward. JWD: A Study of Realism and Romance in Selected Works. So Cal 66.
545 Tabor, Carole S. JWD and the South. Tex Christian 66.

DELL, FLOYD

546 Tanselle, G. Thomas. Faun at the Barricades: The Life and Work of FD. Northwestern 59.

DENNIE, JOSEPH

547 Ellis, H. Milton. JD and His Circle. Harvard 13.

DE SMET, P. J.

548 Magaret, Helene. Father PJDS: Pioneer Priest of the Rockies. Iowa H 40.

DE VOTO, BERNARD

549 Gill, John M. BDV and Literary Anti-criticism: Theory and Experience. NYU 64.
550 Lee, Robert E. The Work of BDV: Introduction and Annotated Check List. Iowa A 57.

DICKINSON, A. E.

550a Young, James H. AED and the Civil War. Ill H 41.

DICKINSON, EMILY

551 Anselmo, Sister Peter M., R.S.M. Renunciation in the Poems and Letters of ED. Notre Dame 65.
551a Arp, Thomas R. Dramatic Poses in the Poetry of ED. Stanford 62.
552 Berlet, Brigitte. Die Bildersprache EDs. Frankfurt.
553 Capps, Jack L. ED's Reading, 1836-1886: A Study of the Sources of Her Poetry. Pa 63.
553a Copple, Lee B. Three Related Themes of Hunger, Homelessness, and Obscurity as Symbols of Privation, Renunciation, and Compensation in the Poems of ED. Mich 54.
554 Davis, William F. The Art of Peace: The Moral Vision of ED. Yale 64.
555 Di Salvo, Leta P. The Arrested Syllable: A Study of the Death Poetry of ED. Denver 65.
556 Ford, Thomas W. The Theme of Death in the Poetry of ED. Tex 59.
557 Frank, Bernhard. The Wiles of Words: Ambiguity in ED's Poetry. Pittsburgh 65.
558 Franklin, Ralph W. Editing ED. Northwestern 65.
559 Gelpi, Albert J. The Business of Circumference: The Mind and Art of ED. Harvard 6
559a Granichstaedten-Czerva, Elisabeth. Bildersprache bei ED. Vienna 40.
559b Gregor, Norman. The Luxury of Doubt: A Study of the Relationship between Imagery and Theme in ED's Poetry. NM 55.
560 Hall, Sister M. Jeremias, O. P. An Analysis of the Relationship of Love and Death in the Poetry of ED. Loyola (Chicago).
561 Higgins, David J. Portrait of ED: The Poet and Her Prose. Columbia 61.
562 Jones, Rowena R. ED's "Flood Subject": Immortality. Northwestern 60.
562a Kelly, Louise K. A Concordance of ED's Poems. Pa State 51.

562b   Kriesberg, Ruth M.   The Poetry of ED.   NYU 65.
563   Marcus, Mordecai.   Nature Symbolism in the Poetry of ED.   Kan 58.
564   Molson, Francis J.   The "Forms" of God: A Study of ED's Search for and Test of God.   Notre Dame 65.
565   Porter, David T.   The Art of ED's Early Poetry.   Rochester 64.
566   Putney, Paula.   ED's Theory of Poetry.   Mo.
567   Sherwood, William R.   Circumference and Circumstance: Stages in the Mind and Art of ED.   Columbia 64.
568   Todd, John E.   ED's Use of the Persona.   Wis 65.
569   Wheatcroft, John S.   ED and the Orthodox Tradition.   Rutgers 60.
570   Wilson, Suzanne M.   Structure and Imagery Patterns in the Poetry of ED.   So Cal 59.
     See also 771.

DICKINSON, JOHN

570a   Powell, John H.   JD: Penman of the American Revolution.   Iowa H 38.
570b   Soler, William.   Some Important Influences upon JD's Thought: Chiefly Bacon, Locke, and Pope.   Temple 53.

DIXON, THOMAS

570c   Cook, Raymond A.   TD: His Books and His Career.   Emory 53.

DOCK, CHRISTOPHER

571   Klassen, Frank H.   CD: Eighteenth Century American Educator.   Ill H 62.

DONNELLY, IGNATIUS

571a   Nydahl, Theodore L.   The Diary of ID, 1859-1884.   Minn H 42.

DOOLITTLE, HILDA

572   Holland, Joyce.   HD: The Shape of a Career.   Brown.
573   Kaufman, J. Lee.   Theme and Meaning in the Poetry of HD.   Ind 59.
573a   Swann, Thomas B., Jr.   The Classical World of HD.   Fla 61.

DOS PASSOS, JOHN

574   Belkind, Allen J.   Satirical Social Criticism in the Novels of JDP.   So Cal 66.
575   Bernardin, Charles W.   The Development of JDP.   Wis 49.
576   Blum, Karl.   Amerikanismen der Regionalmundart und des Slang in JDPs Romantrilogie *U.S.A.*   Mainz 58.
577   Brantley, John D.   The Fiction of JDP.   Tex 61.
578   Canario, John W.   A Study of the Artistic Development of JDP in His Novels from *One Man's Initiation-1917* through *U.S.A.*   Wash 63.
579   Donnell, Richard S.   JDP: Satirical Historian of American Morality.   Harvard 60.
580   Evans, William A.   Influences on and Development of JDP's Collectivist Technique.   NM 66.
581   Fitelson, David.   The Art of JDP: A Study of the Novels through *U.S.A.*   Emory 64.
582   Geissler, Walter.   Das Bild Amerikas in den Romanen von JDP.   Vienna 50.
583   Gorman, Thomas R.   Words and Deeds: A Study of the Political Attitudes of JDP.   Pa A 60.
584   Hoffmann, Hans.   Die Zeit bei JDP.   Cologne 54.
585   Holditch, William K.   Literary Technique in the Novels of JDP.   Miss 61.
586   Lowry, Edward.   "The Writer as Technician":   The Method of JDP, 1925-1936.   NYU 60.
587   Nelson, F. William.   An Analysis of JDP's *U.S.A.*   Okla 57.
588   Neuse, Werner.   Die literarische Entwicklung von JDP.   Giessen 30.
589   Newman, Paul.   The Critical Reputation of JDP, 1920-1950.   Chicago 58.
590   Sihler, Helmut.   Die Zeitstruktur der Romane von JDP.   Graz 53.
591   Winner, Anthony.   The Needs of a Man: A Study of the Formation of Themes, Characters, and Style in the Work of JDP.   Harvard CL 62.
592   Wrenn, John H.   JDP: Artist to Citizen.   Pa 58.

593 Young, Leo V. Values of the Young Characters in the Fiction of JDP,
     Hemingway, and Steinbeck. Stanford E 57.
     See also 2588, 3498, 4388, 4628.

DRAPER, J. W.

594 Fleming, Donald H. JWD and the Religion of Science. Harvard H 48.

DREISER, THEODORE

595 Barracano, Dolores. TD's Social Philosophy. Pa.
596 Biddle, Edmund R. The Plays of TD. Pa 65.
597 Blackstock, Walter. TD: The Aspirant. Yale 52.
598 Bower, Marie H. TD: The Man and His Times; His Work and Its Reception. Ohio
     State 40.
599 Castle, John F. The Making of TD's *An American Tragedy.* Mich 52.
600 Davis, Joe. The Mind of TD: A Study in Development. Emory 60.
601 Davis, Nancy H. The Women in TD's Fiction. Northwestern.
602 Dustman, Marjory P. TD's *An American Tragedy:* A Study. So Cal 65.
603 Elias, Robert H. TD: Apostle of Nature. Pa 48.
604 Elveback, Helen B. The Novels of TD with an Analysis of His Other Writings. Minn 46
605 Hakutani, Yoshinobu. TD Before *Sister Carrie:* French Realism and Early Experience.
     Pa State 65.
606 Horovitz, Sydney. TD: Basic Patterns of His Work. Pittsburgh 51.
607 Hussman, Lawrence E., Jr. The Spiritual Quest of TD. Mich 64.
608 Müller, Irmtraud. Amerikakritik en den Hauptwerken TDs bis zum New
     Deal. Vienna 43.
609 Palmer, Erwin G. Symbolic Imagery in TD's *An American Tragedy.* Syracuse 52.
610 Saalback, Robert P. Collected Poems: TD, Edited with an Introduction and Notes.
     Wash 51.
611 Salzman, Jack. *Sister Carrie:* A History of TD's Novel. NYU 66.
612 Schmidtberger, Loren F. The Structure of the Novels of TD. Fordham 65.
613 Shapiro, Charles. TD and the American Dream: A Study of *Sister Carrie, Jennie
     Gerhardt, The Genius,* and *An American Tragedy.* Ind 54.
614 Staab, Wolfgang. Das Deutschlandbild TDs. Mainz 61.
615 Steinbrecher, George, Jr. TD's Fictional Method in *Sister Carrie* and *Jennie Gerhardt.*
     Chicago 54.
616 Stephanchev, Stephen. TD among the Critics: A Study of American Reactions to the
     Work of a Literary Naturalist, 1900-1949. NYU 50.
617 Wilkinson, Robert E. A Study of TD's *The Financier.* Pa 65.
618 Willen, Gerald. TD's Moral Seriousness: A Study of the Novels. Minn 55.
     See also 397, 494, 3288, 3423, 3498, 4388.

DUBOIS, W. E. B.

619 Broderick, Francis L. WEBD: The Trail of His Ideas. Harvard A 55.

DUNLAP, WILLIAM

620 Coad, Oral S. WD: A Study of His Life and Works and of His Place in
     Contemporary Culture. Columbia 17.
620a Getchell, Charles M. The Mind and Art of WD (1766-1839). Wis 47.
620b Grinchuk, Robert. The Plays of WD: A Study of Popular Culture. Minn.

DUNNE, F. P.

621 Ruddle, James F. FPD: A Critical Study. NM.

DUTTON, C. E.

622 Stegner, Wallace E. CED: Geologist and Man of Letters. Iowa 35.

DUYCKINCK, E. A.

623 Mize, George E.   The Contributions of EAD to the Cultural Development of Nineteenth Century America. NYU 55.

DWIGHT, J. S.

624 Fertig, Walter L.   JSD: Transcendentalist and Literary Amateur of Music. Md 53.

DWIGHT, TIMOTHY

625 Buchanan, Lewis E.   TD, Man-of-Letters: His Ideas and Art. Wis 40.

EATON, W. P.

626 Myers, Norman J.   The Theatre Criticism of WPE, 1905-1930. Ill D 62.
627 Stephenson, Clarence E.   The Theater Criticism of WPE. Mich D 63.

EDMONDS, W. D.
See 3440.

EDWARDS, JONATHAN

628 Alexis, Gerhard T.   Calvinism and Mysticism in JE. Minn 47.
629 Anderson, Wallace E.   Mind and Nature in the Early Philosophical Writings of JE. Minn P 61.
630 Baker, Nelson B.   Anthropological Roots of JE's Doctrine of God. So Cal R 52.
631 Barnett, Das Kelley.   The Doctrine of Man in the Theology of JE (1703-1758). So Baptist R 43.
632 Becker, William H.   The Distinguishing Marks of the Christian Man in the Thought of JE. Harvard R 64.
633 Boorman, John A.   A Comparative Study of the Theory of Human Nature as Expressed by JE, Horace Bushnell, and William Adams Brown, Representative American Protestant Thinkers of the Past Three Centuries. Columbia R 54.
634 Brady, Mother Gertrude V.   Basic Principles of the Philosophy of JE. Fordham P 51.
635 Christian, Curtis W.   The Concept of Life after Death in the Theology of JE, Friedrich Scheiermacher, and Paul Tillich. Vanderbilt R 65.
636 Faust, Clarence H.   JE's View of Human Nature. Chicago 35.
637 Feaver, John C.   JE's Concept of God as Redeemer. Yale R 49.
638 Flynt, William T.   JE and His Preaching. So Baptist R 54.
639 Hankamer, Ernst W.   Das politische Denken von JE. Munich.
640 Hitchcock, Orville A.   A Critical Study of the Oratorical Technique of JE. Iowa S 36.
641 Hoffman, Gerhard.   Seinsharmonie und Heilsgeschichte bei JE. Göttingen R 57.
642 Holbrook, Clyde A.   The Ethics of JE: A Critical Exposition and Analysis of the Relation of Morality and Religious Conviction in Edwardean Thought. Yale R 45.
643 Holtrop, Elton.   JE's Conception of the Will in the Light of Calvinistic Philosophy. Western Reserve P 48.
644 Johnson, Thomas H.   JE as a Man of Letters. Harvard 32.
645 Knopp, Walther T.   JE: The Way of Sanctification. Harvard R 37.
646 Lyttle, David J.   JE's Symbolic Structure of Experience. Pa State 65.
647 MacCracken, John H.   JEs Idealismus. Halle 99.
648 Miller, Raymond C.   JE and His Influence upon Some of the New England Theologians. Temple R 45.
649 Price, Rebecca R.   JE as a Christian Educator. NYU E 38.
650 Rhoades, Donald H.   JE: Experimental Theologian. Yale R 45.
651 Richardson, Herbert W.   The Glory of God in the Theology of JE: A Study in the Doctrine of the Trinity. Harvard R 63.
652 Rudisill, Dorus P.   The Doctrine of the Atonement in JE and His Successors. Duke R 45.
653 Schafer, Thomas A.   The Concept of Being in the Thought of JE. Duke R 49.
654 Schlaeger, Margaret C.   JE's Theory of Perception. Ill P 64.

655 Smith, Claude A. A Sense of the Heart: The Nature of the Soul in the Thought of JE. Harvard R 64.
656 Squires, William H. JE und seine Willenslehre. Leipzig 02 publ.
657 Suter, Rufus O., Jr. The Philosophy of JE. Harvard P 32.
658 Tweet, Ronald D. JE: A Study of the Affecting Style. Chicago.
659 Watts, Emily S. JE and the Cambridge Platonists. Ill 63.
659a Weeks, John S. A Comparison of Calvin and JE on the Doctrine of Election. Chicago 63.

EGAN, M.F.

660 Parant, Sister Mary L., S.M. MFE: Literary Critic. St. John's (Brooklyn) 42.
661 Weitekamp, Raymond. MFE: Writer, Teacher, and Diplomat, 1852-1924. Catholic 62.
     See also 4548.

EGGLESTON, EDWARD

662 Cochran, Bud T. A Definitive Edition of EE's *The Hoosier Schoolmaster.* Ohio State
663 Paine, Stephen C. A Critical Study of the Writings of EE. Duke 61.
664 Randel, William P. EE. Author of *The Hoosier Schoolmaster.* Columbia 45.

EGGLESTON, G. C.

665 Callison, Louise. GCE: A Biographical and Critical Study. Western Reserve.

ELIOT, C. W.

666 Murdock, Mary-Elizabeth. CWE: Crusader for the "New Education." Brown H 62.

ELIOT, JOHN

667 Harling, Frederick F. A Biography of JE, 1604-1690. Boston H 65.

ELIOT, T. S.

668 Andreach, Robert J. The Spiritual Life in Hopkins, Joyce, TSE, and Hart Crane. NYU
669 Austin, Allen C. TSE as a Literary Critic. NYU 56.
670 Barnhill, Viron L. Poetic Context in the Collected Poems (1909-1935) of TSE: A Linguistic Investigation of Poetic Context. Mich 60.
671 Barry, Sister M. Martin. The Prosodic Structure in Selected Poems of TSE. Catholic 4
672 Baun, Elisabeth. TSE als Kritiker: Eine Untersuchung anhand der ungesammelten kritischen Schriften. Freiburg 62 publ.
673 Blau, Herbert. W. B. Yeats and TSE: Poetic Drama and Modern Poetry. Stanford 54
674 Bohnsack, Fritz. Zeit und Ewigkeit im Spätwerk TSEs. Hamburg 51.
675 Bollier, Ernest P. TSE and the Idea of Literary Tradition. Columbia 59.
676 Büdel, Maria. Der Essay Theodor Haeckers und TSEs als Beitrag zur abendländischen Literatur-und Kulturkritik. Marburg 49.
677 Burke, Sister Margaret J., S. S. I. Dryden and TSE: A Study in Literary Criticism. Niagara 45.
678 Butz, Hazel E. The Relation of TSE to the Christian Tradition. Ind 54.
679 Cahill, Daniel J. A Comparative Study of the Criticism of Arnold and TSE. Iowa 66.
680 Calliebe, Gisela. TSE und die Tradition der Mystik. Berlin (F) 55.
681 Costello, Sister M. Cleophas. Between Fixity and Flux: A Study of the Concept of Poetry in the Criticism of TSE. Catholic 47.
682 Darby, James M. An Approach to TSE's Religious Imagery. Harvard 57.
683 Demers, Pierre E. Spiritual Progress in the Poetry of TSE. Harvard 63.
684 Drumm, Sister Robert Mary, O.P. Johnson, Arnold, and TSE as Literary Humanists. Western Reserve 65.
685 Germer, Rudolph. TSEs "Waste Land" (die Geschichte seiner Wirkung und Beurteilung in den Jahren 1922 bis 1956, unter besonderer Berücksichtigung der Rezeption in England, Amerika, Deutschland und Frankreich). Freiburg 57.

686 Graham, James C. The Critical Theories of TSE and I. A. Richards. Wis 41.
687 Greene, Edward J. TSE et la France. Paris 48 publ.
688 Gunter, Bradley. TSE and Anglicanism. Va.
689 Hamalian, Leo. The Voice of This Calling: A Study of the Plays of TSE. Columbia 55.
690 Ishak, F. M. The Philosophical Bearing of Eastern and Western Mysticism on the Poetry of TSE. Liverpool 61-62.
691 Jankowsky, Kurt. Die Versauffassung bei Gerard Manley Hopkins, den Imagisten und TSE: Renaissance altgermanischen Formgestaltens in der Dichtung des 20. Jahrhunderts. Münster 56.
692 Knust, Herbert. The Artist, the King, and "The Waste Land": Richard Wagner, Ludwig II, and TSE. Penn State 61.
693 Koppenhaver, Allen J. TSE's *Murder in the Cathedral:* A Study. Duke 64.
694 Lally, Sister Mary A. A Comparative Study of Five Plays on the Becket Story: by Tennyson, Binyon, TSE, Anouilh, and Fry. Notre Dame 63.
695 Langbaum, Robert W. The Dramatic Monologue and the Poetry of Experience: A Study of Romantic Form [Browning, Tennyson, TSE]. Columbia 54.
696 Lightfoot, Marjorie J. TSE's *The Cocktail Party:* An Experiment in Prosodic Description. Northwestern 64.
696a Lu, Fei-Pai. TSE: The Dialectical Structure of His Theory of Poetry. Chicago 65.
697 Margolis, John D. The Development of the Religious and Social Ideas of TSE. Princeton.
698 Mathewson, George. The Search for Coherence: TSE and the Christian Tradition in English Poetry. Princeton 61.
699 Mayer, John T. The Dramatic Mode of TSE's Early Poetry. Fordham 64.
700 Melchers, Hans J. TSE: Das "Muster" und die Wirklichkeitsprobleme der Dichtung. Cologne 55.
701 Moorman, Charles W. Myth and Modern Literature: A Study of the Arthurian Myth in Charles Williams, C. S. Lewis, and TSE. Tulane 53.
702 Oestreich, Marianne. Das Problem der Schuld bei TSE. Berlin (F) 55.
703 Panicker, Geevarghese T. A Whole of Feeling: A Study of the Place of Emotion and Feeling in the Poetic Theory of TSE. Catholic 59.
704 Rambo, Dorothy E. An Analysis of *Four Quartets* by TSE, with Particular Respect to Its Prosody. Northwestern S 58.
705 Rees, Thomas R. The Orchestration of Meaning: A Study of the Relationship between Form and Meaning in TSE's Early Poetry (1910-1922). Tulane 65.
706 Roby, Robert C. TSE and the Elizabethan and Jacobean Dramatists. Northwestern 50.
707 Rogers, David J. Dramatic Use of the Liturgy in the Plays of TSE: A Secular Evolution. Wis 64.
707a Sando, Ephriam G. Against the Philistines: Literary Orthodoxy in the Criticism of TSE. UCLA 62.
708 Schmidt, Gerd. Die Struktur des Dramas bei TSE. Freiburg 62.
709 Scott, Peter D. The Social and Political Ideas of TSE. McGill 55.
710 Shaw, Sam. TSE's Theory of Tradition. NYU 64.
711 Smith, Carol H. From *Sweeney Agonistes* to *The Elder Statesman:* A Study of the Dramatic Theory and Practice of TSE. Mich S 62.
712 Smith, Grover C., Jr. The Poems of TSE, 1909-1928: A Study in Symbols and Sources. Columbia 50.
713 Sorial, F. I. A Study of Contemporary Verse Drama in England as Exemplified in the Plays of TSE and Christopher Fry. Trinity College, Dublin 59-60.
714 Standop, Ewald. TSEs Kulturkritik. Münster 49.
715 Stead, C. K. The New Poetic: An Investigation into Certain Common Problems Evident in the Work of English-Speaking Poets of the Twentieth Century, the Study Confined Mainly to the Literary Scene in England from 1900 to 1930, and Paying Special Attention to the Work of W. B. Yeats and TSE. Bristol 61-62.
716 Strömsdörfer, Ilse. Der Begriff der Zeit bei TSE. Munich 57.
717 Talley, Jerry B. Religious Themes in the Dramatic Works of George Bernard Shaw, TSE, and Paul Claudel. Denver 64.

718 Terrell, Carroll F. The Bone on the Beach: The Meaning of TSE's Symbols. NYU 56.
719 Thompson, Eric. TSE's *Four Quartets* as a Philosophical Poem. Iowa 51.
720 Thompson, Marion C. The Dramatic Criticsm of TSE. Cornell 53.
721 Uhlmann, Wilfried. Die Dramen TSEs als religiöse Dichtung. Tübingen 62.
722 Vickery, John B. TSE and the Golden Bough: The Archetype of the Dying God. Wis
723 Waters, Leonard A. Coleridge and TSE: A Comparative Study of Their Theories of
     Poetic Composition. Mich 48.
724 Weber, Alfred. Der Symbolismus TSEs: Versuch einer neuen Annäherung an
     moderne lyrik. Tübingen 54.
725 Weiss, Charlotte. Die Sprachkunst in TSEs dichterischen Werken. Hamburg 56.
726 Weiss, Klaus. TSEs *Four Quartets:* Analyse und Interpretation. Freiburg 61.
727 West, William C. Concepts of Reality in the Poetic Drama of W. B. Yeats,
     W. H. Auden, and TSE. Stanford S 64.
728 Williamson, Mervyn W. A Survey of TSE's Literary Criticism: 1917-1956.
     Tex 58.
729 Wingate, Gifford W. Poetic Drama in the 1930's: A Study of the Plays of TSE and
     W. H. Auden. Cornell 54.
730 Wright, George T. Modern Poetry and the *Persona:* The Device and Its
     Aesthetic Context, as Exhibited in the Work of TSE, Yeats, and Pound. UCB 56.
     See also 1246, 1499, 2222a, 2227, 2229, 2243, 2331a, 2897, 4339.

ELLISON, RALPH

See 4285.

EMERSON, R. W.

731 Abbott, John P. RWE and the Conduct of Life: The Early Years. Iowa 39.
732 Adams, John M. The Philosophical Historian: RWE's Theory of History. Kan 60.
733 Amacher, Richard E. The Literary Reputation of RWE, 1882-1945. Pittsburgh 47.
734 Anderson, John Q. RWE's Concept of the Poet. NC 52.
735 Ang, Gertrude R. RWE and Shakespeare. NYU 61.
736 Barrus, Paul W. RWE and Quakerism. Iowa 49.
737 Baumgartner, Alex M. The Mind of RWE: 1817-1832. Pa.
737a Benson, Nelson P. RWE as a Critic of Literature. NYU 19.
737b Bogart, Herbert. RWE: Self and Society, 1850-1870. NYU 63.
738 Bruel, Andrée. RWE et Thoreau. Paris 29 publ.
739 Burns, Harry H. RWE's Judgments on English Literature and the Principles
     which Underlay Them. Wash 36.
740 Burress, Lee A., Jr. The Relationship of Christian Theology to the Idea Content of
     RWE's Poetry. Boston 55.
741 Cannon, Charles W. The Influences Determining RWE's Conception of Jesus. Iowa
     R 37.
742 Carpenter, Frederic I. RWE's Use of Translations from the Oriental. Chicago 29.
743 Carpenter, Hazen C. RWE's Views Concerning Education and the Scholar. Wis 38.
744 Celières, André. The Prose Style of RWE. Paris 36.
745 Charvat, Charles C. RWE and Catholicism. Iowa 40.
746 Clendenning, John. RWE's Response to Skepticism. Iowa A 62.
747 Cobb, Robert P. Society versus Solitude: Studies in RWE, Thoreau, Hawthorne,
     and Whitman. Mich 55.
748 Collins, Christopher. The Uses of Observation: A Study of Correspondental Vision in
     the Writings of RWE, Thoreau, and Whitman. Columbia 64.
748a Cowan, Michael H. RWE and the City: A Case Study in the Urban Tradition in
     American Literature. Yale 64.
749 Crow, Charles R., Jr. The Rhythmic Organization of RWE's Four-Stress
     Verse. Pittsburgh 49.
750 Detweiler, Robert. RWE's Concept of God. Fla 62.
751 Duncan, Jeffrey L. Power and Form: The Theme of Dualism in RWE's Work. Va 65

752 Edrich, Mary W. RWE's Apostasy. Wis 65.
753 Ekhtiar, Mansur A. RWE's Poetic Language: A Linguistic and Literary Investigation. Ind 60.
754 Feidelson, Charles N., Jr. The Idea of Symbolism in American Writing, with Particular Reference to RWE and Melville. Yale 48.
755 Fish, H. M. The Influence of Thomas Carlyle upon RWE. Edinburgh 57-58.
756 Flanagan, John T. RWE and the State. Minn 34.
757 Foster, Charles H. RWE's Theory of Poetry. Iowa 39.
758 Foy, Rena L. W. The Philosophy of RWE and Its Educational Implications. Tex E 62.
759 Friedrich, Gerhard G. The Idea of Internationalism in RWE. Minn 52.
760 Gerber, John C. RWE's Economics. Chicago 41.
761 Gonnaud, Maurice. Individu et société dans l'oeuvre de RWE. Paris 64 publ.
762 Gray, H. D. The Philosophy of RWE. Columbia 04.
763 Grundy, Ernest. RWE and Scotch Common-Sense Philosophy. Denver.
764 Hastings, A. Louise. RWE's Journal at the West, 1850-1853. Ind 42.
765 Henney, Thomas G. The Craft of Genius: A Study of RWE's Development, 1823-1846. Princeton 46.
766 Hildebrand, Hedi. RWEs Verhältnis zur Geschichte. Bonn 36 publ.
767 Hoeltje, Hubert H. RWE in Virginia. Iowa 32.
768 Hopkins, Vivian C. The Aesthetic Theory of RWE. Mich 43.
769 Hotson, Clarence P. RWE and Swendenborg. Harvard 29.
770 Huggard, William A. RWE and the Problem of War and Peace. Iowa 37.
771 Hughes, James. The Dialectic of Death: Transcendentalism and Death in RWE, Poe, Dickinson, and Whitman. Pa.
772 Johnston, Kenneth G. The Organic Tradition in Industrial America: A Study of RWE and Frank Lloyd Wright. Minn.
773 Jordan, Leah E. The Fundamentals of RWE's Literary Criticism. Pa 45.
774 Jyoti, D. D. Mystical and "Transcendental" Elements in Some Modern English and American Writers in Relation to Indian Thought: RWE, H. D. Thoreau, E. M. Forster, T. S. Eliot, A. Huxley. London 56-57.
775 Keller, Hans. RWE in Frankreich: Wirkungen und Parallelen. Giessen 32 publ.
776 Kennedy, Steele M. RWE's "The American Scholar," and the Other Harvard Phi Beta Kappa Orations. NYU 56.
777 Kless, Renate. "Solitude and Society": Ein Grundproblem der Lebensphilosophie RWEs. Hamburg 55.
778 Kloeckner, Albert J. The Moral Sentiment: A Study of RWE's Terminology. Ind 56.
779 Kulot, Brigitte M. Der Schreibstil RWEs. Graz 45.
780 Kurtz, S. Kenneth. The Sources and Development of RWE's *Representative Men*. Yale 47.
781 Lauter, Paul. RWE's Rhetoric. Yale 58.
782 Lawton, John H. A Rhetorical Analysis of Representative Ceremonial Addresses of RWE. Iowa S 57.
783 Lee, Roland F. RWE and Christian Existentialism. Ohio State 52.
784 Lewis, Albert E. RWE: American Educator. Stanford E 43.
785 Link, Franz H. Die Begriffe des "Poet" und des "Writer" in ihres Stellung im Ganzen der Lebensauffassung von RWE auf Grund einer Interpretation der Essays, "Shakespeare; or the Poet" und "Goethe; or the Writer." Frankfurt 50.
786 Lockwood, Francis C. RWE as a Philosopher. Northwestern 96.
787 Lyons, Eleanor. The Parti-Colored Wheel: A Study of RWE's Thought. Va.
788 McGill, Robert A. RWE and His Audience. Pa A 59.
789 MacRae, Donald E. RWE and the Fine Arts. Iowa 34.
790 Maulsby, David L. The Contribution of RWE to Literature. Chicago 09.
791 Mendenhall, Mary. A Transcendental Philosophy of Education: A Study of the Educational Philosophy of Thomas Carlyle and RWE. Yale E 34.
792 Mettke, Edith. Der Dichter RWE. Berlin (F) 63 publ.
793 Miller, Lee W. RWE and the New Testament. La 53.

794   Mohrdiek, Martin.   Demokratie bei RWE.   Berlin 42.
795   Nagy, Gerhard von.   Grundrichtungen im Denken RWEs: Eine psychologische
      Analyse.   Jena 14 publ.
796   Nicoloff, Philip L.   RWE's Thought in *English Traits.*   Columbia 59.
797   Odell, Alfred T.   La Doctrine sociale de RWE.   Paris 31 publ.
798   Orth, Ralph H.   RWE's *Encyclopaedia.*   Rochester 60.
799   Osborne, Clifford H.   RWE's Reading.   Ind 36.
800   Paul, Sherman.   The Angle of Vision and the Arc of the Circle: "Correspondence"
      in RWE's Transcendental Vision.   Harvard A 50.
801   Paulits, Brother F. Joseph.   RWE's Concept of Good and Evil.   Pittsburgh 55.
802   Pettigrew, Richard C.   Milton in the Work of RWE, Lowell, and Holmes.   Duke 30.
803   Pomeroy, Ralph S.   RWE as a Public Speaker.   Stanford S 60.
804   Porte, Joel M.   RWE and Thoreau: Transcendentalists in Conflict.   Harvard 62.
805   Rao, Adapa R.   RWE's Attitude toward Humanitarian Reform.   Wis 64.
806   Reaver, J. Russell.   RWE's Use of Imagery as Seen in a Study of His Poetry.
      Ohio State 42.
807   Roberts, J. Russell.   Seventeenth Century Contributions to RWE's Thought.
      Wash P 40.
808   Rollins, Henry B.   RWE and Practical Affairs.   NC 56.
809   Sandeen, Ernest E.   RWE's Americanism.   Iowa 40.
810   Schiff, Hugo.   RWEs Gestaltung der Persönlichkeit: Versuch einer systematischen
      Darstellung aus seinen Werken.   Erlangen 20 publ.
811   Scudder, Townsend, III.   RWE in England.   Yale 32.
812   Silver, Mildred.   RWE and the Idea of Progress.   Iowa 38.
813   Simon, Julius.   RWE in Deutschland (1852-1932).   Giessen 37 publ.
814   Singh, Man M.   RWE and India.   Pa 47.
815   Slater, Joseph L.   An Introduction to the Correspondence of Carlyle and RWE.
      Columbia 56.
816   Smith, John W.   RWE's *English Traits:*   A Critical and Annotated Study.   Tex 57.
817   Sojka, Raoul.   Untersuchungen über das Vorhandensein grundlegender Ideen RWEs in
      amerikanischen Romanen von Nathaniel Hawthorne.   Vienna 48.
818   Sowder, William J.   RWE's Reputation in English Periodicals from 1840 through the
      Turn of the Century.   Ky 56.
819   Strauch, Carl F.   A Critical and Variorum Edition of RWE's Poems.   Yale 46.
820   Stuart, John A.   RWE's *Nature:*   Its Relation to Coleridge's Transcendental Idealism.
      Northwestern 45.
821   Sutcliffe, E. G.   RWE's Theories of Literary Expression.   Ill 18.
822   Terwilliger, Ernest W.   The Individual and RWE's Concept of Equality.   Cornell 54.
823   Thompson, Frank T.   RWE's Debt to Wordsworth, Carlyle, and Coleridge.   NC 25.
824   Turner, Robert C.   The Influence of French Culture and Literature upon RWE before
      1850.   Yale 35.
825   Turpie, Mary C.   The Growth of RWE's Thought.   Minn 44.
826   Wahr, Frederick B.   RWE and Goethe.   Mich G 15.
827   Whicher, Stephen E.   The Lapse of Uriel: A Study in the Evolution of RWE's
      Thought.   Harvard 42.
828   Wicke, Myron F.   RWE's Mysticism.   Western Reserve 40.
829   Williams, Wallace E.   RWE and the Moral Law.   UCB 63.
830   Wynkoop, William M.   Three Children of the Universe: RWE's View of Shakespeare,
      Bacon, and Milton.   Columbia 62.
      See also 237, 239, 300, 1221, 2698, 3338, 4581, 4595.

ENGLISH, T. D.

831   Gravely, William H., Jr.   The Early Political and Literary Career of TDE.   Va 53.

ERSKINE, JOHN

832   Bautz, Margret.   JE als Parodist.   Würzburg 46.

EVERETT, EDWARD

833 Christian, William K. The Mind of EE. Mich State 53.

EVERSON, WILLIAM

834 Rizzo, Fred F. A Study of the Poetry of WE. Okla 66.

FAIRFIELD, S. L.

835 Patterson, Merrill R. SLF, 1803-1844. Yale 33.

FALKNER, W. C.

836 Duclos, Donald P. Son of Sorrow: The Life, Works, and Influence of Colonel WCF (1825-1889). Mich 62.

FARRELL, J. T.

837 Dyer, Henry H. JTF's Studs Lonigan and Danny O'Neill Novels. Pa 65.
838 Lynch, William J. The Literary Criticism of JTF. Pa 66.
839 Mitchell, Richard. JTF's Scientific Novel. Syracuse 63.
840 Owen, David H. A Pattern of Pseudo-Naturalism: Lynd, Mead, and JTF. Iowa 50.
841 Posselt, Edith. Das Charakterbild in den Werken JTFs als Ausdruck seiner Weltanschauung. Kiel 54.
842 Reiter, Irene M. A Study of JTF's Short Stories and Their Relation to His Longer Fiction. Pa 64.
843 Schmitz, Siegfried. Die Sozialkritik in der Romantrilogie *Studs Lonigan* von JTF. Mainz 56.
     See also 1662, 3317, 3498, 4388, 4628.

FAST, HOWARD
See 3440.

FAULKNER, WILLIAM

844 Baacke, Margareta. WFs Menschen: Charakterdarstellung der Weissen aus Yoknapatawpha County. Marburg 53.
845 Backman, Melvin A. The Pilgrimage of WF: A Study of WF's Fiction, 1929-1942. Columbia 60.
846 Berner, Robert L. The Theme of Responsibility in the Later Fiction of WF. Wash 60.
847 Bradford, M. E. WF's Doctrine of Nature. Vanderbilt.
848 Brady, Emily K. The Literary WF: His Indebtedness to Conrad, Lawrence, Hemingway, and Other Modern Novelists. Brown 62.
849 Brown, William. WF's Use of the Material of Abnormal Psychology in Characterization. Ark 64.
850 Brylowski, Walter M. Man's Enduring Chronicle: A Study of Myth in the Novels of WF. Mich State 64.
851 Callen, Shirley P. Bergsonian Dynamism in the Writings of WF. Tulane 62.
852 Carey, Glenn O. WF: Critic of Society. Ill 62.
853 Carnes, Frank F. The Aesthetics of WF's Fiction. Vanderbilt.
854 Chisholm, William S. Sentence Patterns in *The Sound and the Fury*. Mich 64.
855 Christadler, Martin. Natur und Geschichte im Werk WFs. Tübingen 60 publ.
856 Dike, Donald A. The World of WF's Imagination. Syracuse 54.
857 Doster, William C. WF and the Negro. Fla 55.
858 Dowell, Bobby R. WF's Comic Spirit. Denver 62.
859 Eberly, Ralph D. Immediacy, Suspense, and Meaning in WF's *The Sound and the Fury:* An Experiment in Critical Analysis. Mich 53.
860 Elkin, Stanley L. Religious Themes and Symbolism in the Novels of WF. Ill 61.
861 Emerson, O. B. WF's Literary Reputation in America. Vanderbilt 62.
862 Farnham, James F. They Who Endure and Prevail: Characters in the Fiction of WF. Western Reserve.
863 Fazio, Rocco B. The Fury and the Design: Realms of Being and Knowing in Four Novels of WF. Rochester 64.

864 Franklin, Rosemary F. Clairvoyance in the Works of WF. Emory.
865 Friend, George L. Levels of Maturity: The Theme of Striving in the Novels of WF. Ill 64.
866 Gold, Joseph. The Single Vision: A Study of the Philosophy and the Forms of Its Presentation in the Works of WF. Wis 59.
867 Goren, Leyla Melek. WF: An International Novelist. Harvard A 63.
868 Graves, Wallace. Difficult Contemporary Short Stories: WF, Katherine Anne Porter, Dylan Thomas, Eudora Welty, and Virginia Woolf. Wash 55.
869 Harwick, Robert D. Humor in the Novels of WF. Nebraska 65.
870 Hawkins, E. O., Jr. A Handbook of Yoknapatawpha. Ark 61.
871 Henss, Herbert. WFs Roman *Sartoris* als literarisches Kunstwerk. Mainz 64 publ.
872 Hinteregger, Gerald. Das Land und die Menschen in WFs erzählenden Werken. Graz 53.
873 Hoadley, Frank M. The World View of WF. Okla 55.
874 Hofammann, Albert G., Jr. WF's Conflicting Galaxies: A Study in Literary Polarity. Pa 51.
875 Holmes, Edward M. WF's Twice-Told Tales: His Re-Use of His Material. Brown 62.
876 Hornback, Vernon T. WF and the Terror of History: Myth, History, and Moral Freedom in the Yoknapatawpha Cycle. St. Louis 63.
877 Hunt, John W., Jr. WF's Rendering of Modern Experience: A Theological Analysis. Chicago R 61.
878 Kartiganer, Donald M. The Individual and the Community: Values in the Novels of WF. Brown 64.
879 Kirk, Robert W. An Index and Encyclopedia of the Characters in the Fictional Works of WF. So Cal 59.
880 Knox, Robert H. WF's *Absalom, Absalom!* Harvard 59.
881 Lawson, Richard A. Patterns of Initiation in WF's *Go Down, Moses.* Tulane 66.
882 Lohner, Edgar. Thematik, Symbolik und Technik im Werk WFs. Bonn 50.
883 Longley, John L. WF's Tragic Heroes. NYU 57.
884 Loughrey, Thomas F. Values and Love in the Fiction of WF. Notre Dame 62.
885 Lowery, Perrin H. The Critical Reception of WF's Work in the United States, 1926-1950. Chicago 56.
886 McLaughlin, Carrol D. Religion in Yoknapatawpha County. Denver 62.
887 Malin, Irving M. WF: An Interpretation. Stanford 58.
888 Mascitelli, David. A Study of WF's Intellectual Characters. Duke.
889 Mellard, James M. Humor in WF's Novels: Its Development, Forms, and Functions. Tex 64.
890 Meriwether, James B. The Place of *The Unvanquished* in WF's Yoknapatawpha Series. Princeton 58.
891 Miner, Ward L. The World of WF. Pa A 51.
892 Mirabelli, Eugene, Jr. The Apprenticeship of WF: The Early Short Stories and the First Three Novels. Harvard 64.
893 Moreland, Agnes L. A Study of WF's Presentation of Some Problems that Relate to Negroes. Columbia 60.
894 Nolting-Hauff, Lore. Sprachstil und Weltbild bei WF. Freiburg 58.
895 Overly, Dorothy N. The Problem of Character in the Development of Theme in the Novels and Short Stories of WF. Chicago 50.
896 Penick, Edwin A., Jr. A Theological Critique of the Interpretation of Man in the Fiction and Drama of WF, Ernest Hemingway, Jean-Paul Sartre, and Albert Camus. Yale R 54.
897 Peper, Jürgen. Bewusstseinslage des Erzählens und erzählte Wirklichkeit: Bermuhungen um ein geisteswissenschaftliches und literarhistorisches Verständnis für wirklichkeitsbildendes Erzählen bei WF. Berlin (F) 62.
898 Petesch, Donald. Theme and Structure in WF's Snopes Trilogy. Tex.
899 Player, Raleigh P. The Negro Character in the Fiction of WF. Mich 65.
900 Ploegstra, Henry. WF's *Go Down Moses:* Its Publication, Revisions, Structure, and Reputation. Chicago.

901 Pollock, Agnes S. The Current of Time in the Novels of WF. UCLA 65.
902 Reed, Richard A. A Chronology of WF's Yoknapatawpha Fiction. Emory.
903 Richards, Lewis A. The Literary Styles of Jean-Paul Sartre and WF: An Analysis, Comparison, and Contrast. So Cal 63.
904 Richardson, Harold E. WF: From Past to Self-Discovery, a Study of His Life and Work through *Sartoris* (1929). So Cal 63.
905 Richardson, Kenneth E. Quest for Faith: A Study of Destructive and Creative Force in the Novels of WF. Claremont 62.
906 Rinaldi, Nicholas M. Game-Consciousness and Game-Metaphor in the Work of WF. Fordham 63.
907 Roberts, James L. WF: A Thematic Study. Iowa 57.
908 Rubel, Warren G. The Structural Function of the Christ Figure in the Fiction of WF. Ark 64.
909 Schendler, Sylvan. WF's *A Fable.* Northwestern 56.
910 Serafin, Sister Joan M. WF's Use of the Classics. Notre Dame.
911 Shanaghan, Father Malachy M. A Critical Analysis of the Fictional Techniques of WF. Notre Dame 60.
912 Sidney, George R. WF in Hollywood: A Study of His Career as a Scenarist. NM 59.
913 Simon, John K. The Glance of the Idiot: A Thematic Study of WF and Modern French Fiction. Yale 63.
914 Simpson, Hassell A. The Short Stories of WF. Fla State 62.
915 Slabey, Robert M. WF: "The Waste Land" Phase (1926-1936). Notre Dame 61.
916 Slatoff, Walter J. Emphases and Modes of Organization in the Fiction of WF: A Study in Patterns of Rhetoric and Perception. Mich 56.
917 Stein, Randolph E. The World Outside Yoknapatawpha: A Study of Five Novels by WF. Ohio 65.
918 Steinberg, Aaron. WF and the Negro. NYU 63.
919 Stewart, David H. WF and Mikhail Sholokhov: A Comparative Study of Two Representatives of the Regional Conscience, Their Affinities and Meanings. Mich 59.
920 Sullivan, William P. WF and the Community. Columbia 61.
921 Swiggart, Charles P. Time and Structure in the Novels of WF. Yale 54.
922 Tanner, Jimmie E. The Twentieth Century Impressionistic Novel: Conrad and WF. Okla 64.
923 Taylor, Walter F. The Roles of the Negro in WF's Fiction. Emory 64.
924 Tritschler, Donald H. Whorls of Form in WF's Fiction. Northwestern 57.
925 Ulrey, Pamela A. WF's *Sanctuary* and *Requiem for a Nun:* Songs of Innocence and Experience. Cornell 63.
926 Vickery, Olga W. The Novels of WF: Patterns of Perspective. Wis 54.
927 Wall, Carey G. WF's Rhetoric. Stanford 64.
928 Wigley, Joseph A. An Analysis of the Imagery of WF's *Absalom, Absalom!* Northwestern 56.
929 Wilson, Herman O. A Study of the Humor in the Fiction of WF. So Cal 55.
930 Zink, Karl E. WF: Studies in Form and Idea. Wash 53.
See Also 259, 1141, 1246, 1662, 1848, 1997, 3482, 3487, 4128, 4481.

FAWCETT, EDGAR

931 Harrison, Stanley R. EF: A Minor Writer in the Literary Current of His Time: An Edition of His Unpublished Novel, *The Pride of Intellect.* Mich State 64.

FEARING, KENNETH

932 Rosenthal, Macha L. Chief Poets of the American Depression: Contributions of KF, Horace Gregory, and Muriel Rukeyser to Contemporary American Poetry. NYU 49.

FERBER, EDNA

933 Chisolm, Lawrence W. EF's Interpretation of Far Eastern Civilization in Relation to American Aesthetic Thought, 1870-1920. Yale 58.
934 Giesen, Felicitas. Amerika im Werke der EF. Bonn 35 publ.

FERRIL, T. H.

935 Richards, Robert F. The Poetry of THF. Columbia 61.

FIELDS, J. T.

936 Austin, James C. JTF, Editor and Spokesman of Genteel America. Western Reserve 52.
937 Tryon, William S. The Singing Shepherd: The Life of JTF, Publisher to the Victorian Age, 1817-1881. Harvard H 61.

FISHER, VARDIS

938 Flora, Joseph M. VF's Story of Vridar Hunter: A Study in Theory and Revision. Mich 62.
939 Thomas, Alfred K. The Ideas and Art of VF: A Critical Study. Pa State.

FISKE, H. G.

940 Roten, Paul. The Contributions of HGF to the American Theater as Editor of the *New York Dramatic Mirror*. Mich D 63.

FISKE, JOHN

941 Hazard, Patrick D. JF as American Scholar: A Study in the Testing of a National American Tradition. Western Reserve A 57.
942 Higgins, John. Life of JF. Harvard A.
943 O'Callaghan, Phyllis A. The Philosophy of JF. St. Louis H 57.
944 Pannill, H. Burnell. JF: Cosmic Theist. Duke R 52.

FITCH, CLYDE

945 Masters, Robert W. CF: A Playwright of His Time. Northwestern S 42.
946 Murray, James J. The Contribution of CF to the American Theatre. Boston 50.

FITZGERALD, F. S.

947 Bruccoli, Matthew J. The Composition of FSF's *Tender is the Night:* A Study Based on the Manuscripts. Va 61.
948 Coleman, Thomas C. The Social and Moral Criticism of FSF. So Cal 59.
949 Elliot, James K. The Literary Reputation of FSF. NM 65.
950 Ellis, James N. The Fragmented Hero in the Novels of FSF. Tex 63.
951 Frederick, Kenneth C. The Short Stories of FSF. Mich 63.
952 Goldhurst, William. FSF and His Contemporaries. Tulane 62.
953 Hallam, Virginia. The Popular and Critical Reception of FSF. Pa 66.
954 Harris, Marie. A Critical Study of the Novels of FSF. Md 52.
955 Heseltine, Harry P. The Development of the FSF Hero. La 56.
956 Höcker, Ursula. Darstellung und Kritik der Gesellschaft in den Werken von FSF. Freiburg 61 publ.
957 Hoenisch, Michael. The Development of FSF's Narrative Technique. Berlin (F).
958 Kuehl, John R. FSF: Romantic and Realist. Columbia 58.
959 Miller, James E., Jr. A Study of the Fictional Technique of FSF. Chicago 50.
960 Miller, John N. Romanticism, Irony, and the Novels of FSF. Stanford 64.
961 Milner, Stuart. Social and Economic Background of the Work of FSF. Sussex.
962 Oppelt, Werner. Die Kurzgeschichten FSFs. Erlangen.
963 Piper, Dan. FSF and the Origins of the Jazz Age. Pa A 50.
964 Sklar, Robert A. The Last Laocoon: A Study of FSF. Harvard 65.
965 Staley, Thomas F. FSF: A Study of His Development as a Novelist. Pittsburgh 62.
See also 397, 3288, 4628.

FLETCHER, J. G.

966 Douglass, Thomas E. The Correspondence of JGF: A Catalogue. Ark 65.
967 Osborne, William R. The Poetry of JGF, a Critical Analysis. Peabody 55.
967a Peters, Oliver L. A Name, Works, and Selected Subjects Index of the Correspondence of JGF for Correspondents "A" through "K." Ark 65.
968 Stephens, Edna B. The Oriental Influence in JGF's Poetry. Ark 61.
969 Zur, Bernard P. JGF, Poet: Theory and Practice. Northwestern 58.

FLOWER, B. O.

970 Dickason, David H. The Contribution of BOF and the *Arena* to Critical Thought in America. Ohio State 40.
971 Stallings, Frank L., Jr. BOF and *The Arena:* Literature as an Agent of Social Protest and Reform. Tex 61.

FORBES, ESTHER
See 3440.

FORD, P. L.

972 DuBois, Paul Z. PLF: An American Man of Letters. Western Reserve.

FOX, JOHN

973 Kruger, Arthur N. The Life and Works of JF, Jr. La 41.
See also 495.

FRANK, WALDO

974 Bittner, William A. The Novels of WF. Pa 55.
975 Kloucek, Jerome W. WF: The Ground of His Mind and Art. Northwestern 58.
See also 3360.

FRANKLIN, BENJAMIN

976 Barnes, Jack C. BF and His Memoirs. Md 54.
977 Buxbaum, Melvin. BF and the Presbyterians. Chicago.
978 Currey, Cecil B. BF and the Radicals, 1765-1775. Kan H 65.
979 Davy, Francis X. BF, Satirist: The Satire of BF and Its Rhetoric. Columbia 58.
980 Hausel, Helmut. BF (1706-1790) im literarischen Deutschland seiner Zeit. Erlangen 52.
981 Jankowski, Hans. BF als Publizist. Berlin (F).
982 Keiter, M. R. W. BF as an Educator. Md E 57.
983 MacLaurin, Lois M. The Vocabulary of BF. Chicago 27.
984 Meyer, Gladys E. Free Trade in Ideas: Aspects of American Liberalism Illustrated in BF's Philadelphia Career. Columbia Soc 41.
985 Miles, Richard D. The Political Philosphy of BF: The Beginning of the Pragmatic Tradition in American Political Thought. Mich PS 49.
986 Newcomb, Robert H. The Sources of BF's Sayings of Poor Richard. Md H 57.
987 Pitt, A. Stuart. BF and Religious Sectarianism. Yale 39.
988 Sappenfield, James A. The Growth of the BF Image. Stanford.
989 Seipp, Erika. BFs Religion und Ethik. Giessen 31 publ.
990 Thomas, Macklin. The Idea of Progress in the Writings of BF, Freneau, Barlow, and Rush. Wis 38.
991 Townsend, A. H. BF: Merchant of Ideas. NYU 29.
992 Van Scyoc, Leo L. The Literary Reputation of BF in America, 1790-1860. Kan.
993 Vermont, Adolphe. Les Amis français de BF. Johns Hopkins RL 24.
994 Wetzel, William A. BF as an Economist. Johns Hopkins 95.
995 Wilhite, Virgle G. Some Near Economists of Eighteenth Century America. Wis Econ 40.
996 Zimmerman, John J. BF: A Study of Pennsylvania Politics and the Colonial Agency, 1755-1775. Mich H 56.
See also 108,1100.

FREDERIC, HAROLD

997 Briggs, Austin E. The Novels of HF. Columbia 63.
998 Garner, Stanton B. HF: The Major Works. Brown 63.
999 Haines, Paul. HF. NYU 45.
1000 Hands, Charles B. HF: A Critical Study of the American Works. Notre Dame 59.
1001 Holmes, William J. A Study of the Novels of HF. Iowa 62.
1002 Rogers, Ralph R. HF: His Development as a Comic Realist. Columbia 61.
1003 Woodward, Robert H. HF: A Study of His Novels, Short Stories, and Plays. Ind 57.
1004 Wüstenhagen, Heinz. HFs Romane als Beitrag zur Entwicklung des bürgerlich-kritischen Realismus in der amerikanischen Literatur. Potsdam 63 publ.
See also 1339.

FREEMAN, M. E. W.

1005 Bullard, Marcia M. MEWF and the Popular Fiction in Her Time. UCB.
1006 Foster, Edward R. MEWF: A Critical and Biographical Study. Harvard 37.
See also 4475a.

FRENCH, ALICE (OCTAVE THANET)

1007 McMichael, George L. Minor Figure: A Biography of OT [AF]. Northwestern 59.

FRENCH, L. V.

1008 Peck, Virginia L. Life and Works of LVF. Vanderbilt 40.

FRENEAU, PHILIP

1009 Forman, Samuel E. The Political Activities of PF. Johns Hopkins 97.
1010 Leary, Lewis. That Rascal PF: A Study in Literary Failure. Columbia 40.
1011 Marsh, Philip M. PF, Jeffersonian Publicist. UCLA 46.
See also 990.

FRISBIE, R. D.
See 2020.

FROST, ROBERT

1012 Cook, Charles H., Jr. RF, American Symbolist: An Interpretative Study. Boston 57
1013 Ganz, Robert N., Jr. The Pattern of Meaning in RF's Poetry. Harvard 59.
1014 Hiebel, William R. The Theme of Skepticism in the Works of RF. Northwestern.
1015 Horst, Bernard L., S.M. The Poetry of RF: His Use of Personae. Fordham.
1016 Isaacs, Emily E. RF: The Man and His Art. Wash 57.
1017 Larson, Mildred R. RF as a Teacher. NYU E 49.
1018 Lynen, John F. Pastoralism in the Poetry of RF. Yale 54.
1019 McCoy, Donald. The Reception and Development of RF as a Poet. Ill 52.
1020 Nitchie, George W. Human Values in the Poetry of RF: A Study of a Poet's Convictions. Columbia 58.
1021 Parsons, Thornton H. The Humanism of RF: A Study in Parallels. Mich 59.
1022 Pritchard, William H. The Uses of Nature: A Study of RF's Poetry. Harvard 60.
1023 Roberts, Esther L. The Thought in RF's Poetry. Boston 47.
1024 Ronninger, Lisbeth. Die Kunstform der Dichtung RFs. Vienna 39.
1025 Seibt, Irma. Die Dichtung RFs. Graz 40.
1026 Smith, Mary E. The Function of Natural Phenomena in the Poetry of RF. Iowa 51.
1027 Smythe, Daniel W. RF's Poetry as Self-Clarification. Pa 57.

FULLER, H. B.

1028 Bowron, Bernard R., Jr. HBF: A Critical Study. Harvard A 47.
1029 Griffin, Constance M. A Critical Biography of HBF. Pa 38.
1030 Jackson, Kenny. An Evolution of the New Chicago from the Old: A Study of HBF's Chicago Novels. Pa 61.

1031 Pearce, Richard A. Chicago in the Fiction of the 1890's as Illustrated in the Novels of HBF and Robert Herrick. Columbia 63.
1032 Rosenblatt, Paul. The Image of Civilization in the Novels of HBF. Columbia 60.
1033 Winn, Georgia G. The Works of HBF. Pittsburgh 39.

FULLER, MARGARET

1034 Braun, F. A. MF and Goethe. Ill G 10.
1035 Burton, Roland C. MF's Criticism: Theory and Practice. Iowa 41.
1036 Durning, Russell E. MF, Citizen of the World: An Intermediary Between European and American Literatures. NC 65.
1037 Ebbitt, Wilma R. The Critical Essays of MF from the New York *Tribune,* with Introduction and Notes. Brown 43.
1038 Fay, Sister Francis M. MF. St. John's (Brooklyn) 51.
1038a Kearns, Francis E. MF's Social Criticism. NC 61.

GALE, ZONA

1039 Minor, Delores. The Changing Style in the Novels of ZG. NYU.

GARLAND, HAMLIN

1040 Garvey, Bernadette M. HG's Relationship to the Naturalistic Movement. St. John's (Brooklyn) 42.
1041 Gronewold, Benjamin F. The Social Criticism of HG. NYU 42.
1042 Harris, Elbert L. HG's Use of the American Scene in His Fiction. Pa 59.
1043 Hill, Eldon C. A Biographical Study of HG from 1860 to 1895. Ohio State 40.
1044 Neumann, Edwin J. HG and the Mountain West. Northwestern 51.
1045 Pizer, Donald. HG: A Critical Study of His Early Work and Career (1884-1895). UCLA 55.
1046 Reamer, Owen J. HG: Literary Pioneer and Typical American. Tex 51.
See also 392, 1339, 1374, 3381, 4465.

GARRISON, W. L.

1047 Thomas, John L. Biography of WLG. Brown H 61.

GAYARRÉ, C. E. A.

1048 Saucier, Earl N. CEAG, the Creole Historian. Peabody 34.
1049 Socola, Edward. CEAG, A Biography. Pa 54.

GEORGE, HENRY

1050 Croft, Albert J. The Speaking Career of HG: A Study in Ideas and Persuasion. Northwestern S 53.

GIBBS, WOLCOTT

1051 Bloom, Gilbert L. An Analysis of the Dramatic Theory and Criticism of WG as It Appeared in His *New Yorker* Theatre Reviews. Iowa S.

GILDER, R. W.

1052 Smith, Herbert F. The Editorial Influence of RWG, 1870-1909. Rutgers 61.

GILLETTE, WILLIAM

1053 Sherk, H. Dennis. WG: His Life and Works. Pa State S 61.

GILMER, F. W.

1054 Davis, Richard B. The Life, Letters, and Essays of FWG: A Study in Virginia Literary Culture in the First Quarter of the Nineteenth Century. Va 36.

GLASGOW, ELLEN

1055 Becker, Allen. EG: Her Novels and Their Place in the Development of Southern Fiction. Johns Hopkins 56.
1056 Bressler, Maybelle J. A Critical Study of the Published Novels of EG. Nebraska 65.
1057 Briney, Martha M. EG: Social Critic. Mich State 56.
1057a Derrig, Rev. P. Austin, C.M. EG's Role in American Fiction: A Reinterpretation. St. John's (Brooklyn) 63.
1058 Dillard, Richard H. Pragmatic Realism: A Biography of EG's Novels. Va 65.
1059 Dunn, Norma. EG's Search for Truth. Pa.
1060 Edwards, Herbert W. A Study of Values in Selected Published Prose of EG. NYU 60.
1061 Gore, Luther Y. EG's *Beyond Defeat,* a Critical Edition. (V. 1, Editor's Introduction; V. 2, The Text of *Beyond Defeat.*) Va 64.
1062 Hierth, Harrison E. EG's Ideal of the Lady with Some Contrasts in Sidney Lanier, George W. Cable, and Mark Twain. Wis 56.
1063 Kelly, William W. Struggle for Recognition: A Study of the Literary Reputation of EG. Duke 57.
1064 Kreider, Thomas M. EG: Southern Opponent to the Philistine. Cincinnati 52.
1065 Meyer, Edgar V. The Art of EG. Denver 55.
1066 Moake, Frank B. The Problems of Characterization in the Novels of EG. Ill 57.
1067 Parent, Monique. EG, romancière. Paris 62 publ.
1068 Patterson, Daniel W. EG's Use of Virginia History. NC 59.
1069 Richards, Marion K. The Development of EG as a Novelist. Columbia 61.
1070 Rouse, H. Blair. Studies in the Works of EG. Ill 42.
1071 Santas, Joan F. EG's American Dream. Cornell 63.
1072 Thomas, J. Josef. EG. Ein Beitrag zum Studium des Traditionalismus in der amerikanischen erzählenden Literatur des 20. Jahrhunderts. Cologne 52.
1073 Wehmeier, Helga. Die Widerspiegelung und Entwicklung der ökonomischen und geistigen Struktur des amerikanischen Staates Virginia von 1850 bis 1930 in den Romanen von EG. Berlin (H) 52.
1074 White, James E. Symbols in the Novels of EG. Boston 64.
See also 259, 2617, 4128, 4481.

GLASPELL, SUSAN

1075 Waterman, Arthur E. A Critical Study of SG's Works and Her Contributions to Modern American Drama. Wis 56.

GODKIN, E. L.

1076 Armstrong, William M. ELG and American Foreign Policy, 1865-1900. Stanford H 54.
1077 Christianson, Victor C. ELG as a Utilitarian. Wash 30.
1078 MacLachlin, Mary V. ELG: Utilitarian Editor. Minn 48.
1079 Murray, James G. ELG and the *Nation:* A Study in Political, Economic, and Social Morality. NYU 54.
1080 Rifkin, Lester H. ELG and *The Nation.* Brown 59.

GOLDMAN, EMMA

1081 Drinnon, Richard. EG: A Study in American Radicalism. Minn PS 58.

GOODRICH, S. G.

1082 Roselle, Daniel. SGG, Creator of Peter Parley: A Study of His Life and Work. Columbia 50.

GORDON, CAROLINE

1083 Brown, Samuel A., Jr. CG and the Impressionistic Novel. Vanderbilt 58.
1084 Rocks, James E. The Mind and Art of CG. Duke 66.
See also 259.

GRANT, ROBERT

1085 Obojski, Robert T. RG: Satirist of Old Boston and Intellectual Leader of the New. Western Reserve 55.

GRAYSON, W. J.

1086 Bass, Robert D. WJG's Autobiography. SC 33.
1087 Jarrett, Thomas D. WJG's *The Hireling and the Slave:* A Study of Ideas, Form, Reception, and Editions. Chicago 47.

GREEN, JULIAN

1088 Meyer, Hermann. Die sinnliche und die übersinnliche Welt in den Werken JGs. Hamburg 52.
1089 Stokes, Samuel E. JG and the Thorn of Puritanism. Columbia 54.

GREEN, PAUL

1090 Owens, Henry G. The Social Thought and Criticism of PG. NYU 46.
1091 Treat, Donald R. PG's Concept of Symphonic Drama and Its Application to His Outdoor Plays. Denver 63.

GREEN, ASA

1092 Reed, A. Lachlan. AG, New England Publisher, New York Editor and Humorist, 1789-1838. Minn 53.

GREENE, G. W.

1093 Harrison, Frederick C. The Early Letters of GWG, 1827-1846. Wash 66.

GREENOUGH, HORATIO

See 58, 4595.

GREGORY, HORACE

See 932.

GRIERSON, FRANCIS

1094 Simonson, Harold P. FG: A Biographical and Critical Study. Northwestern 58.

GRISWOLD, R. W.

1095 Bayless, Joy. RWG, Poe's Literary Executor. Columbia 40.

GUINEY, L. I.

1096 Murphy, Sister Mary A. LIG. Fordham 39.
See also 4034.

GUNTER, A. C.

1097 Lowry, Thomas, C. F. A Parallel-Text Edition of *Two Nights in Rome* by ACG. With a Biography and a Check List of ACG's Plays. Chicago 56.

HALE, S. J.

1098 Entriken, Isabelle W. SJH and *Godey's Lady's Book.* Pa 43.

HALIBURTON, T. C.

1099 Chittick, V. L. O. TCH. Columbia 24.

HALL, DAVID

1100 Kany, Robert H. DH: Printing Partner of Benjamin Franklin. Pa State H 63.

HALL, JAMES

1101 Randall, Randolph. JH: A Biography. Columbia 55.

HALL, J. N.
See 2020.

HALLECK, FITZ-GREENE

1102   Adkins, Nelson F.   FGH: An Early Knickerbocker Wit and Poet.   Yale 26.

HAMMETT, DASHIELL

1103   Kenney, William P.   The DH Tradition and the Modern Detective Novel.   Mich 64.

HARLAND, HENRY

1104   Clarke, John J.   HH: A Critical Biography.   Brown 57.

HARRIS, G. W.

1105   Day, Donald.   Life and Works of GWH.   Chicago 42.
1106   Inge, M. Thomas.   The Uncollected Writings of GWH: An Annotated Edition.
Vanderbilt 64.
See also 1743.

HARRIS, J. C.

1107   Brookes, Stella B.   Folklore in the Writing of JCH.   Cornell 46.
1108   Herndon, Jerry A.   Social Comment in the Writing of JCH.   Duke 66.
1109   Ives, Sumner A.   The Dialect of the Uncle Remus Stories.   Tex 50.
1110   Ray, Charles A.   A Study of Realism in the Writings of JCH.   So Cal 52.
1111   Wiggins, Robert L.   JCH: Formative Years.   Va 15.

HART, MOSS

1112   Mason, Richard F.   MH's Plays: The Persistence of a Formula.   Wis T 64.

HARTE, BRET

1113   Brady, Duer S.   A New Look at BH and The *Overland Monthly.*   Ark 62.
1114   Dymke, Irma.   Komik und Humor bei BH.   Berlin (H) 57.
1115   Glover, Donald E.   The Later Literary Career of BH: 1880-1902.   Va 65.
1116   Kessler, Heinrich.   Die Verwendung der Mundart bei BH.   Giessen 28 publ.
1117   Réau, A. Cécile.   La Société californienne de 1850 d'après BH.   Paris 21 publ.
1118   Woods, Hernando J.   A BH Lexicon.   Fla 53.
See also 1619, 3979, 4535, 4541.

HARTLEY, MARSDEN

1119   Burlingame, Robert N.   MH, Painter and Poet.   Brown 54.

HAWTHORNE, JULIAN

1120   Bassan, Maurice.   JH: A Critical Biography.   UCB 60.

HAWTHORNE, NATHANIEL

1121   Abel, Darrel.   The Immortal Pilgrim: An Ethical Interpretation of NH's Fiction.   Mich
1122   Adams, Richard P.   NH: A Study of His Literary Development.   Columbia 51.
1123   Aderman, Ralph M.   NH's English Reputation.   Wis 51.
1124   Arader, Harry F.   American Novelists in Italy: NH, Howells, James,
and F. Marion Crawford.   Pa A 53.
1125   Bales, Allen.   A Study of Point of View in the Novels of NH.   Northwestern 59.
1126   Bangs, Richard F.   The American Criticism of NH: 1949-1964.   St. John's (Brooklyn).
1127   Barnett, Gene.   NH's Use of Setting in His Major Novels.   Wis 61.
1128   Bashore, J. Robert, Jr.   The Villains in the Major Works of NH and Henry James.   Wis 59
1129   Blyth, Marion D.   The Paganism of NH.   So Cal 62.
1130   Boewe, Charles.   Heredity in the Writings of NH, Holmes, and Howells.   Wis 55.
1131   Böhner, Lina.   Brook Farm und NHs *Blithedale Romance.*   Berlin 36 publ.

1132 Bowman, George W. NH and Religion. Ind 54.
1133 Brant, Robert L. NH's Unfortunate Lovers. Wash 60.
1134 Brown, Merle E. The Structure and Significance of NH's *The Marble Faun.* Mich 54.
1135 Campbell, Donald A. A Critical Analysis of NH's *The Blithedale Romance.* Yale 60.
1136 Clay, Edward M. NH's Symbolism as a Synthesis of Permanence and Change. Mo 65.
1137 Cline, John. NH and the Bible. Duke 48.
1138 Coanda, Richard. NH on the Imagination. Wis 60.
1139 Cohen, Benjamin B. Eternal Truth: A Study of NH's Philosophy. Ind 50.
1140 Colacurcio, Michael J. The Progress of Piety: NH's Critique of the Puritan Spirit. Ill 63.
1141 Colson, Theodore. NH and Faulkner: Their Use of Christianity. Mich.
1142 Cook, Larry W. Narrators in the Works of NH. Duke.
1143 Cortissoz, Paul C. The Political Life of NH. NYU 55.
1144 Crane, Maurice A. A Textual and Critical Edition of NH's *Blithedale Romance.* Ill 53.
1145 Crétien, L. E. La Pensée morale de NH (1804-1864), symboliste néo-puritain. Paris 32 publ.
1146 Crowley, Joseph D. NH's *Twice-Told Tales:* A Textual Study Based on an Analysis of the Tales in the Three Major Collections (Volumes I-III). Ohio State 64.
1147 Cuff, Roger P. A Study in Classical Mythology in NH's Writings. Peabody 36.
1148 Curtsinger, E. C. The Byronic Hero and NH's Isolatoes: A Comparative Study. Notre Dame 55.
1149 Cushman, Bigelow Paine. NH's Moral Ambiguity and Bipolarity. Wis 65.
1150 Darnell, Donald G. NH's Emblematic Method. Tex 64.
1151 Davidson, Edward H. The Last Phase of NH's Art. Yale 40.
1152 Dawson, Edward B. NH's Knowledge and Use of New England History: A Study of Sources. Vanderbilt 38.
1153 Denham, Paul. NH's Use of Europe and the Past. Toronto.
1154 Deutsch, Raymond H. NH Periodical Criticism, 1940-1963: An Annotated Bibliography. Loyola.
1155 Dhaleine, L. NH: Sa vie et son oeuvre. Paris 05 publ.
1156 Dolezal, Richard R. The Individual and Society in Selected Novels and Tales of NH: A Study in NH's Use of the Crowd. Loyola (Chicago) 66.
1157 Doubleday, Neal F. NH's Appraisal of New England Life and Thought. Wis 38.
1158 Elder, Marjorie J. Transcendental Symbolists: NH and Melville. Chicago 64.
1159 Fairbanks, Henry G. NH's "Catholic" Critique. Notre Dame 54.
1160 Faust, Bertha B. NH's Contemporary Reputation: A Study of Literary Opinion in England and America, 1828-1864. Pa 37.
1161 Fick, Leonard J. The Theology of NH. Ohio State 51.
1162 Fisher, Arthur W. NH: A Study. Cornell 07.
1163 Flint, Allen D. NH's Political and Social Themes. Minn 65.
1164 Folsom, James K. The Principle of Multiplicity in NH's Fiction. Princeton 59.
1165 Fossum, Robert H. The Inviolable Circle: The Problem of Time in NH's Tales and Sketches. Claremont 63.
1166 Friesen, Menno M. The Mask in NH's Fiction. Denver 64.
1167 Gohlke, Elli. Das Problem der Intersubjektivität in Leben und Werken NHs. Berlin (F).
1168 Gollin, Rita K. Dream and Reverie in the Writings of NH. Minn 61.
1169 Gross, Robert E. A Study of NH's *Fanshawe* and *The Marble Faun:* The Texture of Significance. NYU 60.
1170 Gross, Seymour L. The Technique of NH's Short Stories. Ill 54.
1171 Hall, Lawrence S. NH as a Critic of Nineteenth-Century America. Yale 41.
1172 Hayford, Harrison M. NH and Melville: A Biographical and Critical Study. Yale 45.
1172a Heinitz, Kenneth L. NH's Theory of Art. Loyola (Chicago) 63.
1173 Hollister, Michael A. A Puritan Bouquet: NH's Tales. Stanford.
1174 Hosmer, Elizabeth R. Science and Pseudo-Science in the Writings of NH. Ill 48.
1175 Houston, Neal B. NH and the Eternal Feminine. Tex Tech 65.
1176 Howard, Anne B. NH's Magnetic Chain: The Achievement of Humanity. NM 66.
1177 Hunfeld, Hans. Die Symbolik in NHs Dramen und Erzählungen. Freiburg.

1178 Hunsberger, Claude. The Structural Dimensions of Time and Eternity in NH. Wis.
1179 Janssen, James. NH's Treatment of the Theme of Pride. Wis.
1180 Johnson, Evelyn C. NH and the Supernatural. Stanford 38.
1181 Jones, William B. NH and English Renaissance Allegory. Harvard 62.
1182 Kesterton, David B. Nature in the Life and Works of NH. Ark 64.
1183 Koskelinna, Hazel M. NH and Scott: Parallels and Divergences. Wis.
1184 Kreuter, Kent K. The Literary Response to Science, Technology, and Industrialism:
      Studies in the Thought of NH, Melville, Whitman, and Twain. Wis H 63.
1185 Laser, Marvin. NH and the Craft of Fiction: A Study in Artistic Development.
      Northwestern 48.
1186 Lawson, Alvin H. NH and the Limits of Intellect. Stanford.
1187 Leavitt, Charles. NH's Use of Pageantry. Wis 61.
1188 Leib, Amos P. NH as Scenic Artist. Tulane 63.
1189 Levy, Alfred J. NH's Attitude toward Total Depravity and Evil. Wis 57.
1190 Lundblad, Jane. NH and European Literary Tradition. Uppsala 47.
1191 McInerney, Thomas J. NH, 1825-1850: Literary Apprentice, Magazinist, and
      Experimental Craftsman. Wash 59.
1192 McKiernan, John T. The Psychology of NH. Pa State 58.
1193 McNallie, Robin M. NH and England: His Views on British History and
      Institutions. Princeton.
1194 Magginis, Mary A. NH's Comments on the Arts as Evidence of an Aesthetic
      Theory. NC 48.
1195 Mahan, Helen R. NH's *The Marble Faun:* A Critical Introduction and Annotations.
      Rochester 66.
1196 Marks, Alfred H. NH and Romantic Irony. Syracuse 53.
1197 Masback, Frederic J. The Child Character in NH and James. Syracuse 60.
1198 Mathews, James W. NH and Howells: The Middle Way in American Fiction. Tenn 60.
1199 Meixsell, Anne Bruch. Symbolism in *The Marble Faun.* Pa State.
1200 Miller, Harold P. NH as a Satirist. Yale 36.
1201 Moore, Helen J. The American Criticism of NH, 1938-1948. Pittsburgh 52.
1202 Neff, Merlin. Symbolism and Allegory in the Writing of NH. Wash 39.
1203 Norman, Jean. NH, esquisse d'une analyse de la création artistique. Paris 64 publ.
1204 Ogden, Merlene A. NH and John Bunyan. Neb 64.
1205 Olsen, Frederick B. NH's Integration of Methods and Materials. Ind 60.
1206 Pearson, Norman H. NH's French and Italian Notebooks. Yale 41.
1207 Peters, Leonard J. NH and the Fall of Man. Tulane 53.
1208 Peterson, Annamarie W. NH's Double Focus and Its Use in *The Blithedale Romance.*
      UCLA 65.
1209 Quatermain, P. A. NH and Puritanism: A Study of the Puritan Influences on
      Nineteenth-Century New England Literature. Nottingham 59-60.
1210 Ragan, James. Nature in NH's American Novels. Notre Dame 55.
1211 Rees, John O., Jr. NH and the Emblem. Iowa State 65.
1212 Reid, Alfred S. The Sources of *The Scarlet Letter.* Fla 52.
1213 Resh, Richard. NH's Development of His Major Characters in His Major Novels. Wis.
1214 Reti, Elizabeth. NHs Verhältnis zur Neuenglandtradition. Göttingen 35.
1215 Robey, Richard C. NH's Tales and Sketches. Columbia.
1216 Rodabaugh, Delmer. NH's Use of the English and Italian Past. Minn 51.
1217 Rohrberger, Mary. NH and the Modern Literary Short Story: A Study in Genre.
      Tulane 61.
1218 Rust, R. Dilworth. Character Change and Development in the Major Novels of NH. Wis
1219 Safranek, William P. NH's Use of Setting in His Short Stories. Wis 61.
1220 Sampson, Edward C. The Structure of *The Scarlet Letter* and *The House of the Seven
      Gables.* Cornell 57.
1221 Schlabach, Anne V. A Critical Study of Some Problems Derived from NH's Novels
      and Emerson's *Representative Men.* Wis 47.
1222 Schorer, Calvin E. The Juvenile Literature of NH. Chicago 49.

1223   Schwartz, Arthur M.   The Heart in NH's Moral Vision.   Wis 61.
1224   Schwartz, Joseph M.   NH and Freedom of the Will.   Wis 52.
1225   Smith, Nolan E.   The Image of Puritanism in NH's Fiction.   Yale A.
1226   Stanfield, Elizabeth.   NH's Use of Folklore in His Tales.   Ill.
1227   Stanton, Robert B.   The Significance of Women in NH's American Romances.   Ind 53.
1228   Stein, William B.   The Faust Myth and NH.   Fla 50.
1229   Stewart, Randall.   A Critical Edition of NH's American Notebooks.   Yale 30.
1230   Stock, Ely.   Studies in NH's Use of the Bible.   Brown A 66.
1231   Stubbs, John C.   The Theory of the Prose Romance: A Study in the Background of NH's Literary Theory.   Princeton 64.
1232   Summerhayes, Donald C.   The Relation of Illusion and Reality to Formal Structure in Selected Works of Fiction by NH, Melville, and James.   Yale.
1233   Taylor, J. Golden.   NH's Transmutations of Puritanism.   Utah 58.
1234   Terrell, Horace C.   The NH Problem: Another View.   Wash 39.
1235   Tharpe, Jac L.   Sibyl and Sphinx: Themes of Identity and Knowledge in NH.   Harvard CL 65.
1236   Turcu, Eva.   Der puritanische Geist bei NH.   Vienna 51.
1237   Turner, H. Arlin.   A Study of NH's Origins.   Tex 34.
1238   Vance, William L.   The Comic in the Works of NH.   Mich 62.
1239   Van Pelt, Rachel S.   Folklore in the Tales of NH.   Ill 60.
1240   Veen, Wilhelm.   Die Erzählungstechnik in den Kurzerzählungen NHs.   Münster 38 publ.
1241   Walsh, Thomas F.   NH's Handling of Point of View in His Tales and Sketches.   Wis 57.
1242   Weiffenbach, Rose E.   A Technical Analysis of NH's Style.   Boston 39.
1243   Whelan, Robert E.   The Invisible World of *The Scarlet Letter.*   Mich 61.
1244   White, William M., Jr.   The Personal Philosophy of NH.   Fla 53.
1245   Willauer, George J.   Incongruity in Selected Works of NH.   Pa 65.
1246   Williams, Philip E.   The Biblical View of History: NH, Mark Twain, Faulkner, and Eliot.   Pa 64.
1247   Zaitchik, Joseph A.   NH as Truth-Teller: An Analysis of Moralistic Techniques in the Tales and Sketches.   Boston 65.
       See also 195, 196, 382, 444, 747, 817, 1417, 1426, 1574, 2914, 3423, 3482, 3487, 3523, 4565, 4581.

HAY, JOHN

1248   Ward, Sister Saint Ignatius.   The Poetry of JH.   Catholic 30.

HEARN, LAFCADIO

1249   Briessen, Fritz van.   Stil und Form bei LH.   Giessen 37.
1250   Frost, Orcutt W., Jr.   The Early Life of LH.   Ill 54.
1251   Kitzinger, Angela Mae.   LH and French Literature.   So Cal 58.
1252   Lawless, Ray M.   LH: Critic of American Life and Letters.   Chicago 40.
1253   Morrison, Robert F.   The Growth of the Mind and Art of LH.   Wis 41.
1254   Tuttle, Allen E.   LH and Herbert Spencer.   Northwestern 50.
1255   Wulf, Ingeborg.   Das Japanbild LHs.   Berlin (F) 51.
1256   Yu, Beongcheon.   An Ape of Gods: A Study of LH.   Brown 57.

HEARST, W. R.

1257   Myatt, James A.   WRH and the Progressive Era, 1900-1912.   Fla H 60.

HELLMAN, LILLIAN

1258   Brockington, John.   A Critical Analysis of the Plays of LH.   Yale FA 62.
1259   Haller, C. David.   Social and Moral Themes in the Plays of LH.   Tulane.
1260   Keller, Alvin J.   Form and Content in the Plays of LH: A Structural Analysis.   Stanford 65.
1261   Lederer, Katharine.   LH and the Critics.   Ark.
1262   Triesch, Manfred.   LH: Eine Analyse und Würdigung ihrer Dramen.   Frankfurt 64.

HEMINGWAY, ERNEST

1263 Berendt, Hans D. Die Short-Stories von EH: Entstehung, Form und Stil. (Mit einer EH-Bibliographie.) Bonn 57.

1264 Bobb, Sydney R. Fighter against Loss: The EH Hero. Stanford 54.

1265 Bovie, Verne H. The Evolution of a Myth: A Study of the Major Symbols in the Works of EH. Pa 57.

1266 Brandstätter, Dieter F. Das Problem des Krieges im Werk EHs: Ein Beitrag zur Interpretation der amerikanischen Prosadichtung zwischen den Kriegen (1920-1940). Kiel 51.

1266a Crozier, Rev. Robert D., S.J. A Study of EH's *For Whom the Bell Tolls*. Loyola (Chicago) 65.

1267 Damp, Waldemar. Individuum und Gesellschaft in EHs Romanen. Greifswald 64.

1268 DeFalco, Jospeh M. The Theme of Individuation in the Short Stories of EH. Fla 61.

1269 Doerfel, Hanspeter. EHs Erzählperspektiven. Saarbrucken 64.

1270 Fenton, Charles A. EH's Literary Apprenticeship, 1916-1923. Yale 53.

1271 Fietz, Lothar. Wandlungen der Form im Romanwerk EHs: Untersuchungen zum Wesen des Fiktiven. Tübingen 60.

1272 Gleaves, Edwin S. The Spanish Influence of EH's Concepts of Death, *Nada*, and Immortality. Emory 64.

1273 Gräf, Gerhard, Amerikanische Syntax der Gegenwart bei EH. Jena 56.

1274 Grimes, Sister Mary. EH: The Years with *Esquire*. Ohio State 65.

1275 Gürtler, Lia. Der Bestseller EH. Innsbruck 50.

1276 Halliday, Ernest M. Narrative Technique in the Novels of EH. Mich 50.

1277 Hillebrand-Stadie, Christine. Die Disziplin als ethisches Motiv und stilistisches Prinzip in den Kurzgeschichten EHs. Munich 63.

1278 Kerr, Johnny F. EH's Use of Physical Setting and Stage Props in His Novels: A Study in Craftsmanship. Tex 64.

1279 Killinger, John R., Jr. EH and the Dead Gods. Ky 57.

1280 Lepper, Karl-Hermann. EHs Technik des Erzahlens. Hamburg.

1281 Lewis, Robert W. Eros and Agape: EH's Love Ethic. Ill 63.

1282 Linderoth, Leon W. The Female Characters of EH. Fla State 66.

1283 Linton, Karin. The Literary Reputation of EH in America 1923-1963. UCB.

1284 Longyear, Christopher R. Linguistically Determined Categories of Meanings: A Comparative Analysis of Meaning in "The Snows of Kilimanjaro" in English and German. Mich 61.

1285 Pendleton, Harold E. EH: A Theory of Learning. Ill 59.

1286 Penner, Allen R. EH in Spain. Colo.

1287 Peterson, Richard K. EH: Direct and Oblique. Wash 61.

1288 Ryan, Frank L. *A Farewell to Arms* as Lyric. Catholic.

1289 Schulze, Martin. EH: Werden und Wesen seiner Kunst. Halle 54.

1290 Simon, Charles. The Literary Views and Attitudes of EH. Chicago 56.

1292 Stephens, Robert O. The Escape Motif in the Works of EH. Tex 58.

1293 Stickelmann, Matthias W. View-Point- und Zeitstruktur als Basis morphologischer Interpretation: Eine Darstellung am Roman Gerhart Hauptmanns und EHs. Bonn 55.

1294 Sykes, Robert H. EH's Style: A Descriptive Analysis. Pittsburgh 62.

1295 Sylvester, Bickford. EH's Extended Vision: *The Old Man and the Sea*. Wash 66.

1296 Winkler, Reinhold. Lyrische Elemente in der Prosa EHs. Erlangen.

1297 Wylder, Robert. An Investigation of EH's Fictional Method, Its Sources, and Its Influence on American Literature. Wis 55.

1298 Yokelson, Joseph. Symbolism in the Fiction of EH. Brown 60.

1299 Young, Philip. EH and *Huckleberry Finn:* A Study in Continuity. Iowa A 48.
See also 593, 848, 896, 1662, 1718, 3487, 3872, 4628.

HERGESHEIMER, JOSEPH

1300 Leever, Richard S. JH: Historical Romancer. Ill 61.
1301 Martin, Ronald E. The Achievement of JH in the Art of Fiction. Boston 63.
1302 Napier, James J. JH: A Critical Study. Pa 59.

HERNE, J. A.

1303 Hatlen, Theodore. The Development of JAH as an Exponent of Realism in American Drama. Stanford 50.

HERRICK, ROBERT

1304 Auerbach, Frank L. The Pessimism of RH: A Study of His Postwar Writing. Columbia.
1305 Nevius, Blake R. The Early Novels of RH: A Critical Study. Chicago 47.
1306 Nutley, Grace S. The Social Criticism of RH. NYU 45.
1307 Spangler, George M. The Theme of Salvation in the Novels of RH. UCB 65.
1308 Thompson, Richard J. Themes and Tendencies in the Social Criticism of RH. Buffalo 64.
See also 1031.

HEYWARD, DUBOSE

1309 Durham, Francis M. DH: The Southerner as Artist. Columbia 53.

HIGGINSON, T. W.

1310 Brennan, Sister Thomas C. TWH: Reformer and Man of Letters. Mich State 58.
1310a Edelstein, Tilden G. Strange Enthusiasm: TWH, 1823-1877. Johns Hopkins 62.
1311 Hintz, Howard W. TWH, Disciple of the Newness. NYU 37.
1312 McCormick, Edgar L. TWH as a Literary Critic. Mich 50.

HILDRETH, RICHARD

1313 Emerson, Donald E. RH. Johns Hopkins H 42.
1314 Pingel, Martha M. An American Utilitarian: RH as a Philosopher, with Selections from His Published and Unpublished Works. Columbia 49.
See also 105.

HILLHOUSE, J. A.

1315 Hazelrigg, Charles T. A Biographical Study of JAH. Yale 47.

HOFFMAN, C. F.

1316 Barnes, Homer F. CFH. Columbia 29.

HOLLAND, J. G.

1317 Binney, James A. A Study of the Prose and Editorial Work of JGH. Pittsburgh 47.

HOLLEY, MARIETTA

1318 Blyley, Katherine G. MH. Pittsburgh 37.

HOLMES, O. W.

1319 Goldsmith, Arnold. Determinism, Free Will and Responsibility in the Works of OWH, Henry James, and Frank Norris. Wis 53.
1320 Hayakawa, Samuel I. OWH: Physician, Poet, Essayist. Wis 34.
1321 Kreisman, Arthur. OWH and the Genesis of Naturalism. Boston 52.
1322 Lokensgard, Hjalmar O. A Study of the Essays of OWH. Minn 44.
1323 Phillips, Goldwina N. OWH, Literary Journalist: A Study of the Interpreter of Science for Nineteenth Century America. Denver 65.
1324 Tilton, Eleanor M. Amiable Autocrat: A Biography of Dr. OWH. Columbia 47.

1325 Wallace, Jack E.   The Novels of OWH.   Chicago 60.
1326 Williams, Mentor L.   OWH: The Impact of Science upon Religion in the
      Authentic Brahmin.   Mich 38.
      See also 802, 1130.

HOLMES, O. W., JR.
See 1593.

HOOKER, THOMAS
1327 Denholm, Andrew T.   TH: Puritan Teacher, 1586-1647 (Parts I and II).
      Hartford Seminary Foundation H 61.
1328 Emerson, Everett H.   TH and the Reformed Theology: The Relationship of TH's
      Conversion Preaching to Its Background.   La 55.
1329 Pellman, Hubert R.   TH: A Study in Puritan Ideals.   Pa 58.

HOOPER, J. J.
1330 Smith, Howard W.   An Annotated Edition of JJH's *Some Adventures of Captain
      Simon Suggs.*   Vanderbilt 65.
      See also 1743.

HOPKINSON, FRANCIS
1331 Hastings, George E.   Life and Works of FH.   Harvard 18.

HOVEY, RICHARD
1332 Leffert, Henry.   RH, An American Poet: A Biographical Critique.   NYU 29.
1333 Turner, Katharine C.   RH's Poetry in Its Relation to Certain Dominant Tendencies of
      the 1890's.   Mich 39.

HOWARD, BRONSON
1334 Boyle, Charles J.   BH and the Popular Temper of the Gilded Age.   Wis 57.

HOWARD, SIDNEY
1335 Costy, James O.   A Critical Evaluation of the Selected Plays of SH.   Denver 55.
1336 Housman, A. L.   The Working Methods of SH.   Iowa S 56.
1337 Scott, Charles.   SH.   Yale FA.

HOWE, E. W.
1338 Brune, Ruth E.   The Early Life of EWH.   Colo 49.
1339 Mitchell, Marvin O.   A Study of the Realistic and Romantic Elements in the Fiction of
      EWH, Joseph Kirkland, Hamlin Garland, Harold Frederic, and Frank Norris (1882-1902).
      NC 53.
1340 Ropp, Philip H.   EWH.   Va 49.

HOWELLS, W. D.
1341 Arms, George W.   The Social Criticism of WDH.   NYU 39.
1342 Balcom, Lois.   The Value of a Comparative Analysis of an Author's Autobiographical a
      Fictional Writings for Interpretation of Aspects of His Personality: A Study Based on
      Selected Works of WDH.   NYU Psychology 55.
1343 Baldwin, Marilyn A.   An Edition of WDH's *My Mark Twain:*   Introduction and Notes.
      Rutgers 63.
1344 Ballinger, Richard H.   A Calendar of the WDH Collection in the Library of
      Harvard University.   Harvard 53.
1345 Belcher, Hannah G.   WDH: Magazine Writer (1860-1920).   Mich 42.
1346 Bennett, George N.   WDH: The Boston Years, 1866-1888.   Yale 54.
1347 Boardman, Arthur M.   Social Status and Morality in the Novels of WDH.   UCB 65.
1348 Budd, Louis J.   WDH's Relations with Political Parties.   Wis 49.

1349 Burrows, David J. Point-of-view in the Novels of WDH. NYU 64.
1350 Bush, Charles K. The Effects of Serialization on Structure and Plot in the Novels of WDH. NC.
1350a Butler, Robert E. WDH as Editor of the *Atlantic Monthly*. Rutgers 50.
1351 Buxton, Teresa. A Study of the Relationship of WDH and Samuel Langhorne Clemens. Bucknell 30.
1352 Carrington, George C., Jr. WDH as a Satirist. Ohio State 59.
1353 Carter, Everett. WDH's Theory of Realism in Fiction. UCLA 47.
1354 Coholan, John F. The Portrayal of the Moral World in the Novels of WDH. Notre Dame 51.
1355 Cooke, Delmar G. WDH: A Critical Study. Ill 17.
1356 Cumpiano, Marion. A Study of Artistic Presentation of a Complex, Pluralistic Universe in the Novels of WDH. Columbia.
1357 Daniel, Maggie. WDH's Attitude toward England and English Literature. Wis 53.
1358 Dean, James L. A Comparison of the Earlier and Later Travel Books of WDH. NM.
1359 Dowling, Joseph A. The Reception of WDH. NYU 58.
1360 Eble, Kenneth E. Character and Conscience. A Study of Characterization and Morality in the Novels of WDH. Columbia 56.
1362 Ekstrom, William F. The Social Idealism of William Morris and WDH: A Study of Four Utopian Novels. Ill 47.
1363 Fox, Arnold B. The Progress of Thought in WDH. NYU 47.
1364 Frazier, David L. Symbolism and Realism in the Novels of WDH. NM 65.
1365 Fryckstedt, Olov. WDH and European Literature. Uppsala 58.
1366 Garrow, A. Scott. The Short Novels of WDH. NC 66.
1367 Gauss, Walther. Die Entwicklung von WDH von 1866-1881: WDHs Tätigkeit als Hilfs-und Chefredakteur am *Atlantic Monthly*. Berlin (H) 57.
1368 Goldfarb, Clare R. Journey to Altruria: WDH's Use of Tolstoy. Ind 64.
1369 Hiatt, David F. An Edition of WDH's *Literary Friends and Acquaintance*, with an Introduction Treating Literary Reminiscence as a Genre. NM 60.
1370 Holzschlag, Phyllis-Joyce. WDH's Portraits of Artists. NYU 64.
1371 Hough, Robert L., Jr. WDH: Social Commentator. Stanford 57.
1372 Knickerbocker, M. Robert. WHD and Poetry: Theory, Criticism and Practice. Kan.
1373 Konigsberger, Susanne. Die Romantechnik von WDH. Berlin 33.
1374 Krebsbach, Raymond P. WDH, Mark Twain, Garland and the Agrarian Tradition. Minn.
1375 Kryzanowski, Jerzy R. Turgenev, Tolstoi, and WDH: Transitions in the Development of a Realist. Mich 65.
1376 Lyons, Robert B. The Hero in the Fiction of WDH: 1870 to 1890. Harvard 65.
1377 McMurray, William J. Intention and Actuality in the Fiction of WDH. NM 61.
1378 Malone, Clifton J. The Hitherto Uncollected Critical Opinions of WDH. Okla 47.
1379 Mao, Nathan K. WDH on Evil. Wis 66.
1380 Marshall, Carl L. American Critical Attitudes toward the Fiction of WDH. Ohio State 54.
1381 Marston, Frederic C., Jr. The Early Life of WDH: A Chronicle, 1837-1871. Brown 44.
1382 Meserve, Walter, J., Jr. WDH and the Drama. Wash 52.
1383 Miles, Elton R. WDH: The Impact of Science. Tex 52.
1384 Miller, Charles T. WDH's Theory of the Novel. Chicago 47.
1385 Miloswki, Raymond. WDH: The Promise of a Golden Age and the Quest for Community. Minn.
1386 Moore, Howard K. WDH as a Literary Critic. Boston 50.
1387 Munford, Howard. The Genesis and Early Development of the Basic Attitudes of WDH. Harvard A 51.
1388 Obrecht, Denise M. WDH. Paris 50.
1389 Pattison, Eugene H. WDH's *The Leatherwood God:* Genesis, Artistry, and Reception. Mich 63.
1390 Payne, Alma J. The American Family: WDH. Western Reserve A 56.

1391 Perkins, George B., Jr. The Conflict Between Country and City in the Novels of WDH. Cornell 60.
1392 Reilly, Cyril A. WDH: A Critical Study of *A Modern Instance* and *Indian Summer.* Notre Dame 54.
1393 Renguette, Dale T. The Short Stories of WDH. NC.
1394 Schneider, Clarence E. The Serialized Novels of WDH, 1878-1890. So Cal 57.
1395 Sokoloff, Benjamin A. WDH: The Ohio Years in His Novels. Ill 55.
1396 Stanton, Elizabeth B. WDH: A Study of His Literary Theories and Practices during His *Atlantic Monthly* Years, 1866-1881. Ohio State 43.
1397 Stern, Jerome H. The Late Novels of WDH. NC.
1398 Stiles, Marion L. Travel in the Life and Writings of WDH. Tex 46.
1399 Stronks, James B. The Early Midwestern Realists and WDH. Chicago 56.
1400 Titus, Catherine F. The Depiction of Women in the Novels of WDH. Mo 55.
1401 Walts, Robert W. WDH and the House of Harper. Rutgers 54.
1402 White, Howard H. The Image of Society in the Novels of WDH. Minn 58.
1403 Woodress, James. The Italian Phase of WDH. Duke 50.
      See also 3, 362, 380, 392, 1124, 1130, 1198, 3317, 3423.

HOYT, C. H.

1404 Hunt, Douglas L. The Life and Work of CHH. Vanderbilt 42.
1405 Jones, Leo M. The Structure of the Farces of CHH. Ind.

HUBBARD, ELBERT

1406 Weber, Brom. Spurious Sage: A Study of the Conspiracy Between EH and His Times. Minn 58.

HUGHES, LANGSTON

1407 Emanuel, James A. The Short Stories of LH. Columbia 62.

HUMPHREYS, DAVID

See 413.

HUNEKER, J. G.

1408 Rose, Edgar S. JGH: Critic of the Seven Arts. Princeton 55.
1409 Schwab, Arnold T. The Apprenticeship of a Critic: JGH, 1857-1899. Harvard 51.

HUTCHINSON, ANNE

1410 Battis, Emery J. Troublers in Israel: The Antinomian Controversy in the Massachusetts Bay Colony, 1636-1638. Columbia 58.

IMLAY, GILBERT

1411 Fant, Joseph L. A Study of GI: His Life and Works. Pa.

INGE, WILLIAM

1412 Clarkson, Philip B. The Evolution from Conception to Production of the Dramas of WI. Stanford D 63.
1413 Gobrecht, Eleanor A. A Descriptive Study of the Value Commitments of the Principal Characters in Four Recent American Plays: *Picnic, Cat on a Hot Tin Roof, Long Day's Journey into Night,* and *Look Homeward, Angel.* So Cal D 63.
1414 Lockwood, Patton. The Plays of WI, 1948-1960. Mich State 62.

IRVING, J. T., JR.

1415 Loprete, Nicholas J. The Literary Career of JTI, Jr. Columbia.

IRVING, WASHINGTON

1416 Ballew, Joseph F. The Earlier Letters of WI. Tenn.

1417 Binder, Sister M. Claudia. Studien zur Charakterisierungstechnik in Kurzgeschichten WIs, E.A. Poes, und Nathaniel Hawthornes. Graz 50.

1418 Black, Michael L. A Critical Edition of WI's *History of New York*. Columbia.

1419 Buell, Thomas C. The Professional Idler: WI's European Years—*The Sketch Book* and Its Sequels. Wash 65.

1420 Hedges, William L. The Fiction of History: WI against a Romantic Transition. Harvard A 54.

1421 Künzig, Ferdinand. WI und seine Beziehungen zur englischen Literatur des 18. Jahrhunderts. Heidelberg 11.

1422 McCarter, Pete M. The Literary, Political and Social Theories of WI. Wis 40.

1423 McClary, Ben H. WI and John Murray: An Edited Correspondence. Sussex.

1424 Myers, Andrew B. WI, Fur Trade Chronicler: An Analysis of *Astoria* with Notes for a Corrected Edition. Columbia 64.

1425 Osborne, Robert S. A Study of WI's Development as a Man of Letters to 1825. NC 47.

1426 Pochmann, Henry A. The Influence of the German Tale on the Short Stories of WI, Hawthorne, and Poe. NC 28.

1427 Roth, Martin. Satire and Humor in the Early Writings of WI. Chicago.

1428 Smith, Francis P. WI and France. Harvard RL 38.

1429 Spaulding, Kenneth A. Robert Stuart's *Traveling Memoranda:* A Source for WI's *Astoria*. Iowa 51.

1430 West, Elsie Lee. Gentle Flute: WI as Biographer. Columbia 65.

1431 Young, John P. WI à Bordeaux. Bordeaux 47.
See also 108, 382, 2914.

JACKSON, H. H.

1432 Martin, Minerva L. HHJ, in Relation to Her Time. La 40.

1433 Odell, Ruth. HHJ and Her Times. Neb 37.

JAMES, HENRY

1434 Anderson, Quentin. The American HJ: A Study of the Novelist as a Moralist. Columbia 53.

1435 Arlos, Alma R. "Our Doubt is Our Passion": Ambiguity in Three of the Later Novels of HJ. Radcliffe 62.

1436 Aswell, Edward D. The Art of Aggression: The Short Fiction of HJ, 1888-1898. UCB 64.

1437 Banta, Martha. The Two Worlds of HJ: A Study in the Fiction of the Supernatural. Ind 64.

1438 Bass, Eben E. Ethical Form in the Fiction of HJ. Pittsburgh 61.

1439 Baumgärtel, Werner. HJ im Spiegel moderner englischer Literaturkritik. Tübingen 54.

1440 Beebe, Maurice L. The Alienation of the Artist: A Study of Portraits of the Artist by HJ, Marcel Proust and James Joyce. Cornell 53.

1441 Bennett, Barbara L. The Ethics of HJ's Novels. NC 54.

1442 Bently, Thomas J. The Aesthetics of Discretion: Sexuality in Novels of HJ. Stanford.

1443 Berland, A. HJ and the Nature of Civilization. Cambridge 53-54.

1444 Black, James O. A Novel as a "Work of Art": A Reading of *The Ambassadors*. Ark 58.

1445 Blackall, Jean F. Recurrent Symbolic Elements in the Novels of HJ (1896-1901). Harvard 61.

1446 Bockes, Douglas. The Late Method of HJ. Syracuse 54.

1447 Bogosian, Ezekiel. The Perfect Gentleman: A Study of an Esthetic Type in the Novels of Richardson, Jane Austen, Trollope, and HJ. UCB 37.

1448 Borchers, Lotte. Frauengestalten und Frauenprobleme bei HJ (Ein Beitrag zur amerikanischen Literaturgeschichte). Greifswald 29 publ.

1449 Bosch, Allan. HJ's *American:* The Novel and the Play. Ind.

1450 Bowden, Edwin T., Jr. The Novels of HJ: An Approach Through the Visual Arts. Yale 52.

1451 Brasch, James D. The Relation of Theme and Setting in the Major Novels of HJ. Wis 59.

1452 Buitenhuis, Peter. The American HJ. Yale A 55.

1453 Burstein, Frances B. The Picture of New England Puritanism Presented in the Fiction of HJ. Boston 64.

1454 Büschges, Gisela. Die Kultureinwirkung Europas auf den Amerikaner bei HJ. Freiburg 52.

1455 Byrd, J. Scott. Writers and Artists in the Non-Fiction of HJ. NC.

1456 Chadderdon, Arnold H. Comic Method in HJ's Fiction. Yale 65.

1457 Chen, Lucy M. The Ancestry of *The Wings of the Dove*. Chicago 49.

1457a Clair, John A. The Ironic Dimension in the Fiction of HJ. Western Reserve 64.

1458 Coleman, Elizabeth. HJ's Criticism. Columbia 65.

1459 Coles, Merivan R. Form and Meaning in *The Golden Bowl*. Bryn Mawr 60.

1460 Crotty, Sister M. Madeleine. The Mother in the Fiction of HJ. Fordham 62.

1461 Dankleff, Richard. The Composition, Revisions, Reception, and Reputation of HJ's *The Spoils of Poynton*. Chicago 59.

1461a Deakin, Motley F. The Picturesque in the Life and Work of HJ. UCB 61.

1462 Demel, Erika von Elswehr. Die Wertwelt von HJ. Vienna 44.

1463 De Santis, Alex. The English Fables of HJ: 1895-1900. Princeton.

1464 Diffené, Patricia. HJ. Versuch einer Würdigung seiner Eigenart. Marburg 39.

1465 Donovan, Alan B. The Sense of Beauty in the Novels of HJ. Yale 64.

1466 Dub, Friederike. Die Romantechnik bei HJ. Vienna 33.

1467 Dunbar, Viola R. Studies in Satire and Irony in the Works of HJ. Northwestern 41.

1468 Eakin, Paul J. HJ and the New England Consciousness. Harvard 66.

1469 Edel, Leon. HJ: Les Années dramatiques. Paris 31 publ.

1470 _____. The Prefaces of HJ. Paris 32.

1471 Elderdice, Robert A. HJ's Revisions of His Early Short Stories and Short Novels. Md 52.

1472 Emerson, Donald C. HJ and the Life of the Imagination. Wis 50.

1473 Ferguson, Louis A. HJ and Honoré de Balzac: A Comparative Study in Literary Techniques. Fordham.

1474 Fick, Otto W. The Clue and the Labyrinth: The Mind and Temperament of HJ. Chicago 54.

1475 Finch, George A. The Development of the Fiction of HJ from 1879 to 1886. NYU 4?

1476 Firebaugh, Joseph J. HJ and the Law of Freedom. Wash 52.

1477 Fish, Charles K., Jr. HJ and the Craft of Fiction: The Years of Exploration, 1864-1871. Princeton 64.

1478 Flower, Dean S. The Art of the *Nouvelle:* HJ. Stanford 66.

1479 Foley, Richard N. The Critical Reputation of HJ in American Magazines from 1866 to 1916. Catholic 43.

1480 Forrester, Andrew D. HJ et la France. Lyon 49.

1481 Gale, Robert L. The Caught Image: A Study of Figurative Language in the Fiction of HJ. Columbia 52.

1482 Garnier, Marie-Reine. HJ et la France. Strasbourg 27 publ.

1483 Goldstein, Sallie S. A Critical Study of HJ's *The Wings of the Dove*, *The Ambassadors* and *The Golden Bowl*. Brandeis 63.

1484 Greene, Philip L. HJ and George Eliot. NYU 62.

1485 Grigg, W. Quay. The Technique of Comedy in the Novels of HJ. Pa.

1486 Gutscher, Marianne. HJ und Walter Pater. Vienna 40.

1487 Hall, William F. Society and the Individual in the English Fictions of HJ, 1885-1901. Johns Hopkins 54.

1488 Haney, Charles W. The Garden and the Child: A Study of Pastoral Transformation. Yale 65.

1489 Hart, James S. HJ's Later Novels: The Objectifying of Moral Life. Stanford 54.

1490 Hasler, Jörg. Switzerland in the Life and Work of HJ: The Clare Benedict Collection of Letters from HJ. Basel 66 publ.

1491 Hendrick, Leo T. HJ: The Late and Early Styles. Mich 53.

1492 Heston, Lilla A. A Study of the Point of View in Three Novels by HJ: *The Spoils of Poynton, The Wings of the Dove,* and *The Golden Bowl*. Northwestern 65.

1493 Hicks, Priscilla G. "The Story in It": The Design of HJ's "New York Edition." Boston 60.

1494 Hoag, Gerald B. HJ and Formalist Criticism of the Novel in English in the Twentieth Century. Tulane 65.

1495 Hocks, Richard A. The Problem of Perception in the Late Novels of HJ. NC.

1496 Hofer, Ernest H. The Realization of Conscience in the Later HJ. Cornell 60.

1497 Hoff, Lloyd M. The Revision of *Roderick Hudson:* Its Extent, Nature, and Result. Ohio State 30.

1498 Hofmann, Gert. Interpretationsprobleme bei HJ ("The Turn of the Screw," "The Sacred Fount," "The Figure in the Carpet"). Freiburg 57.

1499 Holder, Alan. Three Voyagers in Search of Europe: A Study of HJ, Ezra Pound, and T. S. Eliot. Columbia 62.

1500 Holland, Laurence B. The Expense of Vision: Essays on the Craft of HJ. Harvard A 65.

1501 Hopkins, Viola. The Art of Seeing: Art Themes and Techniques in the Work of HJ. NYU 60.

1502 Horne, Helen. Basic Ideas of HJ's Aesthetics as Expressed in the Short Stories Concerning Artists and Writers. Marburg 60 publ.

1503 Horowitz, Floyd R. *The Ambassadors:* A Modern Allegory. Iowa 60.

1504 Hughes, Herbert L. Theory and Practice in HJ. Va 23.

1505 Hynes, Joseph A., Jr. HJ's *William Wetmore Story and His Friends:* A Critical Commentary. Mich 61.

1506 Ishizaki, Ayako Tomii. The Psychological Novels of HJ and Matsume Soseki. Pa.

1507 Isle, Walter W. Experiments in the Novel: HJ's Fiction, 1896-1901. Stanford 61.

1508 Johnson, Alice E. A Critical Analysis of the Dislocated Character as Developed in the Major Novels of HJ. Wis 57.

1509 Jones, Walter P. An Examination of HJ's Theory and Practice of Fiction. Cornell 25.

1510 Kaufman, Marjorie R. HJ's Comic Discipline: The Use of the Comic in the Structure of His Early Fiction. Minn 55.

1511 Kelley, Cornelia P. The Early Development of HJ. Ill 30.

1512 Kraft, Quentin G. A Study of Point of View in Selected Short Stories of HJ. Duke 63.

1513 Krause, Sydney J. HJ's Revisions of *The Portrait of a Lady:* A Study of Literary Portraiture and Perfectionism. Columbia 56.

1514 Krehayn, Joachim. HJ und seine Stellung zu England oder der Bürger auf der Suche nach der Bürgerlichkeit. Berlin (H) 51.

1515 Kretzschmar, Helmut. Der Begriff des "consciousness" bei HJ. Hamburg.

1516 Krickel, Edwin F., Jr. HJ and America. Vanderbilt 55.

1517 Küsgen, Reinhardt. Die Kurzgeschichten HJs. Erlangen.

1518 Labrie, Ross. Religion of Consciousness in the Fiction of HJ, 1881-1899. Toronto.

1519 Lebowitz, Naomi. HJ and the Moral Imperative of Relationship. Washington (St. Louis) 62.

1520 Leonard, Vivien R. An Introductory Study of Imagery in the Prefaces to the New York Edition of the Novels and Tales of HJ. Columbia 66.

1521 Levy, Edward R. HJ and the Pragmatic Assumption: The Conditions of Perception. Ill 64.

1522 Levy, Leo B. Versions of Melodrama in the Novels, Tales, and Plays of HJ: 1865-1897. UCB 54.

1523 Lind, Sidney E. The Supernatural Tales of HJ: Conflict and Fantasy. NYU 48.

1524 Lowe, Alma L. The Travel Writing of HJ. Rice 55.

1525 Lucas, John S. HJ's Revisions of His Short Stories. Chicago 49.

1526 McCarthy, Harold T. The Aesthetic of HJ. Harvard 50.

1527 McGinty, Sister Mary C. The Jamesian Parenthesis: Elements of Suspension in the Narrative Sentences of HJ's Late Style. Catholic 64.

1528 McKenzie, Terence J. An Analysis of HJ's Interpretation and Treatment of English Character, Culture, and Morals. Va.

1529 Maixner, Paul R. HJ and the Question of Formal Unity. Columbia 66.

1530 Markow, George. HJ et la France (1843-1876). Paris 52.
1531 Marshall, James M. Patterns of Freedom in HJ's Later Novels. Syracuse 61.
1532 Mays, Milton A. Uptown and Downtown in HJ's America: Sexuality and the Business-Society. Minn 65.
1533 Menikoff, Barry. Narrative Techniques in the Tales of HJ. Wis.
1534 Minter, Elsie G. The Image in the Mirror: HJ and the French Realists. NC 63.
1535 Mintzlaff, Dorothy. The Theme of the Unlived Life in the Fiction of HJ. Mich.
1536 Mlikotin, Anthony M. The International Theme in the Novels of Turgenev and HJ. Ind 60.
1537 Mossman, Robert E. An Analytical Index of the Literary and Art Criticism by HJ. Pittsburgh 66.
1538 Murphy, Edward F. HJ and Katherine Anne Porter: Endless Relations. Ottawa 59.
1539 Murray, Donald M. The Critical Reception of HJ in English Periodicals, 1875-1916. NYU 51.
1540 Nettels, Elsa. The Drama of Consciousness: The Role of the Central Intelligence in Selected Novels of HJ. Wis 60.
1541 Nies, Frederick J. HJ's *The Princess Casamassima:* Its Revisions, Background, and Reception. SC.
1542 Noel, France. HJ, peintre de la femme. Paris 42 publ.
1543 O'Leary, Sister Jeanine, R.H.S.M. The Function of City as Setting in Dickens's *Our Mutual Friend,* Trollope's *The Way We Live Now,* HJ's *The Princess Casamassima,* and Conrad's *The Secret Agent.* Notre Dame 65.
1544 Parquet, Mary E. HJ: The Bliss and the Bale. Neb 59.
1545 Penfield, Lida S. HJ and the Art of the Critic. Boston 38.
1546 Peterich, Werner. HJ und das literarische Experiment. Munich.
1547 Petesch, Natalie M. The Ceremony of Innocence: A Study of Narrative Techniques in HJ. Tex 62.
1548 Poirier, William R. Fiction of Comedy and the Early HJ. Harvard 59.
1549 Powers, Lyall H. HJ and French Naturalism. Ind 55.
1550 Pratt, William C., Jr. Revolution Without Betrayal: HJ, Pound, Eliot, and the European Tradition. Vanderbilt 57.
1551 Prausnitz, Walther G. The Craftsmanship of HJ: A Study of the Critical Reviews, 1864-1884. Chicago 56.
1552 Purdy, Strother B. The Language of HJ with Emphasis on His Diction and Vocabulary. Wis 60.
1553 Ramadan, A. M. The Reception of HJ's Fiction in the English Periodicals Between 1875 and 1890. London 59-60.
1554 Ranald, Ralph A. HJ and the Social Question: "Freedom" and "Life" in the Social Novels of the 1880's. Princeton 62.
1554a Reid, Stephen A. The Role of Technique in HJ's Later Novels. UCB 61.
1555 Roberts, Louise A. HJ's Criticism on Nineteenth-Century America. Chicago 46.
1556 Roberts, Morris. HJ's Literary Criticism. Harvard 28.
1557 Rosenbaum, Stanford P. Studies for a Definitive Edition of HJ's *The Spoils of Poynton* (Vols. I and II). Cornell 60.
1558 Rupp, Henry R. HJ's *The Ambassadors:* Its Text and Evolution. NYU.
1559 Salisbury, Howard E. Wish Fulfillment as Moral Crisis in Fiction of HJ. Wash 62.
1560 Sauer, Edwin H. HJ: The Symbols of Morality in the Novels of the Middle Period, 1881-1900. Cincinnati 51.
1561 Saveson, Marilyn B. The Influence of Emile Zola upon the Theory and Practice of Some English Novelists of His Time [HJ, George Moore, George Gissing, and Arnold Bennett]. Cambridge 56.
1562 Scholes, James B. American and British Criticism of HJ: 1916-1953. NC 61.
1563 Schulte, Rainer O. HJ and Marcel Proust: A Study in Sensibility. Mich 65.
1564 Schwertman, Mary P. HJ's Portraits of Ladies. NC.
1565 Sharp, Sister M. Corona. The Role of the Confidante in HJ. Notre Dame 62.
1566 Sölter, Ursula. Die Romanauffassung bei HJ und in der englischen Literaturkritik der 1920er Jahre. Mainz 56.

1567 Solomon, Jan K. The Puritan, the Gentleman, and the Artist: A Study of the Conflict between Ethics and Aesthetics in the Novels of HJ. Mich 64.

1568 Solotaroff, Theodore. *The Bostonians:* A Social and Literary Study. Chicago.

1569 Spanos, B. The Essential HJ: The American Years, 1843-1870. London 54-55.

1570 Stader, Karl-Heinz. Die Bewusstseinskunst von HJ. Bonn 53.

1571 Stafford, William T. The American Critics of HJ: 1864-1943. Ky 56.

1572 Steinkamp, Egon. Das Fremdheitserlebnis bei HJ: Die Mächte Europa und Amerika im Leben und Werk des Schriftstellers. Münster 56.

1573 Stone, Edward. HJ and His Sense of the Past. Duke 50.

1574 Switzer, John W. HJ's Debt to Hawthorne. Mo.

1575 Tallman, Warren E. Drama of a High Civilization. Preliminary Studies in HJ's Fiction. Wash 58.

1576 Taylor, Christy M. The Pictorial Element in the Theory and Practice of HJ. Stanford 55.

1577 Terrie, Henry L., Jr. Pictorial Method in the Novels of HJ. Princeton 55.

1578 Thomas, William A. HJ: A Study in Realism from the Beginnings in the First Quarter of the Nineteenth Century to 1870. Pa 34.

1578a Tilley, W. H., Jr. The Background, the Writing and the Reception of *The Princess Casamassima.* Chicago 64.

1579 Todasco, Ruth T. The Humanism of HJ: A Study of the Relation between Time and Imagery in the Later Novels. Tex Tech 63.

1580 Traschen, Isadore. HJ: The Art of Revision, a Comparison of the Original and Revised Versions of *The American.* Columbia 52.

1581 Vaid, Krishna B. The Tales of HJ: A Critical Study. Harvard 61.

1582 Volpe, Edmond L. HJ and the Conduct of Life: A Study of the Novelist's Moral Values. Columbia 54.

1583 Von Klemperer, Elizabeth G. The Fiction of HJ and Joseph Conrad in France: A Study in Penetration and Reception. Radcliffe 58.

1584 Ward, Joseph A., Jr. Evil in the Fiction of HJ. Tulane 57.

1585 White, Sidney H. HJ's *The American Scene.* So Cal 62.

1586 Wiesenfarth, Brother Joseph. HJ and the Dramatic Analogy: A Study of the Major Novels of the Middle Period. Catholic 62.

1587 Winslow, Cedric. HJ and the Dilemma of the American Tradition. NYU.

1588 Woelfel, Karl. Dramaturgische Wandlungen eines epischen Themas bei Dramatisierung und Verfilmung, dargestellt an HJs *Washington Square.* Erlangen 55.
See also 195, 392, 1124, 1128, 1197, 1232, 1319, 1591, 1755, 2630, 2681, 3317, 3357, 3423, 3437, 3482, 3517, 3523, 3547, 4167a.

JAMES, WILLIAM

1589 Beard, Robert W. The Concept of Rationality in the Philosophy of WJ. Mich P 62.

1590 Davis, A. R. WJ and the New York Literary Scene, 1837-1855. Columbia.

1591 Gragg, Perry E. The Revelation of Consciousness: The Psychology of WJ and Five Novels of Henry James. Tex 60.

1592 Reilly, William F., Jr. The Pragmatism of WJ as a Religious Philosophy. Fordham P 61.

1593 Silver, Cherry B. WJ, Oliver Wendell Holmes, Jr., Thorstein Veblen: American Intellectual Prose, 1870-1910. Harvard 64.

1594 Tebbe, Margaret M. Contributions of WJ to Speech and Theatre. Ind S 62.
See also 2649.

JEFFERS, ROBINSON

1595 Adams, John H. RJ. A Reinterpretation and Reevaluation. Denver.

1596 Breen, Robert S. Symbolic Action in Oral Interpretation of RJ's *Roan Stallion.* Northwestern S 50.

1597 Brophy, Robert J. The Aesthetics of RJ in Relation to His World View. NC.

1598 Coffin, Arthur B. Ideological Patterns in the Work of RJ. Wis 65.

1599 Kiley, George B. RJ: The Short Poems. Pittsburgh 57.

1600 Powell, Lawrence C. An Introduction to RJ. Dijon 32.

1601   Ridgeway, Ann N.   The Letters of RJ: A Record of Four Friendships.   Corresponden
       with George Sterling, Albert Bender, Benjamin de Casseres, Mark Van Doren.   Bowling
       Green State 66.
1602   Scott, Robert I.   RJ's Poetic Use of Post-Copernical Science.   SUNY (Buffalo) 64.
1603   Spiese, Richard D.   RJ's Aesthetic Theory and Practice.   NM 66.
1604   Squires, James R.   RJ and the Doctrine of Inhumanism.   Harvard 52.
1605   Stephens, George D.   The Narrative and Dramatic Poetry of RJ: A Critical Study.
       So Cal 53.
1606   Weedin, Everett K., Jr.   Ritualism and Naturalism in the Poetry of RJ.   Cornell.
       See also 2504

JEFFERSON, THOMAS

1607   Arnold, Malcolm H.   TJ: A Pioneer in Anglo-Saxon.   Va 15.
1608   Bär, Max.   TJ, eine Entwicklungsgeschichte seiner demokratischen Ideen.
       Erlangen 51.
1609   Colbourn, Harold T.   The Saxon Heritage: TJ Looks at English History.   Johns
       Hopkins H 53.
1610   Coleman, John.   The Concept of Equality as Held by TJ.   Pittsburgh P 34.
1611   Dodd, William E.   TJs Rückkehr zur Politik 1796.   Leipzig 00.
1612   Koch, Adrienne.   The Philosophy of TJ.   Columbia P 44.
1613   Lindley, Thomas F., Jr.   The Philosophical Presuppositions of TJ's Social Theories.
       Boston P 52.
1614   Martin, Edwin T.   TJ and the Idea of Progress.   Wis P 42.
1615   Montgomery, Henry C.   TJ and the Classical Tradition.   Ill H 46.
1616   Peden, William H.   TJ: Book Collector.   Va 42.
1617   Peterson, Merrill D.   The TJ Image in the American Mind, 1826-1861.   Harvard A 50.

JEWETT, S. O.

1618   Bishop, Ferman.   The Mind and Art of SOJ.   Wis 55.
1619   Friedl, Ute.   Die Erziehung des Lokalkolorits in den Werken von SOJ, George
       Washington Cable, und F. Bret Harte.   Graz 53.
1620   Frost, John E.   SOJ.   NYU 53.
1620a Magowan, Robert A.   The Art of the Pastoral Narrative: Sand, Fromentin, Jewett.
       Yale 64.
1621   McGuire, Mary Agnes.   SOJ.   Columbia 64.
1622   Reggio, Kathryn D.   SOJ: A Woman of Compassion.   St. John's (Brooklyn) 53.
1623   Sougnac, Jean.   SOJ.   Paris 37.
       See also 4475a.

JOHNSON, J. W.

1624   Levy, Eugene D.   JWJ: A Study in Negro Leadership.   Yale.
1625   Tate, Ernest C.   The Social Implications of the Writings and the Career of JWJ.   NYU

JOHNSTON, R. M.

1626   Brinson, Lessie B.   A Study of the Life and Works of RMJ.   Peabody 38.

JOHNSTON, W. P.

1627   Shaw, A. Marvin.   The Life and Works of WPJ.   La 41.

JONES, R. M.

1628   Atkins, Gordon C.   A Critical Examination of the Mystical Idealism of RMJ.   So Cal
       R 60.

JUDD, SYLVESTER

1629   Hathaway, Richard D.   The Lapse of Uriel: The Conversions of SJ.   Western
       Reserve 65.

KAUFMAN, G. S.

1630 Lembke, Russel W. The Esthetic Values of Dissonance in the Plays of GSK and His Collaborators. Iowa S 46.

KELLY, GEORGE

1631 Wills, Arthur. The Dramatic Works of GK. Kan.

KELLY, HUGH

1632 Turner, Thomas D. HK as a Dramatist. Iowa S.

KENNEDY, J. P.

1633 Bohner, Charles H. JPK: Novelist and Nationalist. Pa A 57.
1634 Gwathmey, Edward M. JPK. Va 26.
1635 Osborne, William S. JPK: A Study of His Literary Career. Columbia 60.
1636 Pretzer, Wallace L. Eighteenth-Century Literary Conventions in the Fictional Style of JPK (1795-1870). Mich E 63.
1637 Walhout, Clarence P. Religion in the Thought and Fiction of Three Ante-Bellum Southerners: JPK, Caruthers, and Simms. Northwestern 64.

KING, CHARLES

1638 Burton, Wilfred C. The Novels of CK, 1844-1933. NYU 62.
1639 Filipiak, Jack. General CK, Forgotten Novelist of the Frontier Army. Denver.

KING, CLARENCE

1639a Crosby, Harry H. So Deep a Trail: A Biography of CK. Stanford 53.
1640 Wilkins, Thurman. CK: A Biography. Columbia 57.

KING, GRACE

1641 Kelley, Marion. The Life and Works of GK. La.

KIRKLAND, C. S.

1642 Keyes, Langley, C. CSK: A Pioneer in American Realism. Harvard 36.

KIRKLAND, JOSEPH

1643 Henson, Clyde E. The Life and Work of JK: An Introduction to an Edition of *Zury: The Meanest Man in Spring County.* Western Reserve 50.
1644 Holaday, Clayton A. JK: Biography and Criticism. Ind 50.
See also 1339.

KLEIN, CHARLES

1645 Kahn, Leonel L. CK, American Dramatist. Tulane.

KREYMBORG, ALFRED

1646 Weist, Elizabeth M. AK in the Art Theater. Mich 65.

KRUTCH, J. W.

1647 Green, Gordon C. An Analytical Study of the Dramatic Criticism of JWK as Published in *The Nation,* 1924-1952. So Cal S 59.
1648 Green, Joseph G. JWK: Critic of the Drama. Ind 65.
1649 Herrscher, Walter J. JWK: A Critical Study. Wis.

KUMMER, CLARE

1650 Finizio, Victor L. CK: An Analysis of Her Plays and Musicals. Iowa S 65.

LAMPMAN, ARCHIBALD

1651 Connor, Carl Y. AL: Canadian Poet of Nature. Columbia 29.

LA FARGE, OLIVER
See 3872.

LANE, CHARLES

1652 Cummins, Roger W. CL and American Transcendentalism. Minn.

LANIER, SIDNEY

1653 Abernethy, Cecil E. A Critical Edition of SL's *Tiger-Lilies.* Vanderbilt 40.
1654 DeBellis, Jack A. SL and the Morality of Feeling. UCLA 64.
1655 Graham, P. E. SL's Thought in Relation to His Age. Chicago 27.
1656 Havens, Elmer A. SL's Concept and Use of Nature. Wis 65.
1657 Howard, C. Jeriel. SL and His South. Tex Christian.
1658 Niessner, Gertrude. SL als Lyriker und seine metrischen Theorien. Vienna 39.
1659 Norman, Jean. SL, essai de delimitation du domaine poétique. Paris 64.
       See also 1062.

LARDNER, RING

1660 Adams, Dick. RL's America. Minn.
1661 Frakes, James R. RL: A Critical Survey. Pa 53.
1662 Rodnon, Stewart. Sports, Sporting Codes, and Sportsmanship in the Work of RL, James
       T. Farrell, Ernest Hemingway, and William Faulkner. NYU 61.
1662a Webb, Howard W., Jr. RL's Conflict and Reconciliation with American Society.
       Iowa A 53.

LAWSON, J. H.

1663 Brown, Richard P. JHL as an Activist Playwright: 1923-1937. Tulane 64.
1664 McCreath, Harrison W. A Rhetorical Analysis of the Plays of JHL. Stanford S 65.

LAZARUS, EMMA

1665 Zeiger, Arthur. EL: A Critical Study. NYU 51.

LEGARÉ, H. S.

1666 Christophersen, Merrill G. A Rhetorical Study of HSL: South Carolina Unionist.
       Fla S 54.
1667 Rhea, Linda. HSL: A Charleston Intellectual (1797-1843). Vanderbilt 32.

LEGGETT, WILLIAM

1668 Proctor, Page S., Jr. The Life and Works of WL, 1801-1839. Yale 49.

LELAND, C. G.

1669 Lang, Anton. CGL und sein Hans Breitmann. Göttingen 32.
1670 Smith, Ralph C. A Biography of CGL (1824-1903). NM A.

LENNOX, CHARLOTTE

1671 Séjourné, Philippe. CL: America in her Works and Life. Paris 65.

LEWIS, SINCLAIR

1673 Bischof, Liselotte. Frauen bei SL. Vienna 50.
1674 Bucco, Martin. The Serialized Novels of SL: A Comparative Analysis of Periodical
       and Book. Mo 63.
1675 Coleman, Arthur B. The Genesis of Social Ideas in SL. NYU 54.
1676 Conroy, Stephen S. The American Culture and the Individual in the Novels of SL.
       Iowa 66.
1677 Couch, William, Jr. The Emergence, Rise, and Decline of the Reputation of SL.
       Chicago 54.

1678 Daniel, Benne B. SL, Novelist and Speaker: A Comparison of the Themes and Rhetorical Methods Used in Three of His Public Addresses to the Themes and Methods Used in Six of His Novels. Okla S 62.

1679 Edener, Wilfried. Die Religionskritik in den Romanen von SL. Erlangen 63 publ.

1680 Eicke, Gustav. Der Wirtschaftsgeist des Amerikaners im Spiegel von SLs Romanen. Leipzig 39 publ.

1681 Feinberg, Leonard. SL as a Satirist. Ill 46.

1682 Formandl, Hanns. Die sprachlichen Eigentümlichkeiten in den Romanen von SL. Vienna 30.

1683 Grebstein, Sheldon N. SL, American Social Critic. Mich State 54.

1684 Ianni, Laurence. SL's America. Western Reserve.

1685 Kähler, Christa. Die Ideen der Tradition und des Fortschritts im Romanwerk von SL. Freiburg 54.

1686 Kopka, Hans W. Grundlagen und Grenzen der Gesellschaftskritik bei SL. Berlin (H) 51.

1687 Lenk, Walter. Das Amerikabild in den Romanen von SL. Vienna 50.

1688 Light, Martin. A Study of Characterization in SL's Fiction. Ill 60.

1689 Riss, Josefine. Die Amerikakritik bei SL. Graz 48.

1690 Schönfelder, Karl-Heinz. SL als Sozial-und Kulturkritiker. Leipzig 49.

1691 Storch, Willy. SL und das amerikanische Kultur-und Sprachbild. Marburg 38.

1692 Wasmuth, Hans-Werner. Slang bei SL. Hamburg 36 publ.
See also 288, 3352, 3817.

LEWISOHN, LUDWIG

1693 Hespen, Richard C. LL: A Critical Study. Mich.

LINCOLN, ABRAHAM

1694 Basler, Roy P. AL in Literature: The Growth of an American Legend. Duke 31.

1695 Ford, William H. Problems of AL Biography. Pittsburgh 42.

1696 Garner, Wayne L. AL and the Uses of Humor. Iowa 63.

1697 Nary, Bruce L. A Study of Major AL Dramas in Relationship to Selected AL Biographies. Mich S 56.

LINDSAY, VACHEL

1698 Gerstmann, Ilse. Die Technik des Bewegungseindrucks in Gedichten von Edith Sitwell und VL. Greifswald 36.

1699 Heffernan, Miriam M. The Ideas and Methods of VL. NYU 48.

1700 Kuykendall, Radford B. The Reading and Speaking of VL. Northwestern S 52.

1701 Scouffas, George. VL: A Study in Retreat and Repudiation. Ill 51.

1702 Wolfe, Glenn J. VL: The Poet as Film Theorist. Iowa S 64.
See also 1799.

LIPPARD, GEORGE

1703 Greer, Kirk. GL: Novelist and Social Reformer. Pa.

LIPPMANN, WALTER

1704 Forcey, Charles B., Jr. Intellectuals in Crisis: Croly, Weyl, WL, and the *New Republic,* 1900-1919. Wis H 55.

1705 Weingast, David E. WL: A Study in Personal Journalism. Columbia 49.

LIVERIGHT, HORACE

1706 Gilmer, Frank W. HL: Publisher of the Twenties. Northwestern 63.

LONDON, JACK

1707 Baskett, Sam S. JL's Fiction: Its Social Milieu. UCB 51.

1708 Carlson, Roy W. JL's Heroes: A Study of Evolutionary Thought. NM 61.

1709 Holland, Robert B. JL: His Thought and Art in Relation to His Time. Wis 50.
1710 Labor, Earle G. JL's Literary Artistry: A Study of His Imagery and
Symbols in Relation to His Themes. Wis 61.
1711 Margolin, Clara. JLs Short-Stories: Ihre Form und ihr Gehalt. Heidelberg 27.
1712 Pope, Margaret I. JL: A Study in Twentieth-Century Values. Wis 35.
1713 Price, Starling. JL's America. Minn.
1714 Rentmeister, Heinrich. Der Mensch in der Natur und in der Gesellschaft. Das
Weltbild JLs. Leipzig 58.
1715 Rothberg, Abraham. The House that Jack Built: A Study of JL. Columbia 52.
1716 Shivers, Alfred S. Romanticism in JL: A Study of Romantic Qualities in His Life
and in Selected Short Stories and Novels. Fla State 62.
1717 Stadlmann, Ingeborg. JL: Weltanschauung, Schriftstellerisches Werken und
Romantechnik. Vienna 35.
1718 Weltz, Friedrich. Vier amerikanische Erzählungszyklen. JL: *Tales of the Fishpatro*
Sherwood Anderson: *Winesburg, Ohio;* John Steinbeck: *The Pastures of
Heaven;* Ernest Hemingway: *In Our Time.* Munich 53.
1719 Wilcox, Earl J. JL and the Tradition of American Literary Naturalism. Vanderbilt 6
1720 Young, Thomas D. JL and the Era of Social Protest. Vanderbilt 50.
See also 494, 2504, 3317, 4535.

LONGFELLOW, H. W.

1721 Appelmann, Maria. HWLs Beziehungen zu Ferdinand Freiligrath. Münster 16.
1722 Bardacke, Theodore. A Critical Study of HWL's Poetry. Syracuse 50.
1723 Broili, Otto. Die Hauptquellen von HWLs, "Song of Hiawatha." Würzburg 98.
1724 Campbell, Thomas M. HWLs Wechselbeziehungen zu der deutschen Literatur (Teil I:
Deutsche Elemente in HWLs Werken). Leipzig 07.
1725 Crosby, Robert R. HWL as a Dramatist. Ind S 58.
1726 Deiml, Otto. Der Prosastil HWLs: Der Einflusz von Jean Paul auf HWLs
Prosastil. Erlangen 38 publ.
1727 Goggio, Emilio. Italian Influences on HWL's Art. Harvard RL 17.
1728 Hart, Loring E. The Critical Reception of HWL in America, 1834-1856.
Harvard 61.
1729 Hilen, Andrew R., Jr. HWL's Relationship with the Scandinavian Languages and
Literature. Yale 43.
1730 Martin, Ernest. L'Evangéline de HWL et la suite merveilleuse d'un poème. Bordeaux
36 publ.
1731 Morin, Paul. Les Sources de l'oeuvre de HWL. Paris 13 publ.
1732 O'Neill, Joseph E., S.J. Imagery in the Poetry of HWL. Columbia 55.
1733 Salminen, Leena. HWL's Literary Reputation. Helsinki.
1734 Schmidt, Alfred C. HWL's Divine Tragedy. Leipzig 05 publ.
1735 Schulze, Bernard. Das Religiöse bei HWL und dessen Stellung zur Bibel.
Leipzig 13 publ.
1736 Schumacher, J.C.A. Sources of HWL's Poetry. Yale 94.
1737 Silbiger, Josef. HWL als Dramatiker. Vienna 11.
1738 Thompson, Lawrance. Young HWL (1807-1843). Columbia 38.
1739 Ward, Robert S. HWL's Lehrjahre. Boston 51.
1740 Werner, Friedrich. Die Entwicklung des Naturgefühls und der künstlerischen
Wiedergabe desselben bei HWL. Leipzig 10.
1741 Whitman, Iris L. HWL and Spain. Columbia RL 27.
1742 Worden, J. Percy. Über HWLs Beziehungen zur deutshen Literatur. Halle 00.

LONGSTREET, A. B.

1743 Gooch, Margaret M. The Narrator in the Humorous Tales of ABL, Baldwin,
Thompson, Hooper, and G. W. Harris. NC.
1744 Wade, John D. ABL. Columbia 23.

LOWELL, J. R.

1745 Burack, Irving. Étude critique des poèmes inédites de JRL. Paris 39 publ.

1746 Clark, George P. Classical Influences and Background in the Writings of JRL. Yale 48.

1747 De Saegher, William J. JRL and the Bible. UCLA 64.

1748 Downer, James W. Features of New England Rustic Pronunciation in JRL's *Biglow Papers*. Mich 58.

1748a Duncan, Graham H. JRL's Reviews of American Belles-Lettres: An Annotated Anthology. Cornell 53.

1749 Fitz-Gerald, A. Boylan, Jr. The Literary, Political, and Religious Ideas of JRL. Drew 43.

1750 Grommon, Alfred H. JRL's Writings on Liberty, Abolition, and Public Affairs (1836-1861). Cornell 43.

1751 Hanawalt, Murvle H. JRL and Matthew Arnold: A Comparative Study of Their Literary Theories. Iowa 43.

1752 Heil, Johann A. Die Volkssprache im Nordosten der Vereinigten Staaten von Amerika (dargestellt auf Grund der *Biglow Papers* von JRL). Giessen 27 publ.

1753 Hursley, Frank M. The Social Attitudes and Convictions of JRL during His First Creative Period, 1838-1851. Minn 42.

1754 Klibbe, Lawrence H. The Spanish Experiences of JRL. Syracuse 54.

1755 LeClair, Robert C. Three American Travelers in England: JRL, Henry James, and Henry Adams. Pa 44.

1756 McFadyen, Alvan R. The Contemporaneous Reputation of JRL. Fla 55.

1757 Murray, Byron D. JRL's Criticism of Dryden and Pope. Iowa 46.

1758 Nisbet, Ada B. Some Letters of Thomas Hughes to JRL: A Chapter in Anglo-Americana. UCLA 47.

1759 Reilly, Joseph J. JRL as a Critic. Yale 12.

1760 Reinhardt, John E. JRL's Appraisal of American Life and Thought. Wis 50.

1761 Shea, Leo M. JRL's Religious Outlook. Catholic 26.

1762 Smith, Thelma M. The Uncollected Periodical Poems of JRL. Pa A 45.

1763 Voss, Arthur W. The *Biglow Papers* of JRL. Yale 41.
     See also 802.

LOWELL, ROBERT

1763a Mazzaro, Jerome L. The World of RL. Wayne State 63.

LYON, H. M.

1764 Lyon, Zoe. A Comparative Study of Diverse Aspects of Realism and Naturalism in the Short Story Form: Maupassant in France and HML in America. Fla State 65.

LYTLE, ANDREW

1765 Hatley, B. Elizabeth. The Quest Theme in the Fiction of AL. Emory.

MC CONNEL, JOHN

1766 Bain, Robert A. JM and Pre-Civil War Fiction of the Middle West. Ill 64.

MC CULLERS, CARSON

1767 Millichap, Joseph R. The Heart as Center: A Study of CM's Fiction. Notre Dame.

1768 Smith, Simeon M. CM: A Critical Introduction. Pa 64.

1769 Sullivan, Margaret. A Study of the Works of CM. Duke.

MACDOWELL, K. S. B.

1770 Frank, William L. KSBM: A Critical Biography. Northwestern 64.

MC FEE, WILLIAM

1771 Martin, Donald M. The Sea Novels of WM. Mich 58.

MC HENRY, JAMES

1772 Blanc, Robert E.   JM (1785-1845), Playwright and Novelist.   Pa 39.

MACKAYE, BENTON

1773 Bryant, Paul T.   The Quality of the Day: The Achievement of BM.   Ill 65.

MACKAYE, PERCY

1774 Christ, Robert.   PM: The Theories and the Man.   Fla.
1775 Torp, Thaddeus L.   PM: American Masque Maker.   Iowa.
      See also 1954.

MACKAYE, STEELE

1776 Curry, Wade C.   SM: Producer and Director.   Ill S 58.

MACLEISH, ARCHIBALD

1777 Campbell, Colin C.   The Poet as Artist and Citizen: A Study of the
      Life and Writings of AM Through 1958.   Pa 60.
1778 Carrington, Richard H.   AM: A Study of his Prosody for the Oral Interpreter.
      Wis S 65.
1779 Doyle, Esther M.   The Nature of Verse in Drama, with Special Reference to *J.B.,
      A Play in Verse,* by AM.   Northwestern S 64.
1780 Maher, Mary S.   Man and the Natural Condition: Some Aspects of Primitivism in the
      Poetry of AM.   Ariz 65.
1781 Morin, Edward A., Jr.   An Interpretive Study of AM's Plays.   Loyola (Chicago).
1782 Wendt, Viola S.   AM: A Study of His Art and Ideas.   Wis 47.

MAILER, NORMAN

1783 Bickford, George F.   NM: His Critical Reception.   Md.
1784 Scott, James B.   The Individual and Society: NM *versus* William Styron.   Syracuse 6
      See also 3414, 4285.

MALTZ, ALBERT

1785 Brüning, Eberhard.   AM: Ein amerikanischer Arbeitsschriftsteller.   Leipzig 54.

MARCH, WILLIAM

1786 Silva, Frederick.   The Cracked Looking-Glass: A Critical Evaluation of the Fiction of
      WM.   Ind.
      See also 4481.

MARKHAM, EDWIN

1787 Goldstein, Jesse.   Life of EM.   NYU 45.   [Thesis accepted, but degree not granted.]
1788 Synnestvedt, Sigfried T.   Bread, Beauty, and Brotherhood: The Ethical
      Consciousness of EM.   Pa 59.

MARKOE, PETER

1789 Diebels, Sister M. Chrysostom.   PM (1752-1792), A Philadelphia Writer.   Catholic 43.

MARQUAND, J. P.

1790 Abshagen, Hans-Ulrich.   JPM, der Chronist der Oberschicht Neuenglands.   Berlin (H)
1791 Burgstaller, Heimo.   Die Erzähltechnik JPMs.   Graz 62.
1792 Cochran, Robert W.   In Search of Perspective: A Study of the Serious Novels of JPM
      Mich 57.
1793 Elliston, Angela.   The Craftsmanship of JPM.   Ill.
1794 Harris, Bennett.   The Literary Achievement of JPM.   Cincinnati 62.
1795 Johnson, Robert O.   JPM and the Novel of Manners.   Wash 64.
      See also 3447.

MASTERS, E. L.

1796 Flaccus, Kimball. ELM: A Biographical and Critcal Study. NYU 52.

1797 Hartley, Lois T. ELM: A Critical Study. Ill 49.

1797a Narveson, Robert D. ELM's *Spoon River Anthology:* Background, Composition, and Reputation. Chicago 62.

1798 Weeg, Mary Margaret. The Prose of ELM: Its Revelation of His Views and Its Significance in His Canon. Ind 64.

1799 Yatron, Michael. The Influence of Populism on ELM, Vachel Lindsay, and Carl Sandburg. Temple 57.

MATHER, COTTON

1799a Bercovitch, Sacvan. New England Epic: A Literary Study of CM's *Magnalia Christi Americana.* Claremont 65.

1800 Campbell, Philip S. CM. Brown R 55.

1801 McCandlish, George E. Annotations for a New Edition with a Definitive Text of CM's *Magnalia Christi Americana* (1702), Books I and II. Harvard A 63.

1802 Manierre, William R., II. CM and the Plain Style. Mich 57.

1803 Portz, John T. CM and Rationalism. Harvard 58.

MATHER, INCREASE

1804 Murdock, Kenneth B. IM: Foremost American Puritan. Harvard 23.

1805 Watkins, Harold K. The Ecclesiastical Contributions of IM to Late Seventeenth and Early Eighteenth Century Puritan Thought. Pacific School of Religion R 64.

MATHEWS, CORNELIUS

1806 Mahan, Ronald G. A Critical Biography of CM. Tenn.

MATTHEWS, BRANDER

1807 Bender, Jack E. The Theatre of BM. Mich S 54.

MAYHEW, JONATHAN

1808 Lewis, Earl E. The Limits of Power and the Rights of Resistance in the Sermons of JM. Minn.

MELVILLE, HERMAN

1809 Anderson, Charles R. HM in the South Seas. Columbia 36.

1810 Bach, Bert C. Narrative Point-of-View in the Fiction of HM after *Moby-Dick.* NYU.

1811 Bagley, Carol L. HM's Trilogy: Symbolic Precursor of Freudian Personality Structure in the History of Ideas. Wash State 66.

1812 Baird, James R. HM and Primitivism. Yale 47.

1813 Barrett, Laurence N. Fiery Hunt: A Study of HM's Theories of the Artist. Princeton 49.

1814 Barry, Sister Marie. The Problem of Shifting Voice and Point of View in HM's Early Novels and *Moby-Dick.* Catholic 52.

1815 Battenfeld, David H. I Seek for Truth: A Comparative Study of HM's *Moby-Dick* and *Pierre.* Stanford 58.

1816 Beharriell, Stanley R. The Head and the Heart in HM. Wis 54.

1817 Bennett, John. HM's Humanitarian Thought: A Study in Moral Idealism. Wis 56.

1818 Bernstein, John A. Pacifism and Rebellion in the Writings of HM. Pa 61.

1819 Bezanson, Walter E. HM's *Clarel.* Yale 43.

1820 Blansett, Barbara R. HM and Emersonian Transcendentalism. Tex 63.

1821 Boies, Jack J. HM: Nihilist. Wis 59.

1822 Bowen, Merlin S. Self and Experience in the Writings of HM. Chicago 57.

1823 Braswell, William. HM and Christianity. Chicago 34.

1824 Braun, Julie. Spiritual Journey: HM's Use of *Sartor Resartus*. UCLA.

1825 Brodtkorb, Paul, Jr. HM's Symbology. Yale 63.

1826 Camp, James E. An Unfulfilled Romance: Image, Symbol, and Allegory in HM's *Clarel*. Mich 65.

1827 Canaday, Nicholas, Jr. HM and Authority: A Study of Thematic Unity. Fla 57.

1828 Clavering, Rose. The Conflict Between the Individual and Social Forces in HM's Works *Typee* to *Moby-Dick*. NYU 54.

1828a Cockcroft, Geroge P. The Two HMs. Columbia 64.

1829 Cowen, Wilson W. HM's Marginalia. Harvard 65.

1830 Creeger, George R. Color Symbolism in the Works of HM: 1846-1852. Yale 52.

1831 Davis, Frank M. HM and the Churches. Duke.

1832 Davis, Merrell R. HM's *Mardi:* The Biography of a Book. Yale 47.

1833 Dryden, Edgar A. HM's Narrators and the Art of Fiction: A Study in Point of View. Johns Hopkins 65.

1834 Eckardt, Mary E. An Interpretive Analysis of the Patterns of Imagery in *Moby-Dick* and *Billy Budd*. Notre Dame 62.

1834a Elliott, Patrick F. HM's Tragic Vision: An Essay in Theological Criticism. Chicago

1835 Ensslen, Klaus. Stil- und strukturanalytische Untersuchungen von HMs *Tales* (einschl. *Billy Budd*). Munich.

1836 Farnsworth, Robert M. HM's Use of Point of View in His First Seven Novels. Tulane 57.

1837 Fiess, Edward. Byron and Byronism in the Mind and Art of HM. Yale 51.

1838 Fine, Ronald E. HM and the Rhetoric of Psychological Fiction. Rochester 66.

1839 Finkelstein, Dorothee Grdseloff. HM and the Near East. Yale A 57.

1840 Fite, Olive LaRue. The Interpretation of HM's *Billy Budd*. Northwestern 56.

1841 Foster, Elizabeth S. HM's *The Confidence Man,* Its Origins and Meaning. Yale 41.

1842 Franklin, Howard B. HM's Mythology. Stanford 61.

1843 Gilman, William H. HM's Early Life and *Redburn*. Yale 47.

1844 Graves, Robert D. Polarity in the Shorter Fiction of HM. Duke 66.

1845 Grenberg, Bruce L. Thomas Carlyle and HM: Parallels, Obliques, and Perpendiculars. NC 63.

1846 Griffith, Frank C. HM and the Quest for God. Iowa 53.

1847 Gross, John J. HM and the Search for Community. Iowa 55.

1848 Guetti, James L. The Failure of the Imagination: A Study of HM, Conrad, and Faulkner. Cornell 64.

1849 Gupta, Raj Kumar. Form and Style in HM's *Pierre: Or the Ambiguities*. Pittsburgh 64.

1850 Haave, Ethel-Mae. HM's *Pierre:* A Critical Study. Yale 48.

1851 Hall, Joan J. Some Problems of Structure in HM's Novels. Stanford 61.

1852 Hayman, Allen. HM's Theory of Prose Fiction: In Contrast with Contemporary Theories. Ill 61.

1853 Heflin, Wilson L. HM's Whaling Years. Vanderbilt 52.

1854 Helmcke, Hans. Die Funktion des Ich-Erzählers in HMs Roman *Moby-Dick*. Mainz 55.

1855 Hetherington, Hugh. The Reputation of HM in America. Mich 33.

1856 Hillway, Tyrus. HM and Nineteenth-Century Science. Yale 44.

1857 Hoffman, Leonard R. Problems in HM: The Style from the Beginning through *Moby-Dick*. Stanford 54.

1858 Horsford, Howard C. HM's *Journal of a Visit to Europe and the Levant, October 11, 1856-May 6, 1857*. Princeton 52.

1859 Hoyle, Norman E. HM as a Magazinist. Duke 60.

1860 Humbach, Änne. Aspekte der Wortbildung bei HM. Freiburg 59.

1861 Jarrard, Norman E. Poems by HM: A Critical Edition of the Published Verse. Tex 6

1862 Jones, Walter D. A Critical Study of HM's *Israel Potter*. Ala 62.

1863 Kaplan, Sidney. HM and the American National Sin. Harvard.

1864 Kenny, Vincent S. HM's *Clarel*. NYU 65.

1865 Key, Howard C.   The Influence of Travel Literature upon HM's Fictional Technique.
Stanford 53.
1866 Key, James A.   An Introduction to HM's Bird Imagery.   Tulane 66.
1867 Kimpel, Ben D.   HM's Thought after 1851.   NC 42.
1868 Knapp, Joseph G.   Tortured Torturer of Reluctant Rhymes: HM's *Clarel,* an
Interpretation of Post-Civil War America.   Minn 62.
1869 Kosok, Heinz.   Die Bedeutung der Gothic Novel für das Erzählwerk HMs.   Marburg 62
publ.
1870 Lebowitz, Alan L.   HM's Ahab: The Evolution and Extinction of the Hero.   Harvard
64.
1871 Little, Thomas A.   Literary Allusions in the Writings of HM.   Neb 50.
1872 Long, Raymond.   The Hidden Sun: A Study of the Influence of Shakespeare on the
Creative Imagination of HM.   UCLA 65.
1873 Lucas, Thomas E.   HM as Literary Theorist.   Denver 63.
1874 McCarthy, Paul E.   Theme and Structure in the Novels of HM.   Tex 62.
1875 McEniry, William H.   The Young Melville.   Vanderbilt 42.
1876 Magaw, Malcolm O.   HM and the Christian Myth: The Imagery of Ambiguity.
Tulane S 64.
1877 Mahoney, Mother M. Denis.   *Clarel:* An Investigation of Spiritual Crisis.   Catholic 57.
1878 Mangold, Charlotte W.   HM in German Criticism from 1900 to 1955.   Md 59.
1879 Mansfield, Luther S.   HM: Author and New Yorker, 1844-1851.   Chicago 35.
1879a Meldrum, Barbara H.   HM's *Mardi, Moby-Dick,* and *Pierre:* Tragedy in Recoil.
Claremont 64.
1880 Morehead, Barbara.   HM's Use of the Narrator in *Moby-Dick.*   Chicago 51.
1881 Nault, Clifford A., Jr.   HM's Two-Stranded Novel: An Interpretation of *Moby-Dick*
as an Enactment of Father Mapple's Sermon and the Lesser Prophecies, with an Essay on
HM Interpretation.   Wayne State 60.
1882 Newbery, Ilse S.   The Unity of HM's *Piazza Tales.*   British Columbia 64.
1883 Oliver, Egbert S.   HM and the Idea of Progress.   Wash 40.
1884 Packard, Robert.   A Study of HM's *Clarel.*   Columbia 63.
1885 Parker, Herschel C.   HM and Politics: A Scrutiny of the Political Milieux of HM's
Life and Works.   Northwestern 64.
1886 Plumstead, Arthur W.   HM's Concern with Time.   Rochester 60.
1887 Pommer, Henry F.   Milton's Influence on HM.   Yale 46.
1888 Pops, Martin L.   The Winding Quest: A Study of HM.   Columbia 65.
1889 Rasco, Lavon.   The Biographies of HM: A Study in Twentieth-Century Biography.
Northwestern 56.
1890 Roper, Gordon H.   An Index of HM's *Mardi, Moby-Dick, Pierre* and *Billy Budd.*
Chicago 43.
1891 Rosen, Bruce J.   *Typee* and *Omoo:* HM's Literary Apprenticeship.   NYU 65.
1892 Rosen, Roma.   HM's Uses of Shakespeare's Plays.   Northwestern 62.
1893 Rosenberry, Edward H.   The Comic Spirit in the Art of HM.   Pa 53.
1894 Runden, John P.   Imagery in HM's Shorter Fiction: 1853-1856.   Ind 52.
1895 Scott, Sumner W.   The Whale in *Moby-Dick.*   Chicago 50.
1896 Scott, Wilbur S., Jr.   HM's Originality. A Study of Some of the Sources of *Moby-Dick.*
Princeton 43.
1897 Sealts, Merton M.   HM's Reading in Ancient Philosophy.   Yale 41.
1898 Seelye, John D.   The Iridescent Scabbard: HM's Ironic Mode.   Claremont 61.
1899 Seltzer, Leon F.   The Vision of HM and Conrad: A Comparative Study.   SUNY
(Buffalo).
1900 Semmens, John E.   Point of View in the Early and Later Fiction of HM.   Notre
Dame 65.
1901 Shulman, Robert P.   Toward *Moby-Dick:* HM and Some Baroque Worthies.   Ohio
State 59.
1902 Silberman, Donald J.   Form and Point of View in HM's Fiction.   SUNY (Buffalo) 65.
1903 Simon, Jean.   HM, marin, metaphysicien, et poète.   Paris 41 publ.

1904 Sperling, Helmut. HM als Kritiker seiner Zeit. Berlin (H) 54.
1905 Star, Morris. HM's Use of the Visual Arts. Northwestern 64.
1906 Stavig, Richard T. HM's *Billy Budd:* A New Approach to the Problems of
Interpretation. Princeton 53.
1907 Stern, Milton R. Theme and Craft in HM: Fine Hammered Steel. Mich State 55.
1908 Stevens, Sister Mary Dominic, O. P. The Con Man: A Study in HM and Mark
Twain. Loyola.
1909 Sundermann, Karl H. HMs Gedankengut: Eine kritische Untersuchung seiner
weltanschaulichen Grundlagen. Berlin 37.
1910 Sweetser, Margaret S. HM's Conception of the Great Writer and His Experiments in
Literary Manners. Minn 52.
1911 Thurman, Howard K. HM: Humanitarian and Critic of Politics. Iowa 50.
1912 Tick, Stanley. Forms of the Novel in the Nineteenth Century: Studies in
Dickens, HM, and George Eliot. UCSD 66.
1913 Trimpi, Helen P. Romance Structure and HM's Use of Demonology and Witchcraft in
Moby-Dick. Harvard 66.
1914 Vogel, Dan. HM's Shorter Published Poetry: A Critical Study of the Lyrics in *Mardi,*
of *Battle-Pieces, John Marr,* and *Timoleon.* NYU 56.
1915 Ward, Joseph T. HM: The Forms and Forces of Evil. Notre Dame 59.
1916 White, Viola C. Symbolism in HM's Writings. NC 34.
1917 Williams, John B. The Impact of Transcendentalism on the Novels of HM. So Cal 65
1918 Wolpert, Bernard M. The HM Revival: A Study of Twentieth-Century Criticism
through Its Treatment of HM. Ohio State 52.
1919 Wright, Nathalia. HM and the Bible. Yale 49.
1920 Yaggy, Elinor. *Pierre:* Key to HM Enigma. Wash 46.
1921 Zimmerman, Michael P. HM in the 1920's: A Study in the Origins of the HM Reviva
with an Annotated Bibliography. Columbia 63.
1922 Zirker, Priscilla A. The Major and Minor Themes of HM's *White-Jacket.* Cornell 66.
See also 444, 754, 1158, 1172, 1184, 1232, 2150, 2501, 3482, 3523, 3982, 4128, 456.

MENCKEN, H. L.

1923 Hickman, William. Influence of Attitude Toward Religion upon the Writings of HLM
Pittsburgh 63.
1924 Nolte, William H. The Literary Criticism of HLM. Ill 59.
1925 Pickett, Roy G. HLM's Rhetorical Battle. Iowa 60.
1926 Simpson, Herbert M. HLM and Nathan. Md 65.
1927 Singleton, Marvin K. A History of the *American Mercury* under the Editorship of HL
1924 to 1933. Duke 60.
1928 Stenerson, Douglas C. A Genetic History of HLM's "Prejudices," 1880-1926. Minn
1929 Thoma, George N. A Study of the Rhetoric in HLM's Essays, 1917-1927. Chicago 5
1930 Turaj, Frank. A Study of the Significance of HLM. Brown A.
See also 90.

MERRILL, STUART

1931 Henry, Marjorie-Louise. La Contribution d'un américain au symbolisme français:
SM. Paris 27 publ.

MERTON, THOMAS

1932 Campbell, Susan M. The Poetry of TM: A Study in Theory, Influences, and Form.
Stanford FA 54.

MIFFLIN, LLOYD

1933 Criswell, Carl S. LM: His Art and His Poetry. Pa 55.

MILLAY, E. ST. V.

1934 King, Grace H. The Development of the Social Consciousness of ESM as Manifested i
Her Poetry. NYU 43.

1935 Patton, John. ESM as a Verse Dramatist. Colo 62.
1936 Pettitt, Jean. ESM: A Critical Study of Her Poetry in Its Literary and Social Milieu. Vanderbilt 55.

MILLER, ARTHUR

1937 Aaron, Chloe. The Dilemma of the Mid-Twentieth Century Man as Seen in the Plays of AM. Geo Wash.
1938 Calvery, Catherine A. Illusion in Modern American Drama: A Study of Plays by AM, Tennessee Williams, and Eugene O'Neill. Tulane S 64.
1939 Johnson, Robert G. A General Semantic Analysis of Three of AM's Plays: *Death of a Salesman, The Crucible,* and *All My Sons.* Denver S 63.
1940 Johnson, Vernon E. Dramatic Influences in the Development of AM's Concept of Social Tragedy. Peabody 62.
1941 Martin, Robert A. The Major Plays and Critical Thought of AM to the *Collected Plays.* Mich 65.
1942 Murray, Edward J. Structure, Character, and Theme in the Plays of AM. So Cal 66.
1943 Van Allen, Harold. An Examination of the Reception and Critical Evaluation of the Plays of AM in West Germany from 1950-1961. Ark 64.
See also 2030, 3026.

MILLER, HENRY

1944 Baxter, Annette K. Parts of the Mosaic: HM as Expatriate. Brown 58.
1945 Bedford, Richard C. The Apocatastasis of HM. Iowa 60.
1946 Gordon, William A. HM and the Romantic Tradition. Tulane 63.
1947 Mitchell, Edward B. HM: The Artist as Seer. Conn 64.
See also 2694.

MILLER, JOAQUIN

1948 Peterson, Martin S. JM: His Life and Works. Neb 32.
1949 Reade, Frank R. Cincinnatus Hiner Miller: A Critical Biography. Va 26.
See also 4541.

MISTRAL, GABRIELA

1950 Hernandez, Mary F. B. GM and the Standards of American Criticism. NM 63.

MITCHELL, MARGARET

1951 Verdross, Dorothea. Die Darstellung der Verhältnisse des Südens der Vereinigten Staaten zur Zeit des Bürgerkrieges und der Rekonstruktionszeit in MMs *Gone with the Wind.* Innsbruck 46.

MITCHELL, S. W.

1952 Rein, David M. SWM as a Psychiatric Novelist. Western Reserve 50.

MOODY, W. V.

1953 Anderson, Wallace L. Some Critical Attitudes toward Poetry in America as Reflected in the Development of the Reputation of WVM as a Poet, 1900-1912. Chicago 49.
1954 Davis, Charles T. The Poetic Drama of WVM, Robinson, Torrence, and Mackaye, 1894-1935. NYU 51.
1955 Dilworth, Mary L. WVM and the Movement for Poetic Drama in America. Ill 43.
1956 Gilde, Erna. WVM. Berlin 40.
1957 Henry, David D. WVM. Pa State 31.
1958 Lichtenstein, Hyman. WVM: A Poet on the Eve of the American Poetic Renaissance. Columbia 59.

MOORE, J. T.

1959 Green, Claud B. JTM: A Tennessee Man of Letters. Duke 53.

MOORE, MARIANNE

1960 Carey, Sister Mary C. The Poetry of MM: A Study of Her Verse, Its Sources, and Its Influences. Wis 59.
1961 Rees, Ralph. The Imagery of MM. Pa State 56.
1962 Warlow, Francis W. MM: Unfalsifying Sun and Solid Gilded Star. Pa 59.

MORE, P. E.

1962a Connolly, Sister Reginald M., O.P. PEM: An Appreciation of the Critical Theory in the Shelburne Essays. St. John's (Brooklyn) 63.
1963 Davies, Robert M. The Humanism of PEM. Pa 54.
1964 Duggan, Francis X. PEM and the American Tradition. Pa 60.
1965 Mayfield, William H. Platonism and Christianity in the Work of PEM. Ind P 54.
1966 Parsons, Vesta M. The Social Criticism of PEM. NYU Soc 51.
1967 Wise, R. Eugene. Democracy and the Puritan Estimate of Man: An Inquiry into the World and Thought of PEM and Reinhold Niebuhr. Syracuse.
1968 Zoller, William O. The Literary Criticism of PEM. UCB 46.
See also 89, 90, 92, 2897.

MORRIS, G. P.

1969 Auser, Cortland P. The Contribution of GPM to American Journalism. NYU 60.

MORRIS, WRIGHT

1970 Brenner, Jack. WM: Novelist and Critic. NM.

MORSE, JEDIDIAH

1971 Morse, James K. JM: A Champion of New England Orthodoxy. Columbia P 39.

MORTON, THOMAS

1972 Connors, Donald F. Enchanted Wilderness: A Commentary on TM's *New England Canaan.* Columbia.
1973 Major, Minor W. TM and His *New England Canaan.* Colo 57.

MOSHER, T. B.

1974 Huntress, Keith G. TBM: A Biographical and Literary Study. Ill 42.

MOTLEY, J. L.

1975 Gutheim, Marjorie Frye. JLM. Columbia H 55.
1976 Loomis, Edward W. A Study of JLM. Stanford 59.
1977 Lynch, Sister Claire, O.S.B. The Diplomatic Mission of JLM to Austria, 1861-1867. Catholic H 45.
1978 Schantz, Bradford T. The Mind and Art of JLM. Wis 39.
See also 103.

MOWATT, A. C.

1979 Blesi, Marius. The Life and Letters of ACM. Va 38.

MUIR, JOHN

1980 Cosbey, Robert C. JM. Ohio State 49.
1981 Hadley, Edith J. JM's Views of Nature and Their Consequences. Wis 56.
1982 Weber, Daniel B. JM: The Function of Wilderness in an Industrial Society. Minn 64.
See also 238.

MUMFORD, LEWIS

1983 Dow, Eddy W. LM's First Phase: A Study of His Work as a Critic of the Arts in America. Pa 65.
1984 Sclarenco, Carl D. LM: The Utopian Focus. Minn.

NABOKOV, VLADIMIR

1985   Feldman, Leonard.   VN's American Fiction.   Columbia.

NATHAN, G. J.

1986   Rudin, Seymour.   GJN: A Study of His Criticism.   Cornell 53.
1987   Smyth, Richard R.   The Critic and the Playwright: The Influence of GJN on the Playwriting of O'Neill, O'Casey, and Saroyan.   Cornell.

NATHAN, ROBERT

1988   Trachtenberg, Stanley.   RN's Fiction.   NYU 63.

NEAL, JOHN

1989   Lease, Benjamin.   The Literary Theory and Practice of JN.   Chicago 49.
1990   Richards, Irving T.   The Life and Works of JN.   Harvard 33.

NEIHARDT, J. G.

1991   Aly, Lucile F.   JGN as Speaker and Reader.   Mo S 59.
1992   Grant, Paul.   The Poetic Development of JGN.   Pittsburgh 58.

NEMEROV, HOWARD

1993   Meinke, James P.   The Writings of HN.   Minn 65.

NEWCOMB, C. K.

1994   Kennedy, Judith.   The *Journals* of CKN.   Brown 42.

NIEBUHR, REINHOLD

1995   Damhorst, Rev. Donald E.   Social Norms and Protestant Ethics: The Ethical Views of RN and R. Richard Niebuhr.   St. Louis P 63.
1996   Trobaugh, Robert J.   The Nature of Man in the Writings of RN and William Faulkner.   Vanderbilt R 66.
1997   Wright, Palmer.   The "New Liberalism" of the Fifties: RN, Lionel Trilling, David Riesman, and the American Intellectual.   Mich.
   See also 1967.

NOCK, A. J.

1998   Cziraky, J. Sandor.   The Evolution of the Social Philosophy of AJN.   Pa H 59.

NORRIS, FRANK

1999   Beranek, Henriette.   Das "Gilded Age" im Romanwerk des FN.   Vienna 51.
2000   Davison, Richard A.   FN's Aesthetic Theory and Artistic Practice.   Wis 64.
2001   Dillingham, William B.   Themes and Literary Techniques in the Fiction of FN.   Pa 61.
2002   Gardner, Sara J.   Social Thought in the Writings of FN.   Wash State 66.
2003   Hill, John S.   FN's Heroines.   Wis 60.
2004   Johnson, George W.   Romance and Realism in the Novels of FN.   Columbia 60.
2005   Kaplan, Charles.   FN and the Craft of Fiction.   Northwestern 52.
2006   Klein, Karl-Heinz.   FNs Erzählungswerk im Verhältnis zu seiner Kunsttheorie.   Marburg 52.
2007   Lundy, Robert D.   The Making of *McTeague* and *The Octopus*.   UCB 55.
2008   Marchand, Ernest L.   FN: A Study.   Wis 38.
2009   Olafson, Robert B.   FN's Seven Novels: A Study of the Mosaic of Tensions Between Critical Realism and Naturalism in the Works.   Wash 66.
2010   Ramsay, Orrington C.   Setting in FN.   Wis 49.
2011   Ray, Robert J.   Symbolism in the Novels of FN.   Tex 62.
2012   Schloss, Gilbert A.   FN, Form and Development.   Wis 63.
2013   Walker, Frank D.   FN: A Biographical and Critical Study.   UCB 32.
   See also 494, 495, 1319, 1339, 3317, 3381.

NORTON, C. E.

2014 Dubois, Colette. CEN, 1827-1908. Paris 52.
2015 Marsden, Malcolm M. CEN: An Intellectual Biography. Syracuse 51.
2016 Shaffer, Robert B. CEN and Architecture. Harvard FA 51.
2017 Vanderbilt, Kermit. Democracy and Culture: The Ideas and Work of CEN. Minn 56.

NOYES, J. H.

2018 Blankenship, W. Russell. The Perfectionism of JHN in Relation to Its Social Backgroun
Wash 35.

NYE, E. W.

2019 Blair, Walter. The Background of Bill Nye in American Humor. Chicago 31.

O'BRIEN, FREDERICK

2020 Roulston, Charles R. Eden and the Lotus-Eaters: A Critical Study of the South Sea
Island Writings of FO, James Norman Hall, and Robert Dean Frisbie. Md 66.

O'CONNOR, FLANNERY

2021 Asals, Frederick. A Critical Study of the Fiction of FO. Brown.
2022 Blackwell, Louise. The Artistry of FO. Fla State.
2023 Connolly, Janet M. FO: The Writer and Her Country. Columbia.
2024 Keane, Mother Mary St. Jerome, S.H.C.J. Structural Irony in FO. Loyola (Chicago).
2025 Martin, Carter. A Critical Study of the Fiction of FO. Vanderbilt.
2026 Muller, Gilbert. FO and the Catholic Grotesque. Stanford.

ODETS, CLIFFORD

2027 Kaufman, Jack H. A Study of the Plays of CO. Mich State.
2028 Kuryk, David. Love's Thin Awkward Plant: A Study of the Work of CO in
Regard to the Individual and His Relationship to Society. Wis 64.
2029 Mendelsohn, Michael J. CO: A Critical Study. Colo 62.
2030 Sheldon, Neil. Social Commentary in the Plays of CO and Arthur Miller. NYU S 63.
2031 Shuman, R. Baird. Social Concepts in the Stage Plays of CO. Pa 61.
2032 Wagner, Arthur. Technique in the Revolutionary Plays of CO. Stanford D 62.

O'HARA, JOHN

2033 Bassett, Charles W. The Fictional World of JO. Kan 64.
2034 Sedlack, Robert P. Manners, Morals, and the Fiction of JO. Notre Dame 65.
See also 3447.

OLMSTED, F. L.

2035 Mitchell, Broadus. FLO: A Critic of the Old South. Johns Hopkins H 24.

O'NEILL, EUGENE

2036 Adams, William J. The Dramatic Structure of the Plays of EO. Stanford S 57.
2037 Alexander, Doris M. Freud and EO: An Analysis of *Strange Interlude.* NYU 52.
2038 Arbenz, Mary H. The Plays of EO as Presented by the Theatre Guild. Ill D 61.
2039 Arndt, Horst. EOs antitraditionalistische Gesellschaftskritik. Munich 56.
2040 Bernstein, Samuel J. EO: Theatre Artist. A Description of and Commentary upon
Craftsmanship of Four Plays by EO. Brandeis 64.
2041 Burns, Sister M. Vincentia. The Function of Wagner's Theory of the Union of the Art
in the Dramaturgy of EO. Pa 43.
2042 Cook, Thomas E. EO's Use of Dramatic Imagery, 1920-1930: A Study of Six Plays.
Tulane 62.
2043 Dalven, Rae. The Concepts of Greek Tragedy in the Major Plays of EO. NYU 61.
2044 Dawson, William M. The Female Characters of August Strindberg, EO, and Tennessee
Williams. Wis S 64.

2045 Digeser, Andreas. Form-und Darstellungsprobleme bei EO. Freiburg 54.
2046 Dubler, Walter. EO, Wilder, and Albee: The Uses of Fantasy in Modern American Drama. Harvard 64.
2047 Elrod, James F. The Structure of EO's Serious Drama. Ind S 59.
2048 Engel, Edwin A. Recurrent Themes in the Drama of EO. Mich 53.
2049 Falk, Doris V. EO and the Tragic Tension. Cornell 52.
2050 Ficca, John. EO's Critical Reputation in America. Iowa D 62.
2051 Fiskin, Abram M. EO: The Study of a Developing Creed through the Medium of Drama. Minn 64.
2052 Fitch, Polly May. The Language of the Last Three Major Plays of EO. Stanford S 66.
2053 Fox, Josef. Probability in the Plays of EO. Chicago 53.
2054 Fuhrmann, Günther. Der Atridenmythos in modernen Drama: Hauptmann, EO, Sartre. Würzburg 50.
2055 Göttler, Willibald. Tiefenpsychologisches in den Dramen EOs. Erlangen 54.
2056 Hahn, Vera T. The Plays of EO: A Psychological Analysis. La 39.
2057 Hartman, Murray. Strindberg and EO: A Study in Influence. NYU 60.
2058 Herndon, Geneva. American Criticism of EO: 1917-1948. Northwestern 49.
2059 Highsmith, James M. EO: Apprenticeship with Dramatic Presentationalism. NC.
2060 Hill, Charles R. EO's Failures. Kan S.
2061 Hill, Philip G. Irony as a Structural Device in Selected Plays of EO. Tulane S 64.
2062 Itkin, Bella. The Patterns of Verbal Imagery as Found in Ten Major Works of EO. Western Reserve 55.
2063 Kindermann, Maria. Psychologische Probleme in Handlung und Charakteren bei EO. Vienna 38.
2064 Koischwitz, Otto. EO. Berlin 38.
2065 Krämer, Edgar. Freiheit und Notwendigkeit als tragisches Problem bei EO. Kiel 53.
2066 Lee, Robert C. EO: A Grapple with a Ghost. Mich 65.
2067 Lloyd, Helen R. A Study of the Religious Principles in the Plays of EO. Mich State.
2068 Long, Chester C. A Study of the Role of Nemesis in the Structure of Selected Plays by EO. Northwestern D 62.
2069 Miller, Jordan Y. A Critical Bibliography of EO. Columbia 57.
2070 Olson, Esther J. An Analysis of the Nietzschean Elements in the Plays of EO. Minn S 56.
2071 Otto, Wilhelm. EO, T. S. Eliot und die griechische Tragödie. Frankfurt 50.
2072 Peyrouse, John C., Jr. The Use of Stagecraft in the Plays of EO. Northwestern.
2073 Philips, David. The Literary Development of EO: The New England Phase. Pa.
2074 Raghavacharyulu, Dhupaty. The Achievement of EO: A Study of the Dramatist as Seeker. Pa 59.
2075 Ray, Helen Houser. The Relation Between Man and Man in the Plays of EO. Kan 65.
2076 Rohde, Marianne. Bedeutung und innerer Zusammenhang der vier Spätdramen EOs. Freiburg 61.
2077 Schröder, Eva. Frauengestalten bei EO. Berlin 42.
2078 Stierle, Hermann. EOs dramatisches Werk unter dem Einflusz Ibsens und Strindbergs. Tübingen 60.
2078a Stroupe, John H. EO's *Marco Millions:* A Road to Xanadu. Rochester 62.
2079 Törnqvist, Egil. The Dramatic Technique of EO. Uppsala.
2080 Triesch, Gisela. Die Motive in EOs *Thirst* und den anderen frühen Einaktern und ihre weitere Verarbeitung und Umgestaltung in den späteren Dramen. Frankfurt.
2081 Turner, Clarence S. Man's Spiritual Quest in the Plays of EO. Tex 62.
2082 Vunovich, Nancy. The Women in EO's Plays. Kan.
2083 Weiss, Elisabeth. Die Dramen EOs. Vienna 28 publ.
2084 Winchester, Otis W. A Rhetorical Analysis of EO's *Strange Interlude.* Okla S 61.
See also 1413, 1938, 1987, 2927.

O'REILLY, J. B.

2085 Carroll, Martin C., Jr.   The Australian Sojourn of JBO.   Iowa 55.

OTIS, JAMES

2086 Vering, Alice.   JO.   Neb H 54.

PAGE, T. N.

2087 Holman, Harriet R.   The Literary Career of TNP, 1884-1910.   Duke 48.
See also 254.

PAINE, THOMAS

2088 Behling, Siegfried.   TPs Stelling im geistigen Raum seiner Zeit.   Berlin (F) 54.
2089 Elder, Brother Dominic.   The Common Man Philosophy of TP: A Study of the
Political Ideas of TP.   Notre Dame PS 51.
2090 King, Arnold K.   TP in America, 1775-87.   Chicago H 52.
2091 Mercer, Caroline G.   The Rhetorical Method of TP.   Chicago 49.
2092 Metzgar, Joseph V.   TP: A Study in Social and Intellectual History.   NM H 65.
2093 Rabien, Evelyn Schindelmeisser.   TP als Publizist: Mit einem Überblick über sein
gesamtes Schaffen.   Munich 56.

PALFREY, J. G.

2094 Gatell, Frank O.   JGP: His Early Life and Political Career, 1796-1853.   Harvard H 60.

PARKER, H. T.

2095 Canning, Beverly E.   HTP, Drama Critic.   Mich D 60.

PARKER, THEODORE

2096 Dirks, John E.   The Critical Theology of TP.   Columbia R 47.
2097 McCall, Roy C.   The Public Speaking Principles and Practice of TP.   Iowa 37.
See also 4565.

PARKMAN, FRANCIS

2098 Feltskog, Elmer N.   FP's *The Oregon Trail:*   A Textual Edition and Critical Study [with
Facsimile Edition, 1892.   Ill 66.
2099 Reilly, Sister Mary Purissima, O.P.   FP and the Spiritual Factors at Work in New France.
St. Louis H 41.
See also 103.

PARRINGTON, V. L.

2100 Cerveny, George R.   A Study of VLP's Method of Literary Criticism: Its Origin, Its
Content, Its Influence.   NYU 38.
2101 Merikangas, Robert J.   VLP's Method of Intellectual History.   Catholic.
2102 Power, Mary S.   VLP and J. Allen Smith: An American Political Tradition.   Ill
PS 61.

PATTEN, NATHANIEL, JR.

2103 Scroggins, Albert T., Jr.   NP, Jr., and the *Missouri Intelligencer* and the *Boon's Lick
Advertiser.*   Mo J 61.

PAULDING, J. K.

2104 Hall, Harold E.   The Fiction of JKP.   Pa 53.
2105 Hand, Clifford J.   JKP's Literary Practice in Relation to His Political Thought.
Chicago 57.
2106 Herold, Amos L.   Life of JKP.   Columbia 24.
2107 Mason, Melvin R.   The Uncollected Stories of JKP: An Annotated Edition (Volumes
I-III).   Tex 58.

2108   Robertson, James H.   JKP: A Study in Literary Nationalism. Mich 50.
2109   Watkins, Floyd C.   JKP: Humorist and Critic of American Life. Vanderbilt 51.

PAYNE, J. H.

2110   Blakely, Sidney H.   JHP, Dramatic Craftsman. NC 47.
2111   Williams, C. R. McGregor.   JHP. Paris 26 publ.

PEABODY, ELIZABETH

2112   Bilbo, Queenie.   EP. NYU 32.
2113   Roberts, Josephine E.   A New England Family: EP, 1804-1894, Sophia A. Peabody, 1809-1871, Mary T. Peabody, 1806-1887. Western Reserve 37.

PENN, WILLIAM

2114   Dummer, Hans J.   Die Toleranzidee in WPs Schriften. Münster 41.
2115   Hopkins, Jon J.   A Rhetorical Analysis of the Oratory of WP. Pa State S 61.

PERCIVAL, J. G.

2116   Warfel, Harry R.   JGP: A Biographical Study, 1795-1834. Yale 32.

PERKINS, M. E.

2117   Robillard, Ambolena H.   MEP, the Authors' Editor: A Study of a Climate for Creativity. Fla 54.

PERRY, G. S.

2118   Cowser, Robert G.   A Biographical and Critcal Interpretation of GSP (1910-1956). Tex Christian 64.

PERRY, T. S.

2119   Harlow, A. Virginia.   TSP (1845-1928): A Biographical Study. Duke 46.

PETERKIN, JULIA

2120   Henry, Louis L.   JP: A Biographical and Critical Study. Fla State 65.

PHELPS, E. S.

2121   Bennett, Mary A.   ESP, 1844-1911: A Critical Biography. Pa 38.

PHILLIPS, D. G.

2122   McCloskey, John C.   Social Criticism in the Novels of DGP. Stanford 39.
2123   Rodgers, Paul C., Jr.   DGP: A Critical Study. Columbia 55.

PHILLIPS, WENDELL

2124   Sattler, John W.   WP, Speaker and Agitator. Northwestern S 43.
2125   Sherwin, Oscar.   Prophet of Liberty: A Biography of WP. NYU 40.

PIERPONT, JOHN

2126   Ravitz, Abe C.   JP: Portrait of a Nineteenth Century Reformer. NYU 55.

PIKE, ABLERT

2127   Riley, Susan B.   The Life and Works of AP to 1860. Peabody 34.

POE, E. A.

2128   Alexander, Jean A.   Affidavits of Genius: French Essays on EAP from Forgues to Valéry. Wash 60.
2129   Allen, Mozelle S.   EAP's Debt to Gautier, to Pascal, and to Voltaire. Tex 40.
2130   Alterton, Margaret.   Origins of EAP's Critical Principles. Iowa 22.
2131   Anderson, Don Max.   EAP's Influence upon Baudelaire's Style. Iowa 55.

2132   Arnold, John.   EAP: A Handbook to the Tales.   Mass.
2133   Bass, William W.   EAP as Critic of Southern Writers and Literature.   NC 54.
2134   Bierly, Charles E.   *Eureka* and the Drama of the Self: A Study of the Relationship between EAP's Cosmology and His Fiction.   Wash 57.
2135   Bjurman, Gunnar.   EAP: En litteraturhistorisch studie.   Lund 16 publ.
2136   Boussoulas, Nicolas I.   La Peur et l'Univers dans l'oeuvre d'EAP.   Paris 50.
2138   Cain, Henry E.   James Clarence Mangan and the EAP-Mangan Question.   Catholic 29.
2139   Calcott, Emily S.   The Influence of Isaac Disraeli on EAP.   Va 31.
2140   Cambiaire, Célestin P.   The Influence of EAP in France.   Iowa 25.
2141   Carrère, Bertrand.   Dégénérescence et dipsomanie d'EAP.   Toulouse M 08 publ.
2142   Casale, Ottavio M.   EAP and Transcendentalism: Conflict and Affinity.   Mich 65.
2143   Caspari, Heinz.   EAPs Verhältnis zum Okkultismus.   Freiburg 22.
2144   Cobb, Palmer.   The Influence of E.T.A. Hoffman on the Tales of EAP.   Columbia G 08
2145   Dameron, J. Lasley.   EAP in the Mid-Twentieth Century: His Literary Reputation in England and America, 1928-1960, and a Bibliography of EAP Criticism, 1942-1960.   Tenn 62.
2146   Easley, John B.   EAP's *Al Aaraaf:*   Text, Sources, and Interpretation with a History of Its Critical Reception.   NC.
2147   Eberspach, Günter.   Die Natur in der erzählenden Prosa EAPs.   Mainz.
2148   Englekirk, John E.   EAP in Hispanic Literature.   Columbia RL 34.
2149   Fisher, Benjamin F.   EAP and the Tradition of Gothic Romance.   Duke.
2150   Foster, Edward F.   A Study of Grim Humor in the Works of EAP, Melville, and Twain.   Vanderbilt 57.
2151   Fox, Hugh B., Jr.   EAP and Cosmology: The God-Universe Relationship in a Romantic Context.   Ill 58.
2152   Gottschalk, Hans W.   The Imagery of EAP's Poems and Tales: A Chronological Interpretative Study.   Iowa 49.
2153   Grava, Arnolds.   L'Aspect métaphysique du mal dans l'oeuvre littéraire de Charles Baudelaire et d'EAP.   Neb P 54.
2154   Hecht, Harvey E.   Narrator in EAP's Fiction.   Tenn.
2155   Holz, Friedbert.   Das Problem der Wirklichkeit in der Dichtung EAPs.   Freiburg.
2156   Hudson, Ruth L.   EAP's Craftsmanship in the Short Story.   Va 34.
2157   Hull, William D.   A Canon of the Critical Works of EAP with a Study of EAP the Magazinist.   Va 41.
2158   Hutcherson, Dudley R.   One Hundred Years of EAP: A Study of EAP in American and English Criticism, 1827-1927.   Va 36.
2159   Jacobs, Robert D.   EAP's Heritage from Jefferson's Virginia.   Johns Hopkins 53.
2160   Kahn, Ernst.   EAP und Charles Baudelaire: Ein Vergleich ihrer Weltanschauung und Kunstlehre.   Heidelberg 21.
2161   Kelly, George E.   The Aesthetic Theories of EAP: An Analytical Study of His Literary Criticism.   Iowa A 54.
2162   Kennedy, Ralph C., Jr.   The Poems and Short Stories of EAP: Their Compostion, Publication, and Reception.   Ark 61.
2163   Kremenliev, Elva B.   The Literary Uses of Astronomy in the Writings of EAP.   UCLA 63.
2164   **Kühnelt, Harro.**   EAP und Dante Gabriel Rossetti.   Innsbruck 48.
2165   Lauvrière, Emile.   Un Génie morbide: la vie d'EAP.   Paris 04 publ.
2166   Laverty, Carroll.   Science and Pseudo-Science in the Writings of EAP.   Duke 51.
2167   Lemonnier, Léon.   EAP et la critique française de 1845 à 1875.   Paris 28 publ.
2168   _____.   Les Traducteurs d'EAP en France de 1845 à 1875:   Charles Baudelaire.   Paris 28 publ.
2169   Levine, Stuart G.   "The Proper Spirit":   A Study of the Prose Fiction of EAP.   Brown A 58.
2170   Ligon, John F., Jr.   On Desperate Seas: A Study of EAP's Imaginary Journeys.   Wash 61.

2171 Lubbers, Klaus. Die Todesszene und ihre Funktion im Kurzgeschichtenwerk von EAP. Mainz 61 publ.

2172 Lubell, Albert J. EAP, Critic and Reviewer. NYU 51.

2173 Mabbott, Thomas O. An Edition of EAP's *Politian.* Columbia 23.

2174 Maucher, Gisela M. Das Problem der Dichterischen Wirklichkeit im Prosawerk von E. T. A. Hoffmann und EAP. Wash 64.

2175 Menz, Lotte. Die Sinnlichen Elemente bei EAP und ihr Einflusz auf Technik und Stil des Dichters. Marburg 16 publ.

2176 Messac, G. Régis. Influences françaises dans l'oeuvre d'EAP. Paris 29 publ.

2177 Miller, John C. EAP's English Biographer: John Henry Ingram, a Biographical Account and a Study of His Contributions to EAP Scholarship. Va 54.

2178 Mooney, Stephen L. EAP's Grand Design: A Study of Theme and Unity in the Tales. Tenn 60.

2179 Moss, Sidney P. EAP's Literary Battles. Ill 54.

2180 Oppel, Ilse. EAP und Charles Baudelaire. Vienna 50.

2181 Ostrom, John W. A Critical Edition of the Letters of EAP. Va 47.

2182 Patterson, Arthur S. L'Influence d'EAP sur Charles Baudelaire. Grenoble 03 publ.

2183 Peterson, Dewayne A. EAP's Grotesque Humor: A Study of the Grotesque Effects in His Humorous Tales. Duke 62.

2184 Petit, Georges. Étude médico-psychologique sur EAP. Lyon M 06 publ.

2185 Phillips, Elizabeth. EAP: The American Context. Pa 57.

2186 Pollack, Simon. EAP, un génie toxicomane. Paris M 28 publ.

2187 Quinn, Patrick F. The French Face of EAP. Columbia 53.

2188 Reece, James B. EAP and the Literati. Duke 54.

2189 Reilly, John E. EAP in Imaginative Literature: A Study of American Drama, Fiction, and Poetry Devoted to EAP or His Works. Va 65.

2190 Schinzel, Elisabeth. Natur und Natursymbolik bei EAP, Baudelaire und den französischen Symbolisten. Bonn 31.

2191 Schuhmann, Kuno. Die Erzählende Prosa EAPs: Ein Beitrag zu einer Gattungsgeschichte der amerikanischen short story. Frankfurt 57.

2192 Seylaz, Louis. EAP et les premiers symbolistes français. Lausanne 23 publ.

2193 Siebel, Paul. Der Einflusz Samuel Taylor Coleridges auf EAP. Münster 24.

2194 Skaggs, Calvin L. Narrative Point of View in EAP's Criticism and Fiction. Duke 66.

2195 Snider, Harry C. An Edition of the Poems in EAP's Last Collection Based Largely on His Own Critical Principles. Mich 63.

2196 Stauffer, Donald B. Prose Style in the Fiction of EAP. Ind 63.

2197 Stewart, Robert A. Textual Notes for the Tales of EAP, Virginia Edition, Vols. II to VI. Va 01.

2198 Stroer, Ernst. EAPs Lyrick. Vienna 10.

2199 Varnado, Seaborn L. The Numinous in the Work of EAP. Fordham 65.

2200 Vaughan, Joseph L. The Literary Opinions of EAP. Va 40.

2201 Wächtler, Paul. EAP und die deutsche Romantik. Leipzig 11.

2202 Walker, I. M. A Study of EAP. Nottingham 62-63.

2203 Washington, Ruth W. EAP's Indebtedness to Coleridge and Shelley. Ga.

2204 Whipple, William. A Study of EAP's Satiric Patterns. Northwestern 51.

2205 Wolff, Anne L. Tod und Unsterblichkeit, das Leitmotiv von EAPs Werk. Berlin 37 publ.

2206 Wuletich, Sybil. EAP: The Rationale of the Uncanny. Ohio State 61.
See also 196, 442, 771, 1417, 1426, 2501, 2546, 2914, 3338.

POLLARD, PERCIVAL

2207 Kummer, George N. PP: Precursor of the "Twenties." NYU 47.

POOLE, ERNEST

2208 Black, Henry C. EP: The Liberal and the Ideal of Social Change. Minn.

2209 Keefer, Truman F. The Literary Career and Literary Productions of EP, American Novelist. Duke 60.

PORTER, K. A.

2210 Adams, Robert H. The Significance of Point of View in KAP's *Ship of Fools*. So Cal 65.
2211 Hertz, Robert N. Rising Waters: A Study of KAP. Cornell 64.
2212 Nance, Brother William L. The Principle of Rejection: A Study of the Thematic Unity in the Fiction of KAP. Notre Dame 63.
2213 Redden, Dorothy Sue. The Legend of KAP. Stanford 65.
2214 Schwartz, Edward. The Fiction of KAP. Syracuse 53.
2215 Yosha, Lee W. The World of KAP. Mich 61.
See also 868, 1538, 3437.

PORTER, W. S. (O. HENRY)

2216 Kreiter, Wolfgang. Zur Frage des Realismus in den Short Stories OHs. Berlin (H) 56.
2217 Long, E. Hudson. OH, a Biographical Study. Pa 42.
2218 Noack, Heinz. OH als Mystiker. Berlin 37 publ.
2219 Patek, Hertha. OH: Erzählungskunst, Probleme, literarische Stellung. Vienna 40.
2220 Ross, Crystal R. Le Conteur américain OH et l'art de Maupassant. Strasbourg 25 publ.

PORTER, W. T.

2221 Yates, Norris. WTP and the Development of Frontier Writing, 1831-1861. NYU 53.

POUND, EZRA

2222 Baisch, Dorothy R. London Literary Circles, 1910-1920, with Special Reference to Ford Madox Ford, EP, D. H. Lawrence, and Virginia Woolf. Cornell 50.
2222a Bullaro, John J. The Dantean Image of EP, T. S. Eliot, and Hart Crane. Wis 62.
2223 Coffman, Stanley K., Jr. Imagism: The Contribution of T. E. Hulme and EP to English Poetry, 1908-1917. Ohio State 48.
2224 Davenport, Guy M., Jr. A Reading of I-XXX of *The Cantos* of EP. Harvard 61.
2225 Edwards, John H. A Critical Biography of EP, 1885-1922. UCB 52.
2226 Glenn, Edgar M. Association and *The Cantos* of EP. Stanford 55.
2227 Gross, Harvey S. The Contrived Corridor: A Study in Modern Poetry and the Meaning of History [EP, Eliot, Yeats]. Mich 55.
2228 Halperen, Max. The Structural Reading of *The Cantos* of EP. Fla State 59.
2228a Jung, Angela Chih-ying. EP and China. Wash 55.
2229 Kelly, Robert G. The Premises of Disorganization: A Study of Literary Form in EP, T. S. Eliot, James Joyce, and Dorothy Richardson. Stanford 52.
2230 Landini, Richard G. A Guide to the Economic Thought in EP's *Cantos*. Fla 59.
2231 Lenberg, Lore. The Coherence of the *Pisan Cantos* and Their Significance in the Context of EP's *Poem of Some Length*. Freiburg 58.
2232 Lennig, Arthur G. An Analysis of *The Cantos* of EP. Wis 61.
2233 Manganaris-Decavalles, Andonis. EP and the Mediterranean World. Northwestern 60.
2234 Meyer, Peter. Die Finanz- und wirtschaftspolitische Auffassung EPs und ihre Bedeutung für seine Dichtung. Freiburg.
2235 Puckett, Walter S. The Nineteenth-Century Foundations of the Robert Browning-EP Bridge to Modernity in Poetry. St. Louis 61.
2236 Racey, Edgar F. EP's *Cantos:* The Structure of a Modern Epic. Claremont 63.
2236a Reed, Victor B. Toward *The Cantos* of EP. Columbia 65.
2237 Rowe, Hershel D. Basic Elements in the Criticism of EP. Fla 59.
2238 Schneidau, Herbert N. EP's Criticism and the Influence of His Literary Relationships in London, 1908-1920. Princeton 63.
2239 Slatin, Myles. A Study of the Works of Robert Browning and EP. Yale A 58.

2240 Ueda, Makoto. Zeami, Bashō, Yeats, EP: A Study in Japanese and
English Poetics. Wash 61.
2241 Vasse, William W. The Structure of History in EP's *Cantos*. UCB.
2242 Von Hendy, Andrew J. The Form and Principal Themes of EP's *Cantos*. Cornell 63.
2243 Woodard, Charles R. Browning and Three Modern Poets: EP, Yeats, and Eliot. Tenn 53.
See also 730, 1499, 4339.

PRESCOTT, W. H.
See 103.

PRIESTLEY, JOSEPH
2244 Park, Mary C. JP and the Problem of Pantisocracy. Pa 47.

PRINCE, THOMAS
2245 Van de Wetering, John E. TP, Puritan Polemicist. Wash H 59.

PULITZER, JOSEPH
2246 Siebert, Horst. JP als Journalist und Verleger. Munich 56.

RALPH, JAMES
2247 Kenny, Robert W. JR, Author by Profession. Brown 34.

RANSOM, J. C.
2248 Greene, Joseph A. The Evolution of JCR's *Selected Poems*. Mich.
2249 Karanikas, Alexander. JCR and Allen Tate: A Study of the Southern Agrarian
Theory of Literature. Northwestern 53.
2250 Knight, Karl F. Diction, Metaphor, and Symbol in the Poetry of JCR. Emory 62.
2251 Mills, Gordon H. Myth and Ontology in the Thought of JCR. Iowa 42.
2252 Stocking, Fred H. Poetry as Knowledge; the Critical Theory of JCR and Allen Tate.
Mich 46.

RASCOE, BURTON
2253 Hensley, Donald M. BR as Literary Editor and Critic. Pa 63.

READ, OPIE
2254 Baird, Reed M. The Works of OR: A Study in Popular Culture. Mich.

READ, T. B.
2255 Keller, Isaac C. TBR. Pittsburgh 32.

REEDY, W. M.
2256 Wolf, Fred W. WMR: A Critical Biography. Vanderbilt 51.

REESE, L. W.
2257 Klein, L. Ruth. LWR: A Critical Biography. Pa 43.

REPPLIER, AGNES
2258 Stokes, George S. AR: A Critical Biography. Pa 46.
2259 Vaughn, Ann C. AR: Social Critic. Mich State 57.

RHODES, E. M.
2260 Fife, Jim L. EMR: Spokesman for Romantic Frontier Democracy. Iowa 65.

RICE, C. Y.
2261 Berry, Brother C. Cornelius. A Comparative Study of the Revised Poetic Dramas of
CYR with Other Outstanding American Poetic Dramas. St. John's (Brooklyn) 49.

RICE, ELMER

2262 Allison, James D. A Study of Some Concepts of Social Justice in the Published Plays of ER. Denver 53.
2263 Fleischhaker, Daniel. The Significance of ER in the American Theatre Between the Two World Wars. Mich State.

RICHARDS, I. A.

2264 Guth, Hans P. Threat as the Basis of Beauty: Pragmatist Elements in the Aesthetics of IAR, Dewey, and Burke. Mich 56.
See also 686, 2882.

RICHTER, CONRAD

2265 Edwards, Clifford D. CR's Ohio Trilogy: Its Ideas, Themes, and Relationship to Literary Tradition. Mich 63.
2266 LaHood, Marvin J. A Study of the Major Themes in the Work of CR and His Place in the Tradition of the American Frontier Novel. Notre Dame 62.
2267 Young, David L. The Art of CR. Ohio State 64.

RIDDLE, A. G.

2268 Wehner, Ralph. The Life and Works of AGR. Western Reserve.

RIGGS, LYNN

2269 Aughtry, Charles E. LR, Dramatist: A Critical Biography. Brown 59.
2270 Wilson, Eloise. LR: Oklahoma Dramatist. Pa 57.

RILEY, J. W.

2271 Kellermann, Friedrich. JWR: Ein Beitrag zur Geschichte der neuesten amerikanischen Literatur. Marburg 18.

RIPLEY, GEORGE

2272 Crowe, Charles R. GR, Transcendentalist and Utopian Socialist. Brown P 55.
2273 Riggs, Lisette. GR and Sophia R. Md 42.
2274 Rittenhouse, Caroline S. The Testimony of Man's Inward Nature: A Study of GR's Transcendentalism. Harvard 65.
2275 Wilson, Howard A. GR, Social and Literary Critic. Wis 41.

ROBERTS, E. M.

2276 Lockwood, Isabel A. EMR: Her Development as Self-Conscious Narrative Artist. NC
2277 Rovit, Earl H. EMR: Her Symbolism and Philosophic Perspective. Boston 57.
2278 Spears, Woodridge. EMR: A Biographical and Critical Study. Ky 53.

ROBERTS, KENNETH

2279 Kitch, John I. From History to Fiction: KR as an Historical Novelist. Ill 65.
See also 3440.

ROBINSON, E. A.

2280 Ayo, Nicholas. EAR and the Bible. Duke 66.
2281 Baumgärtner, Alfred. Das lyrische Werk EARs. Mainz 52.
2282 Betsky, Seymour. Some Aspects of the Philosophy of EAR: Self-knowledge, Self-acceptance, and Conscience. Harvard 43.
2283 Burton, David H. Christian Conservatism in the Poetry of EAR. Georgetown 53.
2284 Crowder, Richard H. Three Studies of EAR: His Male Characters, His Emergence, and His Contemporaneous Reputation. Iowa 44.
2285 Dauner, Margaret L. Studies in EAR. Iowa 44.
2286 Dechert, Peter. EAR and Alanson Tucker Schumann: A Study in Influences. Pa 55.
2287 Foy, John V. Character and Structure in EAR's Major Narratives. Cornell 61.

2288 Fryxell, Lucy D. EAR as Dramatist and Dramatic Poet. Ky 55.
2289 Fussell, Edwin S. The Early Poetry of EAR. Harvard 49.
2290 Grohs, Elisabeth. EARs langere Verserzählungen. Vienna 36.
2291 Isley, Elise. The Imagery in the Poetry of EAR. Ark.
2292 Joyner, Nancy. EAR's Theory of Poetry. NC.
2293 Kaplan, Estelle. Philosophy in the Poetry of EAR. Columbia P 40.
2293a Malof, Joseph F. The Engaging Mask: Isolation in the Early Poems of EAR.
      UCLA 62.
2294 Moon, E. Samuel. Organic Form in the Shorter Poems of EAR. Mich 56.
2295 Morrill, Paul H. Psychological Aspects of the Poetry of EAR. Northwestern 56.
2296 Mott, Sara L. The Happy Ending as a Controlling Comic Element in the Poetic
      Philosophy of EAR. SC 65.
2297 Perrine, Laurence D. EAR and Arthurian Legend. Yale 48.
2298 Robinson, William R. EAR: The Poetry of the Act. Ohio State 62.
2299 Stephens, Alan A., Jr. The Shorter Narrative Poems of EAR. Mo 54.
2300 Stevick, Robert. EAR: The Principles and the Practice of His Poetry. Wis 56.
2301 Zietlow, Paul N. The Shorter Poems of Thomas Hardy and EAR: A Study in Contrasts.
      Mich 65.
      See also 1954.

ROETHKE, THEODORE

2302 Maloff, Karl. The Poetry of TR. Columbia 65.

ROGERS, WILL

2303 Alworth, E. Paul. The Humor of WR. Mo 58.
2304 Brown, William R. The Rhetorical Techniques of WR. Okla 64.

RØLVAAG, O. E.

2305 Gvåle, Gudrun H. OER: Nordman og amerikanar. Oslo 62 publ.
2306 Reigstad, Paul M. The Art and Mind of OER. NM 58.
2307 Stevens, Robert L. OER: A Critical Study of His Norwegian-American Novels. Ill 55.
      See also 163, 4465.

ROOSEVELT, THEODORE

2308 Behl, William A. The Speaking and Speeches of TR. Northwestern S 42.
2309 Dornbusch, Clyde H. TR's Literary Taste and Relationships with Authors. Duke 57.
2310 Zyskind, Harold. The Rhetorical Principles of TR. Chicago S 65.

RUKEYSER, MURIEL

See 932.

RUNYON, DAMON

2311 Wagner, Jean. Runyonese, a Short Inquiry into the Mind and Craft of DR. Paris 63 publ.

RUSH, BENJAMIN

2312 d'Elia, Donald J. BR: An Intellectual History. Pa State H 65.
2313 Good, H. G. BR and His Services to American Education. Pa H 15.
      See also 990.

SAFFIN, JOHN

2314 Sands, Alyce E. JS: Seventeenth Century American Citizen and Poet. Pa State 65.

SALINGER, J. D.

2315 Fort, Keith. Beyond Despair: A Comparative Study of Four Novels. Minn 64.
2316 Jordan, Joseph W. JDS as a Writer of Fiction for Students in Senior High School.
      Ohio State E 62.

2317 Schröder, Bernhard.   Das Problem des Jugendlichen bei JDS.   Freiburg.
      See also 2566, 3414.

SALTUS, EDGAR

2318 Stephenson, Ruth D.   ES.   Wis 53.

SANBORN, F. B.

2319 Clarkson, John W., Jr.   The Life and Letters of FBS.   Columbia.
2320 Hickok, Benjamin B.   The Political and Literary Careers of FBS.   Mich State 53.

SANDBURG, CARL

2321 Durnell, Hazel B.   The America of CS.   Geneva 63.
2322 Green, Jerome.   CS as Poet: A Study of the Criticism and Other Factors Contributing
      to His Reputation as a Poet through 1960.   NYU 63.
2323 Stroud, Parry.   CS: A Biographical and Critical Study of His Major
      Works.   Northwestern 56.
      See also 1799.

SANDYS, GEORGE

2324 Grüninger, Günther H.   GS als Übersetzer des Christus Patiens von Hugo Grotius.
      Freiburg 28.
2325 Ingalls, Beatrice K.   GS's Translations of Ovid's *Metamorphoses*.   Radcliffe 50.
2326 Overly, Floyd E.   Preliminary Studies in the Ovidian Mythography of GS.   Chicago 50.

SANTAYANA, GEORGE

2327 Ballowe, James C.   The Art and Criticism of GS's *The Last Puritan*.   Ill 63.
2328 Grossman, Morris.   GS as Dramatist and Dialectician: A Critical Estimate
      Made with the Help of Unpublished Manuscripts.   Columbia P 60.
2329 Howgate, George W.   GS: Man of Letters.   Pa 33.
2330 Obendieck, Edzard.   GSs Roman *The Last Puritan* und seine Literaturtheorie.   Bonn 57
2330a Sherman, Frank E.   GS as a Critic of America.   UCB 62.
2331 Wermuth, Paul C.   GS as a Literary Critic.   Pa State 55.
2331a Wilbur, Robert H.   GS and Three Modern Philosophical Poets: T. S. Eliot, Conrad
      Aiken, and Wallace Stevens.   Columbia 65.
2332 Wilson, Douglas.   GS: The Poet in America.   Pa 64.
      See also 2414.

SAROYAN, WILLIAM

2333 Morris, David W.   A Critical Analysis of WS.   Denver D 60.
2334 Petricek, Walter A.   WS als Dramatiker.   Vienna 49.
      See also 1987, 3026.

SCHOOLCRAFT, H. R.

2335 Freeman, John.   Biography of HRS: Relationship of Anthropology and American
      Life.   Harvard A 60.

SCOTT, EVELYN

2336 Welker, Robert L.   ES: A Literary Biography.   Vanderbilt 58.

SEABURY, SAMUEL

2337 Steiner, Bruce E.   SS and the Forging of the High Church Tradition: A Study in the
      Evolution of New England Churchmanship, 1722-1796 (Vols. I-II).   Va H 62.

SEDGWICK, A. D.

2338 Swanson, Grace E.   A Critical Study of the Novels of ADS.   NYU 56.

SEDGWICK, C. M.

2339　Gidez, Richard B.　A Study of the Works of CMS.　Ohio State 58.
2340　Welsh, Sister M. Michael.　CMS:　Her Position in American Literature and Thought up to 1860.　Catholic 37.

SETON, E. T.

2341　Reindorf, Konrad.　Die Tierbücher des ETS.　Vienna 39.

SEWALL, SAMUEL

2342　Blackmon, Joab L.　Judge SS, 1652-1730:　A Biography.　Wash E 64.
2343　Highfill, Robert D.　The Vocabulary of SS from 1673 to 1699.　Chicago 27.
2344　Strandness, Theodore B.　SS:　The Man and His Work.　Mich State 51.

SHAW, IRWIN
See 3026.

SHELDON, EDWARD

2345　Cohn, Albert.　The Plays of ES.　Northwestern.

SHEPARD, THOMAS

2346　Hasler, Richard A.　TS:　Pastor-Evangelist (1605-1694), a Study in the New England Puritan Ministry.　Hartford Seminary Foundation R 64.
2347　Olsson, Karl A.　Theology and Rhetoric in the Writings of TS.　Chicago 49.

SHERMAN, S. P.

2348　McDowell, Frederick P.　The Career and Criticism of SPS.　Harvard 49.
See also 90.

SHERWOOD, R. E.

2349　Harris, Paul C., Jr.　The Relation of Dramatic Structure to the Ideas in RES's Dramatic Works.　Stanford S 60.
2350　McCray, William E.　The Place of RES in American Drama.　NYU S 63.

SILL, E. R.

2351　Ferguson, Alfred R.　A Study of the Life and Works of ERS.　Yale 48.

SIMMS, W. G.

2352　Argo, Iris S.　The Influences of the Elizabethan Dramatists on the Novels of WGS.　Ga.
2353　Deen, Floyd H.　WGS:　Novelist, Romanticist, and Short Prose Fictionist.　Ind 40.
2354　Guilds, John, Jr.　WGS as a Magazine Editor, 1825-1845:　With Special Reference to His Contributions.　Duke 54.
2355　Herbert, Edward T.　WGS as Editor and Literary Critic.　Wis 57.
2356　Holman, C. Hugh.　WGS's Theory and Practice of Historical Fiction.　NC 49.
2357　Jarrell, Hampton M.　WGS:　Realistic Romancer.　Duke 32.
2358　Kane, Katherine.　WGS:　A Biographical and Critical Study, 1806-1841.　Yale 43.
2359　McDowell, David A.　WGS's Place in American Fiction:　A History of His Literary Reputation from 1833 through 1865.　Vanderbilt.
2360　Palmer, Raymond C.　The Prose Fiction Theories of WGS.　Ind 47.
2361　Popp, Klaus-Jürgen.　Die Stellung von WGS in der amerikanischen Literatur.　Tübingen 65.
2362　Ridgely, Joseph V.　WGS:　The Novelist as Southerner.　Johns Hopkins 56.
2363　Wakelyn, Jon L.　WGS:　The Artist as Public Man, A Political Odyssey, 1830-1860.　Rice E 66.
2364　Welsh, John R., Jr.　The Mind of WGS:　His Social and Political Thought.　Vanderbilt 51.

2365 Wimsatt, Mary Ann. The Comic Sense of WGS: A Study of the Humor in His Fiction and Drama. Duke 64.
See also 1637.

SINCLAIR, UPTON

2366 Biella, Arnold. US: Crusader. Stanford 54.
2367 Blinderman, Abraham. US's Criticism of Higher Education in America: A Study of *The Goose-Step,* Its Sources, Critical History, and Relationship to Subsequent Criticism of Higher Education. NYU E 63.
2368 Eastman, Norton B. US: A Social Crusader Views American Education. SUNY (Buffalo) E 65.
2369 Gottesman, Ronald. US: An Annotated Bibliographical Catalogue, 1894-1932. Ind 64.
2370 Litto, Frederic M. The Plays of US. Ind.
2371 Lockard, Earl N. Technique in the Novels of US. Chicago 48.
2372 McIntosh, Clarence F. US and the EPIC Movement. Stanford H 55.

SLOCUM, JOSHUA

2373 Teller, Walter M. The Voyages of JS. Rutgers 59.

SMITH, C. H.

2374 Christie, Annie May. CHS, "Bill Arp": A Biographical and Critical Study of a Nineteenth Century Georgia Humorist, Politician, Homely Philosopher. Chicago 53.

SMITH, E. H.

2375 Cronin, James E. The Life of EHS. Yale 46.

SMITH, E. O.

2376 Wyman, Mary. Seba and EOS: Two American Pioneers. Columbia 26.

SMITH, R. P.

2377 McCullough, Bruce W. The Life and Writings of RPS with a Reprint of *The Deformed.* Pa 17.
2378 Westlake, Neda. Definitive Edition of *Caius Marius* by RPS, with Critical and Historical Introduction. Pa.

SMITH, SEBA
See 2376.

SMITH, THORNE

2379 Blotner, Joseph L. TS: A Study in Popular Fiction. Pa 51.

SMITH, WILLIAM

2380 Gegenheimer, Albert F. Provost WS and His Group. Pa 40.

SNELLING, W. J.

2381 Woodall, Allen E. WJS. Pittsburgh 32.

SNIDER, D. J.

2382 Huenemann, Calvin V. DJS: A Critical Study. Wis 53.

SOUTHWORTH, E.D.E.N.

2383 Boyle, Regis L. Mrs. EDENS, Novelist. Catholic 38.

SPINGARN, J. E.

2384 Van Deusen, L. Marshall. JES and American Criticism. Pa A 53.

SPOFFORD, H. P.

2385 Halbeisen, Elizabeth K. HPS: A Romantic Survival. Pa 34.

STEDMAN, E. C.

See 4019.

STEFFENS, LINCOLN

2386 Brandes, Werner. Studien zu LS. Munich.
2387 Cheslaw, Irving G. An Intellectual Biography of LS. Columbia 52.
2388 Hinds, George L. The Speeches and Speaking of LS. Northwestern S 53.
2389 Shapiro, Herbert. LS: The Evolution of an American Radical. Rochester H 64.

STEIN, GERTRUDE

2390 Garvin, H. R. GS: A Study of Her Theory and Practice. Mich 50.
2391 Hoffman, Michael J. The Development of Abstractionism in the Writing of GS to 1913. Pa 63.
2392 Leach, Wilford. GS and the Modern Theatre. Ill S 56.
2393 Lowe, Frederick W., Jr. Gertrude's Web: A Study of GS's Literary Relationships. Columbia 57.
2394 McMillan, Samuel H. GS, the Cubists, and the Futurists. Tex 64.

STEINBECK, JOHN

2396 Alexander, Stanley G. Primitivism and Pastoral Form in JS's Early Fiction. Tex 65.
2397 Casimir, Louis J. Human Emotion and the Early Novels of JS. Tex 66.
2398 Freel, Eugene L. A Comparative Study between Certain Concepts and Principles of Modern Psychology and the Writings of JS. NYU 47.
2399 **Gärtner, Heinz. JS: eine Monographie. Berlin (F) 56.**
2400 Haas, Paula. JS et la Californie. Rennes 52.
2401 Kutz, Hermann. Die Erfahrungen des Menschen in den Romanen und Erzählungen JSs. Kiel 54.
2402 Levant, Howard S. A Critical Study of the Longer Fiction of JS. Cornell 62.
2403 Lisca, Peter. The Art of JS: An Analysis and Interpretation of Its Development. Wis 55.
2404 Maier, Wolfgang C. Die Grundformen der menschlichen Existenz in den Romanen von JS. Munich 60.
2405 Maresch, Gertrud M. JSs literarisches Schaffen, seine sozialen Romane und sein Symbolismus. Vienna 49.
2406 Marks, Lester J. A Study of Thematic Continuity in the Novels of JS. Syracuse 61.
2407 Meyer, Helga. Das Menschenbild im Werk JSs. Freiburg.
2408 Rahn, Walter. Die Funktion der kalifornischen Landschaft im epischen Frühwerk JSs. Mainz 62 publ.
2409 Rauter, Herbert. Bild und Symbol im Werke JSs. Cologne 60.
2409a Schumann, Hildegard. Zum Problem des Kritischen Realismus bei JS. Berlin (H) 55.
2410 Taylor, Horace P., Jr. The Biological Naturalism of JS. La 61.
2411 Wallis, Prentiss B. JS: The Symbolic Family. Kan 66.
See also 593, 1718.

STEPHENS, C. A.

2412 Cutts, Richard. A Study of CAS. Penn State 58.

STEVENS, WALLACE

2413 Betar, George V., Jr. Imagination and Reality in WS's Prose and Early Poetry. So Cal 62.
2414 Burney, William A. WS and George Santayana. Iowa 62.

2414a Buttel, Robert W. Prelude to *Harmonium:* The Development of Style and Technique in WS's Early Poetry. Columbia 62.

2414b Forslund, David E. The Function of Allusions in the Poetry of WS. Ariz 65.

2415 Fuchs, Daniel. The Comic Spirit of WS: An Aspect of the Poet's Mind. Columbia 6

2416 Gilbertson, Mary J. WS's Meditative Poems. Cornell 65.

2417 Hamlin, William C. A Thematic Study of Reality, Death, Order, and Imagination in the Poetry of WS. Mo 63.

2418 Hammond, Mac S. Sound and Grammar in WS's *The Man With the Blue Guitar.* Harvard 62.

2419 Heringman, Bernard. WS: The Reality of Poetry. Columbia 55.

2420 Heyen, William. WS: Theme and Structure in the Verse Plays. Ohio State.

2421 Lauter, Estella L. "The World Must be Measured by Eye": The Presentational Poetry of WS. Rochester 66.

2422 Lawless, Sister Mary K. The Ceramics of WS: Aspects of Imagery and Theme. Notre Dame 63.

2423 Lensing, George S., Jr. The Aspiring Clown of WS: A Study of "The Comedian as the Letter C" as Preliminary Statement. La 66.

2424 Lentricchia, Frank, Jr. The Poetics of Will: WS, W. B. Yeats, and the Theoretic Inheritance. Duke 66.

2425 Lord, Georgianna W. The Annihilation of Art in the Poetry of WS. Ohio State 62.

2426 Lovell, James H., Jr. Form and Structure in the Poetry of WS. Vanderbilt 63.

2427 Mitchell, R. S. WS's Supreme Fiction. Manchester 62-63.

2428 Morse, Samuel F. An Examination of the Practice and Theory of WS. Boston 52.

2429 Murphy, Frances E. The Concept of Nature in the Poetry of WS. Harvard 60.

2430 Nassar, Eugene P. WS: An Anatomy of Figuration. Cornell 62.

2431 O'Neal, Charles R. WS and the Arts. Ind 64.

2432 Peterson, Margaret Wilson. WS and the Idealist Tradition: A Study of the Philosophical Background of WS's Poetry. Stanford 65.

2433 Powell, Grosvenor E. Romantic Mysticism and the Poetry of WS. Stanford 65.

2434 Rice, Oliver L. The Dilemma of Reality in WS's *Harmonium.* Ill 65.

2435 Riddel, Joseph N. The Never-Ending Meditation: A Study of Myth Metaphor and the Poetry of Order in the Works of WS. Wis 60.

2436 Robillard, Richard H. The Rhetoric of WS: He That of Repetition is Most Master. Brown 63.

2437 Rosenfeld, Norman. Definitions of Poetry in The Essays and Poems of WS. Pittsburgh 65.

2438 Schneider, Daniel J. WS: The Application of His Theory of Poetry to His Poems. Northwestern 57.

2439 Stern, Herbert J. Art of Uncertainty: Studies in the Early Career of WS. Ind 65.

2440 Sukenick, Ronald. A WS Handbook: A Reading of His Major Poems and an Exposition of His Theory and Practice. Brandeis 62.

2440a Sweitzer, Ronald L. WS: A Study of His Theory of Imagination. Yale 62.

2441 Whitbread, Thomas B. The Later Poems of WS. Harvard 59.

2442 Williamson, Julian M. An Annotated Bibliography of the Criticism of the Works of WS, 1900-1965. Columbia.
    See also 2331a.

STICKNEY, TRUMBULL

2443 Riggs, Thomas, Jr. TS (1874-1904). Princeton 49.

STITH, WILLIAM

2444 Tsuruta, Toshiko. WS, Historian of Colonial Virginia. Wash H 57.

STOCKTON, F. R.

2445 Griffin, Martin I. A Critical Biography of FRS. Pa 38.

STODDARD, C. W.

2446 Stroven, Carl G. A Life of CWS. Duke 39.

STODDARD, R. H.
See 4019.

STOLL, E. E.

2447 Morgan, George A. Illustrations of the Critical Principles of EES. Iowa 57.

STOWE, H. B.

2448 Adams, John R. The Literary Achievement of HBS. So Cal 39.
2449 Cooper, Alice A. HBS: A Critical Study. Harvard A 64.
2449a Jackson, Frederick H. *Uncle Tom's Cabin* in Italy. Syracuse H 52.
2450 Lucas, Edith E. La Littérature anti-esclavagiste au XIXe siècle. Étude sur Madame HBS et son influence en France. Paris 30.
2451 Maclean, Grace E. *Uncle Tom's Cabin* in Germany. Heidelberg 10 publ. *See also 4475a.*

STRIBLING, T. S.

2452 Eckley, Wilton E. The Novels of TSS: A Socio-Literary Study. Western Reserve 65. *See also 259, 4481.*

STROTHER, D. H.

2453 Eby, Cecil D., Jr. A Critical Biography of DHS ("Porte Crayon"). Pa 58.

STUART, JESSE

2453a Blair, Everetta L. JS: A Survey of His Life and Works. SC 64.
2454 Leavell, Frank H. The Literary Career of JS. Vanderbilt 65.
2455 Washington, Mary L. The Folklore of the Cumberlands as Reflected in the Writings of JS. Pa 60.

STUART, R. M.

2456 Fletcher, Mary F. A Biographical and Critical Study of RMS. La 55.

STURGIS, H. O.

2457 Borklund, Elmer. HOS, 1855-1920. Chicago 59.

STYRON, WILLIAM

2458 Nigro, Augustine J., Jr. WS and the Adamic Tradition. Md 64. *See also 1784, 2566, 4285.*

SUCKOW, RUTH

2459 Kissane, Leedice. RS: Interpreter of the Mind of Mid-America. Minn.
2460 Stewart, Margaret. A Critical Study of RS's Fiction. Ill 60.

TABB, JOHN B.

2461 Litz, Francis E. Father JBT: A Study of His Life and Works, with Uncollected and Unpublished Poems. Johns Hopkins 21.
2462 Williams, John J. A Critical Study of the Poetry of JBT. Ga 66.

TARKINGTON, BOOTH

2463 Fennimore, Keith. A Case Study of BT as a Novelist. Mich State 56.
2464 Van Nostrand, Albert D. The Novels and Plays of BT: A Critical Appraisal. Harvard 51.

TATE, ALLEN

2465 Eder, Ursula. The Poetry of AT. Wis 55.
2466 Gerlach, Lee F. The Poetry and "Strategies" of AT. Mich 55.
2467 McDonald, James L. The Literary Theory of a Modern Man of Letters: The Critical Principles of AT. Northwestern 65.
2468 Meiners, Roger K. The Last Alternatives: The Poetry and Criticism of AT. Denver 61.
2469 O'Dea, Richard J. To Make the Eye Secure: The Criticism, Fiction, and Poetry of AT. La 64.
See also 2249, 2252, 2882.

TAYLOR, BAYARD

2470 Haskell, Juliana. BT's Translation of Goethe's *Faust.* Columbia G 08.
2471 Krumpelmann, John T. BT as a Literary Mediator between Germany and America. Harvard G 24.
See also 4019.

TAYLOR, EDWARD

2472 Epperson, William R. The Meditative Structure of ET's *Preparatory Meditations.* Kan 65.
2473 Fender, S. A. ET and the Sources of American Puritan Wit. Manchester 62-63.
2474 Gilman, Harvey. A Study of Image Patterns and Clusters in ET's *Preparatory Meditations.* Duke.
2475 Grabo, Norman S. ET's *Christographia* Sermons: Edited from the Manuscript with a Discussion of Their Relationship to His "Sacramental Meditations." UCLA 58.
2476 Junkins, Donald A. An Analytical Study of ET's *Preparatory Meditations.* Boston 6.
2477 Mignon, Charles W., Jr. The American Puritan and Private Qualities of ET, the Poet. Conn 63.
2478 Nicolaisen, Peter. Die Bildlichkeit in ETs *Preparatory Meditations.* Kiel 64.
2479 Shepherd, Emma L. The Metaphysical Conceit in the Poetry of ET. NC 60.
2480 Stanford, Donald E. An Edition of the Complete Poetical Works of ET. Stanford 53
2481 Wack, Thomas G. The Imagery of ET's *Preparatory Meditations.* Notre Dame 61.
2482 Wiley, Elizabeth. Sources of Imagery in the Poetry of ET. Pittsburgh 62.

TAYLOR, PETER

2483 Schuler, Mother Cor Mariae. The House of PT: Vision and Structure. Notre Dame

TERHUNE, M. V. H.

2484 Wright, Mary Hudson. MVHT ("Marion Harland"): Her Life and Works. Peabody 3

THAXTER, CELIA

2485 de Pizá, Mary D. CT: Poet of the Isles of Shoals. Pa 55.

THOMAS, AUGUSTUS

2486 Bergman, Herbert. AT: Dramatist of His Age. Wis 53.
2487 Bynum, Lucy Scott. The Economic and Political Ideas of AT. NC 54.

THOMPSON, BENJAMIN

See 413.

THOMPSON, D. P.

2488 Flitcroft, J. E. DPT: The Novelist of Vermont. NYU 27.

THOMPSON, J. R.

2489 Miller, Joseph R. JRT: His Place in Southern Life and Literature: A Critical Biography. Va 30.

THOMPSON, MAURICE

2490 Wheeler, Otis. MT: A Biographical and Critical Study. Minn 52.

THOMPSON, W. T.

2491 Miller, Henry P. The Life and Works of WTT. Chicago 42.
See also 1743.

THOREAU, H. D.

2492 Adams, Raymond W. HDT's Literary Theory and Criticism. NC 28.
2493 Baym, Nina Z. The Paradoxical Hero in HDT's Writings. Harvard 63.
2494 Becker, Klaus. Der Stil in den Essays von HDT. Marburg 53.
2495 Bode, Carl J. HDT as a Poet, with a Critical Edition of the Poems. Northwestern 41.
2496 Broderick, John C. HDT's Principle of Simplicity as Shown in His Attitudes toward Cities, Government, and Industrialism. NC 53.
2497 Cheruvelil, Joseph M. The Influence of Indian Philosophy on HDT. Miss.
2498 Christie, John. HDT, Traveler. Duke 56.
2499 Cochnower, Mary E. HDT and Stoicism. Iowa 38.
2500 Craig, George D. Literary Criticism in the Works of HDT. Utah 52.
2501 Culhane, Mary J. HDT, Melville, Poe, and the Romantic Quest. Minn 45.
2502 Eisenlohr, Herman L. The Development of HDT's Prose. Pa 66.
2503 Elligen, Betty J. HDT: His Literary Theory and Criticism. Okla.
2504 Fairbanks, Jonathan. The Impact of the Wild on HDT, Jack London, and Robinson Jeffers. Otago (New Zealand).
2505 Ford, Arthur L. A Critical Study of the Poetry of HDT. Bowling Green 64.
2506 Freniere, Emil A. HDT: 1837-1847. Vols. I and II. Pa State 61.
2507 Glick, Wendell P. HDT and Radical Abolitionism: A Study of the Native Background of HDT's Social Philosophy. Northwestern 50.
2508 Gozzi, Raymond D. Tropes and Figures: A Psychological Study of HDT. NYU 57.
2509 Gruber, Christian P. The Education of HDT, Harvard, 1833-1837. Princeton 53.
2510 Gruenert, Charles F. HDT's Humor in Theory and Practice. Chicago 57.
2511 Guthrie, Harold N. The Humor of HDT. Iowa 53.
2512 Hamilton, Franklin W. HDT's Ideas for Self-Education of the Individual, as Expressed in His Journal, 1837-1862. Kan E 61.
2213 Harding, Walter. The Correspondence of HDT, 1836-1849. Rutgers 50.
2514 Hendrick, George. HDT and Gandhi: A Study of the Development of "Civil Disobedience" and Satyragraha. Tex 54.
2515 Hoblitzelle, Harrison. The War against War in the Nineteenth Century: A Study of the Western Backgrounds of Gandhian Thought. Columbia 59.
2516 Hovde, Carl F. The Writing of HDT's *A Week on the Concord and Merrimack Rivers:* A Study in Textual Materials and Techniques. Princeton 56.
2517 Howarth, William L. HDT's Journal: A Study of Transcendental Craftsmanship. Va.
2518 Huffert, Anton M. HDT as a Teacher, Lecturer, and Educational Thinker. NYU E 52.
2519 Innerhofer, Helga. HDT, seine Stellung zu seiner Zeit, zu Mensch und Natur. Innsbruck 51.
2520 Irsiegler, Leopold. Naturbeobachtung und Naturgefühl bei HDT. Vienna 51.
2521 Jaques, John F. HDT's *The Maine Woods.* Columbia.
2522 Kirchner, William H. HDT as a Social Critic. Minn 38.
2523 Kopp, Charles C. The Mysticism of HDT. Pa State 63.
2524 Lacey, James F. The Reception and Critical Reputation of HDT in Germany. Munich.
2525 Lorch, Fred W. HDT and the Organic Principle in Poetry. Iowa 36.
2526 Magnus, John L. HDT's Poetic Cosmos and Its Relation to Tradition: A Study of His Reading and His Writings, 1837-1854. Johns Hopkins 65.
2527 Moldenhauer, Joseph J. The Rhetoric of *Walden.* Columbia 64.
2528 Nichols, William W. HDT and Science. Mo.
2529 Poger, Sidney B. HDT: Two Modes of Discourse. Columbia 65.
2530 Rohman, David G. An Annotated Edition of HDT's *Walden.* Syracuse 60.

2531   Seybold, Ethel L.   HDT and the Classics.   Yale 47.
2532   Shear, Walter L.   HDT's Imagery and Symbolism.   Wis 61.
2533   Smith, John S.   The Philosophic Naturalism of HDT with Special Reference to Its Epistemological Presuppositions and Theological Implications.   Drew R 48.
2534   Snyder, Helena A.   HDT's Philosophy of Life.   With Special Consideration of the Influence of Hindoo Philosophy.   Heidelberg 02.
2535   Stoller, Leo.   HDT and the Economic Order: The Later Years.   Columbia 56.
2536   Thomas, Robert K.   HDT and the Sense of the Past.   Columbia.
2537   Thompson, Wade C.   The Aesthetic Theory of HDT.   Columbia 59.
2538   Whaling, Anne.   Studies in HDT's Reading of English Poetry and Prose, 1340-1660.   Yale 46.
2539   Willson, Lawrence S.   The Influence of Early North American History and Legend on the Writings of HDT.   Yale 44.
2539a Woodson, Thomas M.   HDT's Prose Style.   Yale 63.
2540   Zwanzig, Karl J.   HDT als Kritiker der Gesellschaft.   Berlin (F) 56.
       See also 237, 444, 738, 747, 748, 774, 804, 2914, 4595.

THORPE, T. B.

2541   Rickels, Milton H.   TBT: His Life and Work.   La 53.

THURBER, JAMES

2542   Black, Stephen A.   JT: His Masquerades.   Wash 64.
2543   Morsberger, Robert E.   The Predicaments and Perplexities of JT.   Iowa 56.

TICKNOR, F. O.

2544   Brockman, Allan A.   FOT: A Biographical Study.   Pa.

TIETJENS, EUNICE

2545   Love, Willie N.   ET: A Biographical and Critical Study.   Md 60.

TOMLIN, JOHN

2546   Phillips, Elizabeth C.   The Literary Life of JT, Friend of Poe.   Tenn 54.

TORRENCE, RIDGELY

2547   Clum, John M.   RT: A Literary Biography.   Princeton.
2548   Leathers, Lyman L.   RT and the Search for an American Identity.   Pa 63.
       See also 1954.

TOURGÉE, A. W.

2549   Dibble, Ray F.   AWT.   Columbia 21.
2550   Gross, Theodore L.   AWT: Reporter of the Reconstruction.   Columbia 60.
2551   Hillger, Martin E.   AWT: Critic of Society.   Ind 59.
       See also 4128.

TRAUBEL, HORACE

2552   Stoddard, Donald R.   HT: A Critical Biography.   Pa.

TRENT, W. P.

2553   Walker, Franklin T.   WPT, a Critical Biography.   Peabody E 43.

TRILLING, LIONEL
       See 1997, 2588.

TROWBRIDGE, J. T.

2554 Coleman, Rufus A.   JTT.   Boston 38.

2555 Griffith, William W. A Study of the Writings of an American Magazinist, JTT. Pittsburgh 41.

TRUMBULL, JOHN

2556 Cowie, Alexander. JT: A Biographical Study. Yale 30.

TRUMBULL, JONATHAN

2557 Weaver, Glenn. JT: Connecticut's Merchant Magistrate. Yale H 53.

TUCKER, GEORGE

2558 McLean, Robert C. GT: Moral Philosopher and Man of Letters. Wash (St. Louis) 60.

TUCKER, N. B.

2559 Turrentine, P. W. Life and Works of NBT. Harvard 52.

TUCKER, S. G.

2560 Prince, William S. SGT as a Poet of the Early Republic. Yale 54.

TUCKERMAN, F. G.

2561 Momaday, Navarre S. An Edition of the Complete Poems of FGT. Stanford 63.

TUCKERMAN, H. T.

2562 Ellsworth, Richard G. HTT as Revealed in His Published Works. Md 59.
2563 McLean, Sidney R. HTT to 1860. Yale 33.

TURNER, J. A.

2564 Huff, Lawrence. JAT: A Study in the Culture of Ante-Bellum Middle Georgia. Vanderbilt 58.

TYLER, M. C.

2565 Casady, Thomas E. MCT: A Critical Biography. Mich 29.

UPDIKE, JOHN

2566 Galloway, David D. The Absurd Hero in Contemporary American Fiction: The Works of JU, William Styron, Saul Bellow, and J. D. Salinger. Buffalo 62.
      See also 3414.

VAN DYKE, HENRY

2567 Bos, William H. A Study of the Preaching of HVD. Mich S 55.

VAN VECHTEN, CARL

2568 Davis, Robert M. The Externalist Method in The Novels of Ronald Firbank, CVV, and Evelyn Waugh. Wis 64.
2569 Lueders, Edward G. CVV and the Twenties: Literature, Society, and the Arts. NM A 52.

VEBLEN, THORSTEIN

2570 Caraker, Catherine. TV and the American Novel. Mich.
      See also 1593.

VERPLANCK, G. C.

2571 Harvey, Sara K. GCV: A Forgotten Knickerbocker. Chicago 34.
2572 July, Robert W. The Essential New Yorker: GCV. Columbia H 52.

VERY, JONES

2573 Bartlett, William I. JV: His Life and Works. Va 36.

2573a Gittlemen, Edwin. Resurrection Verified: The Effective Life of JV, 1833-1840. Columbia 65.
2574 Lyons, Nathan R. Selected Poems by JV. Mich 63.

VILLARD, O. G.

2575 Wrezin, Michael. OGV: Pacifist Editor at War. Brown.

WALLACE, H. B.

2576 Hatvary, George E. HBW: A Critical Biography. NYU 57.

WALSH, ROBERT, JR.

2577 Woodall, Guy R. RW, Jr., as an Editor and Literary Critic: 1797-1836. Tenn 66.

WARD, NATHANIEL

2578 Bohi, Mary J. NW, Pastor Ingeniosus, 1580?-1652. Ill H 59.
2579 Harvey, Shirley W. NW: His Life and Works together with an Edited Text of His *Simple Cobler.* Boston 35.

WARD, S. G.

2580 Baldwin, David. Puritan Aristocrat in the Age of Emerson: A Study of SGW. Pa 6▌

WARNER, C. D.

2581 Gottschalk, Jane. CDW and the American Scene, 1873-1900. Wis 65.

WARREN, R. P.

2582 Casper, Leonard. The Lost Sense of Community and the Role of the Artist in RPW. Wis 53.
2583 Clark, Marden J. Symbolic Structure in the Novels of RPW. Wash 57.
2584 Justus, James H. The Concept of Gesture in the Novels of RPW. Wash 61.
2585 Lane, Calvin W. Narrative Art and History in RPW's *World Enough and Time.* Mich 56.
2586 Linenthal, Mark, Jr. RPW and the Southern Agrarians. Stanford 57.
2587 Moore, Littleton H. RPW and History: "The Big Myth We Live." Emory 64.
2588 Platzker, Doris A. Politics and Literature in America after World War II: A Study of RPW, Lionel Trilling, James Gould Cozzens, and John Dos Passos. Yale.
2589 Poenicke, Klaus. RPW: Kunstwerke und kritische Theorie. Berlin (F) 57 publ.
2590 Ross, Joe C. RPW and the Negro. Vanderbilt.
2590a Samuels, Charles T. RPW: The End and the Beginning. UCB 62.
2591 Shepherd, Allen G., III. A Critical Study of the Fiction of RPW. Pa 65.
2592 Strandberg, Victor. RPW as Poet: A Close Analysis of *Selected Poems, Brother to Dragons, Promises,* and *You, Emperors, and Others.* Brown 62.

WEBSTER, NOAH

2594 Shoemaker, Ervin C. NW, Pioneer of Learning. Columbia E 36.
See also 3908.

WELTY, EUDORA

2595 Appel, Alfred. The Short Fiction of EW. Columbia.
2596 Bredenförder, Elke. Die amerikanischen Südstaaten in Werk von EW. Mainz.
2597 Folsom, Gordon R. Form and Substance in EW. Wis 60.
2598 Griffith, Albert J., Jr. EW's Fiction. Tex 59.
2599 Opitz, Kurt. Travelers for Love: Neo-Romantic Substance Finding a Form in EW's Fiction. Berlin (F) 57.
2600 Rouse, Sarah A. Place and People in EW's Fiction: A Portrait of the Deep South. Fla State 62.

2601 Wild, Rebecca Smith. Studies in the Shorter Fiction of Elizabeth Bowen and EW. Mich 65.
See also 868.

WESCOTT, GLENWAY

2602 Kahn, Sy M. GW: A Critical and Biographical Study. Wis 57.

WEST, NATHANAEL

2603 Comerchero, Victor. NW: The Tuning Fork. Iowa 61.
2603a Edenbaum, Robert I. NW: The Idiom of Violence. UCB 62.
2604 Light, James. NW: A Critical Study. Syracuse 53.
2605 Locklin, Gerald I. A Critical Study of the Novels of NW. Ariz 64.
2606 Lorch, Thomas M. The Peculiar Half-World of NW. Yale 65.
2607 Reid, Randall C. NW: No Redeemer, No Promised Land. Stanford 66.
2608 Smith, Marcus. The Art and Influence of NW. Wis 64.

WHARTON, EDITH

2609 Askew, Melvin W. EW's Literary Theory. Okla 57.
2610 Bell, Millicent L. EW: Studies in a Writer's Development. Brown 55.
2611 Brown, E. K. EW, étude critique. Paris 35 publ.
2612 Fritz, Alphonse J. The Use of the Arts of Decoration in EW's Fiction: A Study of Her Interests in Architecture, Interior Decoration, and Gardening. Wis 56.
2613 Greenwood, Florence J. V. A Critical Study of EW's Short Stories and *Nouvelles.* Stanford 62.
2614 Greenwood, Walter B. EW: Her Materials and Methods. Cincinnati 41.
2615 Hemmer, Sister Jean M. A Study of Setting in the Major Novels of EW. Fordham 64.
2616 Horton, Rod W. Social and Individual Values in the New York Stories of EW. NYU 45.
2617 Jessup, Josephine L. The Fate of Our Feminists: EW, Ellen Glasgow, and Willa Cather. Vanderbilt 48.
2618 Johnson, Sylvia. EW and the Social Novel in America. Minn.
2619 Klampferer, Helga. Die New Yorker Aristokratie in den Werken EWs. Vienna 51.
2620 Leach, Nancy R. EW: Critic of American Life and Literature. Pa 52.
2621 Lindberg, Gary H. EW and the Rhetoric of Manners. Stanford.
2622 Löwy, Julius. EW and Her Relationship to France. Vienna 49.
2623 Lyde, Marilyn J. The Theory and Treatment of Morality in the Work of EW. Chicago 56.
2624 Patrice, Sister Mary, O.P. Comic Techniques in EW's Later Novels. Stanford.
2625 Pitlick, Mary L. EW's Narrative Technique: The Major Phase. Wis 65.
2626 Plante, Patricia R. The Critical Reception of EW's Fiction in America and England with an Annotated Enumerative Bibliography of EW Criticism from 1900 to 1961. Boston 62.
2627 Rice, Mary Lund. The Moral Conservatism of EW. Minn 53.
2628 Saunders, Thomas. Moral Values in the Novels of EW. Pittsburgh 54.
2629 Tuttleton, James W. EW and the Novel of Manners. NC 63.
2630 Weissmann, Leopoldine. EWs Romankunst und ihre Beeinflussung durch Henry James. Vienna 47.
See also 3288.

WHIPPLE, E. P.

2631 Peacock, Leishman A. EPW: A Biography (1819-1886). Pa State 42.

WHITE, E. B.

2632 Fuller, John W. Prose Styles in the Essays of EBW. Wash 59.

WHITE, J. B.

2633 Partridge, Paul H. JBW: The Gentleman-Amateur in Republican Charleston, 1781-1859. Pa 51.

WHITE, S. E.

2634 Butte, Rosemary. SEW: His Life and Literary Career. So Cal 60.

WHITE, W. A.

2635 Cuthbertson, William W. WAW and the *Emporia Gazette,* 1895-1944. Rochester 62
2636 Johnson, T. Walter. WAW. Chicago H 41.
2637 Rich, Ora E. A Biography of WAW. Western Reserve 40.
2638 Riley, Donn C. WAW: The Critical Years. An Analysis of the Changing Political Philosophy of WAW during the Period 1896-1908. St. Louis H 60.
2639 Wilhoit, Robert L. The Rhetoric of the Folk Hero: WAW. Ill 62.

WHITLOCK, BRAND

2640 Kytle, Juanita S. BW: His Life and His Fiction. NM 58.
2641 Pyle, Everett G. The Fictional Writings of BW. Iowa 61.
2642 Steffens, Eleanor. The Novels and Other Literary Writings of BW. Western Reserve.
2643 Tager, Jack. The Search for Freedom: BW and Urban Reform. Rochester H 65.
2644 Thorburn, Neil A. BW: An Intellectual Biography. Northwestern H 65.

WHITMAN, S. H.

2645 Varner, John G., Jr. SHW, Seeress of Providence. Va 41.

WHITMAN, WALT

2646 Asselineau, Roger. L'Evolution de WW après la Ière édition des *Feuilles d'Herbe.* Paris 53 publ.
2647 Azarnoff, Roy S. WW's Rhetorical Theory and Practices. Mo S 65.
2648 Baker, Portia. The Development of WW's Literary Reputation in the United States and in England from 1855-92. Chicago 33.
2649 Balasz, Mary E. WW and William James: Stirrers of the Long Silent American Mind. Pa State 65.
2650 Beaver, Joseph C. WW, Poet of Science. NYU 50.
2651 Bernbrock, John E., S.J. WW and "Anglo-Saxonism." NC 61.
2652 Blodgett, Harold. WW in England. Cornell 29.
2653 Bozard, John F. WW in America: 1855-1892. Cornell 37.
2654 Brady, Sister Mary W. WW's Revisions of the "Song of Myself". Chicago 48.
2655 Brasher, Thomas L. "To All the People of Brooklyn": WW as Editor of *The Brookly Daily Eagle.* La 56.
2656 Burke, Charles B. The Open Road, or the Highway of the Spirit: An Inquiry into WW's Absolute Selfhood. Cornell 01.
2657 Carlisle, Ervin F. *Leaves of Grass:* WW's Epic Drama of *The Soul and I.* Ind 63.
2658 Carr, Harry L. The Comparison of Poetry and Painting: WW's "Out of the Cradle Endlessly Rocking" and Some Paintings of Albert Pinkham Ryder. So Cal 59.
2659 Catel, Jean. Rythme et language dans la Ière édition des *Leaves of Grass* (1855). Paris 31 publ.
2660 _____ WW, la naissance du poète. Paris 31 publ.
2661 Chupack, Henry. WW in Camden: The Formation of a Literary Circle and the Growth of a Poet's Reputation. NYU 52.
2662 Clark, Leadie M. WW's Concept of the American Common Man. Ill 52.
2663 Cooke, Alice L. WW's Background in the Life and Thought of His Times. Tex 33.
2664 Crawley, Thomas E. The Structure of *Leaves of Grass.* NC 65.
2665 Daggett, Gwynne H. WW's Poetic Theory. NC 41.
2666 Davidson, Loren K. WW's "Song of Myself." Duke 59.

2667   Faner, Robert D.   Operatic Music and the Poetry of WW.   Pa 47.

2668   Forrest, John K.   WW's Naturalism.   Wash 42.

2669   Freedman, Florence B.   WW Looks at the Schools.   Columbia E 48.

2670   Fulghum, Walter B., Jr.   Quaker Influences on WW's Religious Thought.
Northwestern 43.

2671   Gibbons, Robert F.   Ocean's Poem: A Study of Marine Symbolism in *Leaves of Grass*.
Tulane 57.

2672   Glicksberg, Charles I.   WW and the Civil War.   Pa 32.

2673   Golden, Arthur.   A Glimpse into the Workshop: A Critical Evaluation and Diplomatic
Transcription of the 'Blue Book,' WW's Annotated Copy of the 1860 Edition of *Leaves
of Grass* (Parts I and II).   NYU 62.

2674   Gonzales, Louis.   WW's Hispanic Fame.   Columbia 60.

2675   Grier, Edward F.   WW's Democratic Idealism.   Pa A 49.

2676   Grimmeiss, Joseph.   WW im Lichte objektiver Forschung.   Munich 19.

2677   Hesser, Dale.   The Religion of WW.   Kan.

2678   Hoople, Robin P.   *Leaves of Grass* (1860) As Opinion: A Study of WW's
Understanding of the Major Problems of 1860 American Culture as Reflected
in the Third Edition of *Leaves of Grass*.   Minn 63.

2679   Howard, P. Leon.   WW's Evangel of Democracy.   Johns Hopkins 29.

2680   Hubach, Robert R.   WW and the West.   Ind 43.

2681   Jellema, R. H.   Victorian Critics and the Orientation of American Literature, with
Special Reference to the Reception of WW and Henry James.   Edinburgh 62-63.

2682   Jellicorse, John L.   WW and Public Speaking.   Northwestern S.

2683   Kallsen, Theodore J.   *Leaves of Grass:*   A Study of Structure.   Iowa 49.

2684   Kanes, Martin.   La Fortune de WW en France.   Paris 53.

2685   Kisler, Karl M.   WW: seine persönlichen und künstlerischen Beziehungen zu Österreich
und Deutschland.   Vienna 50.

2686   Knosp, Engelbert.   WWs Demokratie.   Vienna 49.

2687   Law-Robertson, Harry.   WW in Deutschland.   Giessen 35.

2688   Malone, Walter K.   Parallels to Hindu and Taoist Thought in WW.   Temple 64.

2689   Matle, John.   The New Poetry in WW's *Drum Taps*.   Wayne State.

2690   Mercer, Dorothy F.   *Leaves of Grass* and the *Bhagavad Gita:*   A Comparative Study.
UCB 33.

2691   Moe, Sigrid.   WW and Wergeland: A Comparative Study.   NYU 51.

2692   Mohrmann, Gerald P.   The Impact of Rhetorical Theory and Practice upon the Poetry
of WW.   Fla 65.

2693   Nelson, Herbert B.   WW and the Westward Movement.   Wash 45.

2694   Nicholson, Homer K., Jr.   O Altitudo: A Comparison of the Writings of WW, D. H.
Lawrence, and Henry Miller.   Vanderbilt 57.

2695   Oakes, Frances E.   The WW Controversy in France.   Fla State 55.

2696   Ogilvie, John T.   The Art of *Leaves of Grass:*   A Critical Analysis of the Final Text,
with Particular Attention to Imagery, Symbolism, and Structure.   Ind 58.

2697   Posey, Meredith N.   WW's Debt to the Bible with Special Reference to the Origins of
His Rhythm.   Tex 38.

2698   Pressley, Ruth P.   WW's Debt to Emerson.   Tex 30.

2699   Pucciani, Oreste F.   The Literary Reputation of WW in France.   Harvard RL 43.

2700   Roesler, Sister Miriam C.   The Sea and Death in WW's *Leaves of Grass*.   Catholic 63.

2701   Rubin, Joseph J.   The Early Years of WW.   Yale 40.

2702   Sanderlin, W. Stephen, Jr.   The Growth of *Leaves of Grass*, 1856-1860:   An Analysis
of the Relationship of the Valentine-Barrett Manuscripts to the Third Edition.   Va 55.

2703   Satyanarayana, T. V.   WW, Poet and Prophet.   Andhra, India.

2704   Schönwälden, Karl.   WWs Versuch einer Erneuerung der Religion.   Berlin (F) 50.

2705   Schyberg, Frederick.   WW.   Copenhagen 33 publ.

2706   Sharma, Som P.   A Study of Themes, Self, Love, War, and Death, in Relationship to
Form in the Poetry of WW.   Wis 64.

2707   Shephard, Esther.   WW's Pose.   Wash 38.

2708   Shoemaker, G. Brant, Jr.   WW's Biographers.   Pa.
2709   Sixbey, Goerge L.   WW's Middle Years.   Yale 41.
2710   Smith, Thomas K.   WW's *Leaves of Grass:*   Style and Subject-Matter with Special Reference to *Democratic Vistas.*   Königsberg 14.
2711   Swayne, Mattie.   Structural Unity in *Leaves of Grass.*   Tex 38.
2712   Tanner, James T.   WW: Poet of Lamarckian Evolution.   Tex Tech 65.
2713   Townsend, Frank H.   Literary Nationalism in WW's Theory and Practice of Poetry.   Chicago 53.
2714   Tuttle, Robert C.   The Identity of WW: Motive, Theme, and Form in *Leaves of Grass.*   Wash 65.
2715   Van Egmont, Peter G.   WW's Knowledge of Oratory and Uses of It in *Leaves of Grass.*   NC.
2716   Wankhade, Manohar N.   WW and Tantrism: A Comparative Study.   Fla 65.
2717   Warner, Ella.   A History of WW's Reception in the British Isles.   Yale 16.
2717a   Waskow, Howard J.   WW and the Problem of Literary Form.   Yale 63.
2718   Weissgärber, Alfred.   WW und die psychologischen Grundlagen seiner Dichtung.   Vienna 51.
2719   Westerfield, Hargis.   WW's Reading.   Ind 49.
2720   Willard, Charles B.   The Growth of WW's Reputation in America after 1892.   Brown 4
2721   Willingham, John R.   The WW Tradition in Recent American Literature.   Okla 53.
See also 237, 747, 748, 771, 1184, 2767, 4434, 4595.

WHITTIER, J. G.

2722   Eastburn, Iola K.   JGW's Relation to German Life and Thought.   Pa G 13.
2723   Ernest, Joseph F., Jr.   JGW and the American Writers.   Tenn 52.
2724   Fercalek, Elfriede.   Die Wertwelt JGWs.   Vienna 46.
2725   Garrison, Theodore R.   JGW: Pioneer Regionalist and Folklorist.   Wis 60.
2726   Holmes, J. Welfred.   JGW's Prose on Reforms other than Abolition.   Pittsburgh 45.
2727   Krugmann, Siegfried.   JGWs Kampf gegen die Sklaverei.   Erlangen 53.
2728   Marcy, Clara P.   The Literary Criticism of JGW.   Boston 46.
2729   Pickard, John B.   The Artistry of JGW.   Wis 54.
2730   Pollard, John A.   JGW's Early Years, 1807-1836.   Yale 37.
2731   Pray, Frances M.   JGW's Poetical Apprenticeship.   Pa State 29.
2732   Tegan, Charles R.   The Religious Poetry of JGW.   Ga.
2733   Tharp, Charles D.   The Frontier in the Poetry of JGW.   Pittsburgh 40.
2734   Williams, Cecil B.   Historicity of JGW's *Leaves from Margaret Smith's Journal.*   Chicago 34.

WIGGLESWORTH, MICHAEL

2735   McCleary, Stella M.   A Definitive Edition of MW's *The Day of Doom,* Based on the 1701 Text.   Kent State.

WILDE, R. H.

2736   Graber, Ralph S.   The Fugitive Poems of RHW, with an Introduction.   Pa 59.
2737   Tucker, Edward L.   RHW: Life and Selected Poems.   Ga 57.

WILDER, THORNTON

2738   Barland, Peter M.   TW: The German Phase.   Pa.
2739   Beaver, Walter S.   A Critical Study of the Apprentice Plays of TW and Their Relationship to His Major Dramatic Works.   So Cal S 66.
2740   Burbank, Rex J.   TW: A Critical Study.   Mich 60.
2741   Clüver, Claus.   Studien zum Drama und zur dramatischen Theorie TWs.   Hamburg.
2741a   Haberman, Donald C.   TW: A Study of His Theatrical Style.   Yale 62.
2742   Sartori, Lucia.   Stil und Erzählungstechnik in den Werken TWs.   Graz 51.
2743   Stock, Gisela.   Das Erzählwerk TWs: Entwicklung seines Welbildes von *The Cabala* zu *The Ides of March.*   Mainz 56.

2744 Vos, Nelvin. Three Structures of Modern Comedy: The Drama of TW, Ionesco, and Fry. Chicago.

2745 Voss, Renate. Die Umsetzung von TWs *The Skin of Our Teeth* im deutschsprachigen Raum: Übersetzungen und Aufführungen. Kiel 63.
See also 2046.

WILLARD, SAMUEL

2746 Van Dyken, Seymour. SW, 1640-1707: Preacher of Orthodoxy in an Era of Change. Princeton Theological Seminary 63.

WILLIAMS, ESPY

2747 Rickels, Patricia K. The Literary Career of EW: New Orleans Poet and Playwright (1852-1908). La 61.

WILLIAMS, ROGER

2748 Brockunier, Sam H. RW: A Study of His Life and Career to 1657. Harvard H 37.
2749 Ernst, James E. The Political Thought of RW. Wash 26.
2750 Roddy, Clarence S. The Religious Thought of RW. NYU R 48.

WILLIAMS, STEPHEN

2751 Medlicott, Alexander, Jr. The Journals of the Rev. SW: 1775-1777. Wash 62.

WILLIAMS, TENNESSEE

2752 Asral, Ertem. The Relations of Stage to Moving Picture in the Plays of TW. Pa 61.
2753 Britton, Joe S. Extra-Literary Accents in the Dramas of TW. So Ill.
2754 Clayton, John S. The Themes of TW. Yale FA 60.
2755 Dillard, Robert L. The TW Hero: An Analytic Survey. Mo S 65.
2756 Fedder, Norman J. The Influence of D.H. Lawrence on TW. NYU 62.
2757 Friedrich, Jutta. Individuum und Gesellschaft in den Dramen von TW. Jena 63.
2758 Hurley, Paul J. TW: Critic of American Society. Duke 62.
2759 Jackson, Esther M. The Emergence of a Characteristic Contemporary Form in the American Drama of TW. Ohio State S 58.
2760 Patterson, Nancy M. Patterns of Imagery in the Major Plays of TW. Ark 57.
2761 Quirino, Leonard S. The Darkest Celebrations of TW: A Study of *Battle of Angels, Orpheus Descending, A Streetcar Named Desire, Camino Real, Cat on a Hot Tin Roof,* and *Suddenly Last Summer.* Brown 64.
2762 Starnes, Leland. The Comic and TW. Yale.
2762a Steiner, Robert J. Toward an Integrated Personality: A Study of the Dramas of TW. St. John's (Brooklyn) 65.
2763 von Dornum, Jack H. The Major Plays of TW, 1940 to 1960. So Cal 62.
2764 Warren, Clifton L. TW as a Cinematic Writer. Ind 63.
2765 Wolf, Morris P. Casanova's Portmanteau: A Study of *Camino Real* in Relation to the Other Plays and Stories of TW. Ga 59.
See also 1413, 1938, 2044, 3026.

WILLIAMS, W. C.

2766 Bouma, J. Gysbert. A Study of the Prose Style of WCW. Pa 56.
2767 Breslin, James E. The Poetry of Celebration, WCW and Walt Whitman. Minn 64.
2768 Dupeyron-Marchessou, Hélène. WCW et le renouveau du lyrisme dans la poésie américaine. Poitiers 64 publ.
2769 Guimond, James K. WCW: A Developmental Study. Ill 65.
2770 Massie, Lillian E. Narrative and Symbol in *Paterson.* Ark 55.
2771 Ostrom, Alan B. The Poetic World of WCW. Columbia 59.
2772 Slate, Joseph E. WCW's Image of America. Wis 57.
2773 Wagner, Linda W. Imagery, Measure, and Design in the Poems of WCW. Bowling Green 63.

2773a Wallace, Emily M. A Bibliographical Study of WCW. Bryn Mawr 65.
2774 Willard, Nancy M. An Experiment in Objectivity: The Poetic Theory and Practice of WCW and Rainer Maria Rilke. Mich 63.

WILLIS, N. P.

2775 Daughrity, Kenneth L. The Life and Work of NPW. Va 34.
2776 Goffee, Lewis C. The Fiction of NPW. Boston 61.
2777 Huguenin, Charles A. NPW: His Literary Criticism and His Contemporaries. St. John's (Brooklyn) 40.

WILSON, ALEXANDER

2778 Wilson, Gordon. AW, Poet-Essayist-Ornithologist. Ind 30.

WILSON, A. E.

2779 Fidler, William P. The Life and Works of AEW. Chicago 48.

WILSON, EDMUND

2780 Dabney, Lewis M. EW: The Early Years. Columbia 65.
2781 Frank, Charles P. The Fiction of EW. Mich 64.
2782 Kriegel, Leonard. The Politics of EW. NYU 60.
2783 Schlesinger, Lorraine A. EW on American Literature. Md.

WINTER, WILLIAM

2784 Ludwig, Richard M. A Critical Biography of WW. Harvard 50.
2785 McGaw, Charles J. An Analysis of the Theatrical Criticism of WW. Mich S 40.
2786 Rubenstein, Gilbert M. The Shakespearean Criticism of WW: An Analysis. Ind 51.

WINTERS, YVOR

2787 Sexton, Richard J. The Complex of YW's Criticism. Fordham 65.
See also 89, 2897.

WINTHROP, THEODORE

2788 Martin, Willard E., Jr. The Life and Works of TW. Duke 44.
2789 Propst, Harold D. TW: His Place in American Literary and Intellectual History. Peabody 64.
2790 Woolf, Eugene T. TW: Portrait of an American Author. Utah 65.

WIRT, WILLIAM

2791 Cauble, Frank P. WW and His Friends: A Study in Southern Culture, 1772-1834. NC 34.

WISE, JOHN

2792 Cook, George A. JW: Early American Democrat. Columbia 53.
2793 Ericson, Jon M. JW: Colonial Conservative. Stanford H 61.
2794 Taylor, Douglas. JW and the Development of American Prose Style. UCD 67.

WISTER, OWEN

2795 Watkins, George T. OW and the American West, A Biographical and Critical Study. Ill 59.

WOLFE, THOMAS

2796 Bärsch, Hans G. Das Epos TWs. Wesen und Gehalt. Mainz 52.
2797 Blackwelder, J. Ray. Literary Allusions and Quotations in *Look Homeward, Angel.* Emory 67.
2798 Boyle, Thomas E. TW's Myth of America. Ill 64.

2799 Delakas, Daniel L.   TW et les romanciers français.   Paris 50 publ.
2800 Finney, Frank F., Jr.   A Critical Examination of the Transition from a Psychological
       Vision of Life to an Increasingly Christian Awareness of Evil in the Fiction of TW.
       Okla 61.
2801 Fleming, Delmont F.   Humor in the Works of TW.   Pa 66.
2802 Gatlin, Jesse C., Jr.   The Development of TW as a Literary Artist.   Denver 61.
2803 Halperin, Irving.   The Basis and Nature of Unity in the Novels of TW.   Wash (St. Louis) 57.
2804 Hurt, Lester E.   A House Divided: A Study of Theme in TW's Novels.   Minn 56.
2805 Idol, John.   TW's Satire: A Study of Objects, Motives, and Artistry.   Ark 65.
2806 Johnson, Stanley L.   A Critical Study of the Works of TW.   So Cal 55.
2807 Kennedy, Richard S.   A Critical Biography of TW to His Thirty-Fourth Year.
       Harvard 53.
2808 Kilburn, Patrick E.   Ulysses in Catawba: A Study of the Influence of James Joyce
       on TW.   NYU 54.
2809 Kracht, Fritz.   Die TW-Kritik in den Vereinigten Staaten und Deutschland.   Munich 53.
2810 Larras, Horst.   TW: Zur Problematic des bürgerlichen Dichters im Zeitalter des
       Imperialismus.   Greifswald 61 publ.
2811 LaSalle, Claude W., II.   TW: The Dramatic Apprenticeship.   Pa 64.
2812 Lawrence, Oliver C.   TW: From Individual to Man-Swarm.   Wash 61.
2813 Linder, Wolfgang.   Die epische Struktur des Romanwerkes von TW.   Bonn 51.
2814 McCormick, John O.   TW, André Malraux, Hermann Hesse: A Study in Creative
       Vitality.   Harvard 51.
2815 Maddock, Lawrence H.   The Critical Image of TW.   Peabody 65.
2816 Oertel, Ferdinand.   Die Europa-Erfahrung TWs.   Cologne 54.
2817 Pfister, Karin.   Zeit und Wirklichkeit bei TW.   Marburg 53 publ.
2818 Reeves, Georges M.   TW et l'Europe.   Paris 53.
2819 Reeves, Walter P., Jr.   Race and Nationality in the Works of TW.   Duke 63.
2820 Rubin, Larry.   Image and Theme in the Tetralogy of TW.   Emory 56.
2821 Rubin, Louis D., Jr.   The Weather of His Youth: A Study of the Form of
       Autobiographical Fiction in the Work of TW.   Johns Hopkins 54.
2822 Schulte, Wolfgang.   Die romantischen und realistischen Elemente im Werk TWs.   Kiel 56.
2823 Skipp, Francis E.   TW and His Scribner's Editors.   Duke 62.
2824 Smith, Eleanor G.   TW's Unfinished Symphony: A Study of Form in the Novels of
       TW.   Wis 48.
2825 Sprowles, Harry D., Jr.   The Search for TW, with Particular Stress upon the Meaning of
       the Amatory Theme.   Pa 56.
2826 Stanton, Edgar E., Jr.   Hegel and TW.   Fla State 60.
2827 Stanzel, Franz.   Das Amerikabild TWs (1900-1938).   Graz 50.
2828 Strozier, Robert I.   The Anatomy of TW: A Study of the Question of Unity in the
       Gant-Webber Saga.   Fla State 65.
2829 Voigt, Walter.   Die Bildersprache TWs mit besonderer Berücksichtigung der
       amerikanischen Englisch.   Munich 60 publ.
       See also 4628.

WOOLMAN, JOHN

2830 Altman, Walter F.   JW's Reading.   Fla State 57.

WOODBERRY, G. E.

2831 Doyle, Joseph.   GEW.   Columbia 52.

WOODWORTH, SAMUEL

2832 Taft, Kendall B.   SW.   Chicago 37.

WOOLSON, C. F.

2833 Gray, Stella Clifford.   The Literary Achievements of CFW.   Wis 57.
2834 Kern, John D.   CFW.   Pa 33.

WRIGHT, RICHARD

2835 Bakish, David J. The Works of RW: The Exile Years. Del.
2836 Brignano, Russell. RW: Art and Idea in His Fiction and Non-Fiction. Wis.
2837 Kinnamon, Kenneth. The Emergence of RW: A Literary, Bibliographical, and Social Study. Harvard 66.
2838 Margolies, Edward L. A Critical Analysis of the Works of RW. NYU 64.

WYLIE, ELINOR

2839 Collura, Ida M. EW's Prose: A Study in Conflict. Pittsburgh 62.
2840 Farr, Judith B. "Language from Spirit": The Art of EW. Yale 66.
2841 Potter, Nancy A. EW: A Biographical and Critical Study. Boston 54.
2842 Wright, Elizabeth V. A Bibliographic Study of EW. Loyola (Chicago) 54.

YOUNG, STARK

2843 Drexter, Malcolm B. SY's Ideas of Theatre Practice. Ill S 64.
2844 Lumianski, Robert M. SY and His Dramatic Criticism. Mich State 55.
2845 Miller, John M. SY's Principles of Theater Art. Tulane T 63.
2846 Thurman, Bedford. SY: A Bibliography of His Writings with a Selective Index to His Criticism of the Arts. Cornell S 54.

ALMANACS, ANNUALS, AND GIFT BOOKS

2847 Goldberg, Joseph P. The Eighteenth-Century Philadelphia Almanac and Its English Counterpart. Md 62.
2848 Perrine, F. J. Significance of the English and American Almanacs of the Seventeenth and Eighteenth Centuries. NYU 17.
2849 Shelley, Philip A. The German Heritage of the American Annuals and Gift-Books. Harvard 38.
2850 Sidwell, Robert T. The Colonial American Almanacs: A Study in Non-Institutional Education. Rutgers E 65.
2851 Thompson, Ralph. American Literary Annuals and Gift Books, 1825-1865. Columbia 37.
2852 Wechsler, Louis K. New York Almanacs, 1694-1793: Their Significance and Influence. Harvard 36.
      See also 3855.

AMERICAN REVOLUTION

2853 Bushey, Glenn L. A Bibliography of Controversial Literature Published in the American Revolutionary Period, 1750-1785, Found in the Historical Society of Pennsylvania. Temple 39.
2854 Culp, Ralph B. Drama-and-Theater as a Source of Colonial American Attitudes toward Independence, 1758-1776. Cornell D 62.
2855 Delmage, Rutherford E. The Theory of the Future: A Study of the Idea of Progress in the Literature of the American Revolution. Cornell 37.
2856 Granger, Bruce I. Political Satire in the American Revolution (1763-1783). Cornell
2857 Heilman, Robert B. The English Novel, 1760-1800, and the American Revolution. Harvard 35.
2858 Korn, Harold. The Oratory of the American Revolution. NYU 14.
2859 Leemhuis, Roger P. The Revolutionary and Federalist Age in American Fiction, Historiography, and Social Thought, 1885-1910. Wis.
2860 Leffler, Margarete. Der amerikanische Unabhängigkeitskrieg in der englischen Literatur (1765-1790). Freiburg 23.

2861 Patterson, Samuel W. The Spirit of the American Revolution as Revealed in the Poetry of the Period: A Study of American Patriotic Verse from 1760 to 1783. NYU 13.

2862 Smith, Glenn C. Pamphleteers and the American Revolution in Virginia, 1752-1776. Va H 41.

2863 Strong, Clinton A. The Political Verse of the Revolution as Represented in Newspapers and Magazines of Massachusetts. Pa 11.
See also 570a, 2948, 3546, 3614, 4161.

CIVIL WAR

2864 Babcock, Havilah. Some Aspects of the Literary Influence of the Civil War. SC 27.

2865 Ellinger, Esther P. The Southern War Poetry of the Civil War. Pa 18.

2866 Fife, Iline. The Theatre during the Confederacy. La FA 49.

2867 Fredrickson, George M. The Inner Civil War: Northern Intellectuals and the War for the Union. Harvard A 64.

2868 Hecht, Walter. Der amerikanische Bürgerkrieg und seine Behandlung in einigen der bekanntesten literarischen Werke. Vienna 50.

2869 Hitt, Ralph E. Controversial Poetry of the Civil War Period: 1830-1878. Vanderbilt 55.

2870 Kimball, William J. The Civil War in American Novels: 1920-1939. Pa State 58.

2871 Most, Ralph C. Civil War Fiction, 1890-1920. Pa 51.

2872 Rudolph, Earle L. Confederate Broadside Verse. Harvard 47.

2873 Sine, Edward W. The Civil War Poetry of the North (1861-1865). Pa 31.

2874 Skinner, Donald T. The Civil War as a Subject for American Drama. Northwestern 49.

2875 Smith, Rebecca W. The Civil War and Its Aftermath in American Fiction, 1861-1899, with a Dictionary Catalogue and Indexes. Chicago 32.

2876 Waller, John O. The American Civil War and Some English Men of Letters: Carlyle, Mill, Ruskin, Arnold, Kingsley, Hughes, Trollope, Thackeray, and Dickens. So Cal 54.

2877 Weissbuch, Ted N. Literary and Historical Attitudes toward Reconstruction Following the Civil War. Iowa 65.
See also 132, 135, 550a, 1951, 2672, 2943, 3543, 3546, 3990, 4266, 4368, 4585.

CRITICISM

2878 Ball, Roland C., Jr. Literary Criticism and Theory in the American Little Magazines. UCB 53.

2879 Boaz, Martha T. A Qualitative Analysis of the Criticism of Best Sellers: A Study of the Reviews and Reviewers of Best Selling Books from 1944 to 1953. Mich LS 55.

2880 Bradbury, John M. The Fugitive Critics: A Critical History. Iowa 48.

2881 Browne, Robert M. Theories of Convention in Contemporary American Criticism. Catholic 56.

2882 Burgauner, C. Der Realitätsbezug von Dichtung als Element und als Kriterium literarischer Theorien im amerikanischen New Criticism (Richards, Brooks, Tate). Munich.

2883 Calhoun, Richard J. Literary Criticism in Southern Periodicals, 1828-1860. NC 59.

2884 Cauger, Richard E. The Concept of the Puritan in American Literary Criticism, 1890-1932. Northwestern 64.

2885 Charvat, William. The Origins of American Critical Thought, 1810-1835. Pa 34.

2886 Clecak, Pete E. Marxism and American Literary Criticism. Stanford 65.

2887 Current-Garcia, Eugene. Criticism and the Problem of Literary Expression in a Democratic Society. Harvard A 47.

2888 Darling, Richard L. Reviewing of Children's Books in American Periodicals, 1865-1881. Mich LS 60.

2889 Dolan, Paul J. Tradition in Modern Literary Criticism. NYU 66.

2890 Eby, Edwin H. American Romantic Criticism, 1815 to 1860. Wash 27.

2891 Flewelling, Howard L. Literary Criticism in American Periodicals, 1783-1820. Mich 3

2892 Foster, Richard J. Modern Critics and Romantic Sensibility: A Study of the Romanticism of the New Criticism. Syracuse 57.

2893 Fourier, Ruth G. The Literary Criticism of the *Dial*, 1920-1929. Vanderbilt 59.

2894 Fraiberg, Louis. The Use of Psychoanalytic Ideas by Literary Critics. Mich 56.

2895 Garcia, Daniel P. Theories of Catharsis in Modern Literary Criticism: The Influences of Psychoanalysis, Anthropology, and the New Criticism. Ore 62.

2896 Geier, Norbert J. The Problem of Aesthetic Judgment and Moral Judgment of Literary Value in the Critical Theories of Irving Babbitt, Paul Elmer More, Yvor Winters, and T. S. Eliot. Wis 64.

2897 Gomme, A. H. Some Presuppositions in Modern Literary Criticism in Britain and the U. S. A. Cambridge 62-63.

2898 Haefner, Gerhard. Das antiromantische Denken in der modernen amerikanischen Literaturkritik. Freiburg 61.

2899 Harwood, C. Edwin. An Analysis of Literary Criticism in America between 1899 and 1914. Colo 58.

2900 Heidinger, Maurice M. "Intrinsic" Kafka Criticism in America (1949-1963). Ind 65.

2901 Jones, Arthur E., Jr. Early American Literary Criticism: A Study of American Literary Opinions and Attitudes, 1741 to 1820. Syracuse 50.

2902 Kibel, Alvin C. After Such Knowledge: Modern Criticism and Its Ideology. Columbia 63.

2903 Lang, Hans-Joachim. Studien zur Entstehung der neueren amerikanischen Literaturkri Hamburg 61.

2904 Lawler, John J. Comments on Art and Literature from the Personal Writings of a Group of Well-Traveled Early American Writers and Artists: A Critical Collation. Fla State 60.

2905 Lutwack, Leonard I. The Dynamics of Conservative Criticism: Literary Criticism in American Magazines, 1880-1900. Ohio State 50.

2906 McDonald, Florin L. Book Reviewing in the American Newspaper. Mo 37.

2907 McMahon, Helen M. Criticism of Fiction in the *Atlantic Monthly*, 1857-1898. Iowa

2908 Manning, Charles. American Literary Culture, 1865-1886, by Selected Critics. NC 5(

2909 Minter, David L. The Interpreted Design: A Study in American Prose. Yale 65.

2910 Morrison, Claudia C. Depth Psychology in American Literary Criticism, 1900-1926. NC 64.

2911 Mounts, David L. The Validity of the New Humanist Criticism of Romanticism. So Cal 39.

2912 Passe, Martha E. Criticism of Poetry in America during the Nineties. Ohio State 57.

2913 Pedigo, Frances M. Critical Opinions of Poetry, Drama, and Fiction in *The Christian Examiner*, 1824-1869. NC 53.

2914 Pfenning, Hazel T. Periodical Literary Criticism, 1800-1865: A Study of the Book Reviews from 1800 to the Close of the Civil War, Dealing with the Successive Works of Irving, Cooper, Bryant, Poe, Hawthorne, and Thoreau, Which Appeared in American Publications within the Lifetime of the Individual Authors. NYU 32.

2915 Rathbun, John W. The Development of Historical Literary Criticism in America, 1800-1860. Wis 56.

2916 Rooney, Rev. William J. The Problem of "Belief" in Contemporary English and American Criticism. Catholic 45.

2917 Sedgwick, William E. The Problem of American Literature as Seen by Contemporary Critics, 1815-1830. Harvard 34.

2918 Smith, Hubert H. Some American Fiction Writers and Their Reviewers: A Study of the Reviews and Reviewers in Connection with Eight Representative Fiction Writers, 1918-1941. Pa 49.

2919 Smith, Thomas F. Contemporary Criticism of the Novel: The Four Basic Approach Pittsburgh 62.

2920 Speckbaugh, Paul F. Some General Canons of Literary Criticism Determined from an Analysis of Art. Catholic 36.
2921 Stafford, Arnold J. The Literary Criticism in Three New York Political Periodicals, 1837-1850. Tex 48.
2922 Stedtfeld, Wolfgang. Aspects of the New Criticism. Freiburg 56.
2923 Tomas, Vincent A. The Criticism of Literature. Brown P 41.
2924 Weeks, Lewis E., Jr. Nineteenth Century British and American Periodical Criticism of American Literature: A Comparative Study. Boston.
2925 Weimann, Robert. New Criticism und die Entwicklung bürgerlicher Literaturwissenschaft: Zur Geschichte und Kritik des modernen Interpretationsbegriffs in der Anglistik. Berlin (H) 60.

See also 211, 215, 233, 235, 660, 669, 672, 679, 686, 728, 773, 838, 1035, 1312, 1386, 1458, 1537, 1545, 1759, 1924, 1968, 2100, 2130, 2157, 2158, 2161, 2172, 2237, 2238, 2252, 2331, 2355, 2384, 2467, 2468, 2469, 2492, 2500, 2503, 2728, 2777, 2783, 2787, 3550, 3690, 3748, 4096, 4284, 4324, 4337.

DRAMA

CHARACTERS, CHARACTER TYPES AND THEMES

2926 Bloore, J. Stephen. The Jew in American Dramatic Literature, 1794-1930. NYU 50.
2927 Corrigan, Robert W. The "Electra" Theme in the History of Drama. Minn 55.
2928 Davis, Blanche E. The Hero in American Drama, 1787-1900: A Critical Appraisal of American Dramas through a Consideration of the Hero. Columbia 51.
2929 Dell, Robert M. The Representation of the Immigrant on the New York Stage: 1881 to 1910. NYU S 60.
2930 Denning, Dennis F. The Theme of Poverty as Reflected in Plays by Six Depression Playwrights. Kan S 66.
2931 Dusenbury, Winifred L. The Theme of Loneliness in Modern American Drama. Fla 56.
2932 Fisch, Mortimer L. The Politician on the American Stage, from 1870 to 1915. NYU S 59.
2933 Floyd, Virginia H. The Role of *Hubris* in the Spiritual Environment of Selected British and American Plays. Northwestern S.
2934 Gallagher, Kent G. The Foreigner in American Drama to 1830: A Study in Attitudes. Ind D 62.
2935 Goodrich, George. Characterization of the Protagonist in Serious One-Hour (or Longer) Dramas for Television. Iowa D.
2936 Hyde, Stuart W. The Representation of the West in American Drama from 1849 to 1917. Stanford 54.
2937 Klein, Elaine S. The Development of the Leading Feminine Character in American Musical Comedy from 1900 to 1959. Columbia Teachers College.
2938 Klein, Ralph. An Analysis of the American Military Hero in Representative American Plays. Denver.
2939 Koster, Donald N. The Theme of Divorce in American Drama, 1871-1939. Pa 41.
2940 Leonard, Mother Dymphna. Mary Stuart: The Historical Figure in English and American Drama. Columbia D 64.
2941 Logan, Winford B. An Investigation of the Theme of the Negation of Life in American Drama from World War II to 1958. Ohio State D 61.
2942 Lown, Charles R., Jr. Business and the Businessman in American Drama Prior to the Civil War. Stanford S 57.
2943 McGraw, Rex T. The Villain in Civil-War Melodrama. Ind.
2944 Marcuson, Lewis R. The Irish, the Italians, and the Jews: A Study of Three Nationality Groups as Portrayed in American Drama Between 1920 and 1960. Denver 66.
2945 Pettit, Paul B. The Important American Dramatic Types to 1900: A Study of the Yankee, Negro, Indian, and Frontiersman. Cornell 49.

2946 Quinn, James J., Jr. The Jonathan Character in the American Drama. Columbia 55.
2947 Ruffner, Sydney J. The American Theme in Selected Dramas of the Golden Age.
      So Cal 54.
2948 Shirk, Samuel. The Characterization of George Washington in American Plays since
      1875. Pa 48.
2949 Smalley, Webster L. The Characterization of the Male Protagonist in Serious America
      Drama from 1920 to 1940. Stanford S 60.
2950 Thurman, William R. Anxiety in Modern American Drama. Ga 64.
2951 Tillson, M. W. The Frontiersman in American Drama: An Analytical Study of
      Characters and Plays Reflecting the Phenomenon of Westward Expansion. Denver 51.
2952 Vincent, James E. Freedom and Responsibility: An Introductory Essay on
      Existential Themes in American Drama. Wis D 62.
2953 von Tornow, Georgiana J. The Heroine in American Drama and Theatre Down to
      the Civil War, and Her Relation to "Life" and the Novels of the Times. Cornell 44.
2954 Welsh, Willard, Jr. The Characterization of the Male Protagonist in Serious American
      Drama from 1867 to 1920. Stanford 54.

CRITICISM

2955 Angotti, Vincent. A Critical Survey of American Dramatic Criticism, 1800-1835.
      Kan S.
2956 Blymyer, Louise A. Journalistic Dramatic Criticism: A Survey of Theater Reviews
      in New York, 1857-1927. La 39.
2957 Gearhart, Sally M. Aristotle and Modern Theorists on the Elements of Tragedy.
      Ill S 56.
2958 Greenberg, Edward. Dramatic Criticism of the Professional New York Theater, 1929
      to 1940. NYU S.
2959 Gregoric, Michael T. Principles and Practice in Modern Dramatic Criticism. Cornell I
2960 Hunter, Frederick J. Clayton Hamilton and the Technical Mode in American Dramati
      Criticism. Stanford S 54.
2961 Jasspé, Arthur. Critical Theory and Playwriting Practice of Contemporary American
      Playwrights: A Study of the Relationship of Critical Theory to Playwriting Practice as
      Evidenced in the Prize Winning Plays of Contemporary Playwrights during the Years
      1920 to 1940. NYU S 58.
2962 Knapp, Daniel B. Early Twentieth Century Dramatic Criticism and the Idea of Progre
      UCB 55.
2963 Norton, Hugh Z. Studies in the Theatre Criticism of Arthur Bingham Walkley (1855-
      1926). Mich FA 47.
2964 Rottsolk, James E. Criticism of the Drama in the Twenties. Chicago 51.
2965 Sederholm, Frederic L. The Development of Dramatic Comic Theory in America to
      1850. Iowa S.
2966 Walters, Walter H. Representative Trends in American Theatrical Criticism from
      1900 to 1940. Western Reserve 50.
      See also 720, 1986, 2095, 2785, 2786, 2844, 2846, 2913, 3648, 3699, 3702.

FOREIGN RELATIONSHIPS

2967 Abood, Edward. The Reception of the Abbey Repertory Theatre in America, 1911-
      1914. Chicago D 64.
2968 Bauland, Peter M. German Drama on the American Stage: 1894-1961. Pa 64.
2969 Beachboard, Robert. Le Théâtre de Maeterlinck aux États-Unis. Paris 51.
2970 Bilgray, Ruth. The Foreign Plays Popular in the United States, 1870-1900. Chicago
2971 Brédé, Charles F. The German Drama in English on the Philadelphia Stage from 1794
      to 1830. Pa 05.
2972 Costello, Brother Raymond. Le Théâtre français devant la critique américaine, 1900-
      1950. Laval 54.
2973 Edwards, Christine E. The Contributions of Stanislavsky and the Moscow Art Theatr
      to the American Theatre. NYU S 60.

2974   Gergely, Emro J.   Adaptations of Hungarian Plays upon the New York Stage.   Pa 38.
2975   Haugen, Ralph H.   American Drama Critics' Reactions to Productions of August
        Strindberg.   Minn S 59.
2976   Henry, Donald R.   The American Theatre as Viewed by 19th Century British Travellers,
        1860-1900.   Wis 64.
2977   Hudson, Virginia O.   Charles Dickens and the American Theatre.   Chicago 26.
2978   Lazenby, Walter S.   Stage Versions of Dickens's Novels in America to 1900.   Ind D 62.
2979   Leuchs, Frederick A.   The Early German Theater in New York, 1840-1872.
        Columbia 28.
2980   Lyman, Kenneth C.   Critical Reaction to Irish Drama on the New York Stage: 1900-
        1958.   Wis S 60.
2981   Mason, Hamilton.   French Theatre in New York: A List of Plays, 1899-1939.
        Columbia RL 39.
2982   Moehlenbrock, Arthur H.   The German Drama on the New Orleans Stage.   Iowa G 41.
2983   Muldrow, Blanche.   The American Theatre as Seen by British Travellers, 1790-1860.
        Wis S 54.
2984   Nolle, Alfred H.   The German Drama on the St. Louis Stage.   Pa 15.
2985   Risley, Herbert J.   The Reception of American Drama in America and in England, 1900-
        1915:   A Comparative Study with Emphasis on the Reactions of English Critics.   Ind 58.
2986   Robertson, Alice M.   Eight Plays of Jean Cocteau Translated from French into English
        with an Analysis of the Problems Encountered in Making These Translations.   Utah 60.
2987   Rothfuss, Hermann E.   The German Theater in Minnesota.   Mich G 49.
2988   Schlossmacher, Stephan G.   Das deutsche Drama im amerikanischen College-und
        Universitätstheater.   Cologne 38 publ.
2989   Schoenberger, Harold W.   American Adaptations of French Plays on the New York
        and Philadelphia Stages from 1790 to 1833.   Pa 24.
2990   Shoemaker, Robert W.   Russian Drama on the New York Stage from the Beginning
        to 1920.   Pa 51.
2991   Steene, Kerstin B.   The American Drama and the Swedish Theater, 1920-1958.
        Wash S 60.
2992   Stever, Brother Declan.   Le Théâtre américain à Paris.   Laval 54.
2993   Waldo, Lewis P.   The French Drama in America in the Eighteenth Century and Its
        Influence on the American Drama of That Period, 1701-1800.   Mich 40.
2994   Ware, Ralph H.   American Adaptations of French Plays on the New York and
        Philadelphia Stages from 1834 to the Civil War.   Pa 30.
2995   Zuther, Gerhard.   Problems in Translation: Modern American Dramas in German.
        Ind 59.

HISTORY

2996   Carmichael, Herbert K.   The Best Representative Short Plays in the United States:
        1900-1940.   Minn S 43.
2997   Curvin, Jonathan W.   The Realistic Tradition in American Art and Drama.   Cornell S 41.
2998   Ernst, Earle.   Cycles in the Development of the Dramatic Arts.   Cornell S 40.
2999   Hartman, John G.   Development of American Social Comedy from 1787 to the
        Present Day.   Pa 37.
3000   Havens, Daniel F.   The Development of a Native Tradition in Early American Social
        Comedy, 1787-1845.   Mich 65.
3001   Hruby, Norbert J.   Successful American Plays, 1919-1929:   Patterns and Their
        Implications.   Loyola (Chicago) 51.
3002   Ketels, Arthur O.   The American Drama of the Twenties: A Critical Evaluation.
        Northwestern S 60.
3003   Laufe, Abe.   The Long-Running Plays on the New York Stage, 1918-1950:   A Literary
        Evaluation.   Pittsburgh 52.
3004   McCormick, Robert A.   A Study of Original American Fantasy Presented on the New
        York Stage from 1920 to 1950.   Denver 55.
3005   Meneely, John H.   A Study of the American Drama Prior to 1825.   NYU 11.

3006 Nickel, Gerhard. Der kulturelle, politische und soziale Hintergrund der Comedy of Manners in Amerika von 1787-1845. Erlangen 52.

3007 Obee, Harold B. A Prompt Script Study of Nineteenth-Century Legitimate Stage Versions of *Rip Van Winkle*. Ohio State D 61.

3008 Plessow, Gustav. Das amerikanische Kurzschauspiel zwischen 1910 und 1930. Halle 33.

3009 Riley, Donald W. A History of American Radio Drama from 1919 to 1944. Ohio State S 44.

3010 Smith, Irvine N. American Plays and Playwrights of the 19th Century. Denver 59.

3011 Smith, Ross D. A Survey of Native American Serious Drama from 1900 to 1918. Utah 52.

3012 Sturcken, Francis W. An Historical Analysis of Live Network Television Drama from 1938 to 1958. Minn D 60.

MISCELLANEOUS SPECIAL TOPICS

3013 Bassage, Rev. Harold E. The Moral Price of Freedom: Problems of Personal Freedom Reflected in Modern American Drama. Columbia 52.

3014 Bauer, Gero. Tradition und Experiment in der Gestaltung des amerikanischen Dramas des zwanzigsten Jahrhunderts. Vienna 62.

3015 Bell, Richard H. A Study of the Image of the American Character as Presented in Selected Network Television Dramas. Ohio State E 61.

3016 Blackburn, Clara B. Influences on American Expressionistic Drama. Ohio State 38.

3017 Bradley, Robert. Proposals for Reforms in the Art of the Theatre as Expressed in General American and British Periodicals. Ill.

3018 Burke, William M. American Playwrights' Treatment of War, 1914-1949. Pa A 50.

3019 Chinoy, Helen K. The Impact of the Stage Director on American Plays, Playwrights, and Theatres: 1860-1930. Columbia S 63.

3020 Crandall, Frederic O. Three Studies in Propaganda in the American Theatre. Mich S 40.

3021 Damaser, Henry. The Uses of the Past in American Drama from 1919 to 1963. Pa.

3022 Decker, Phillip. Elements of Classical Myth in Twentieth Century English and American Drama from 1900 to 1960. Northwestern.

3023 Devi, K. Lakshmi. Modern American Drama and the Image of Man. Andhra, India.

3024 Dickinson, Donald H. Problems of Religion and Myth in Modern Drama: 1914-1950. Northwestern D 61.

3025 Edyvean, Alfred R. A Critical Appraisal of American Dramas (1935-1949) in the Light of the Christian View of Man. Northwestern 52.

3026 Fisher, William J. Trends in Post-Depression American Drama: A Study of the Works of William Saroyan, Tennessee Williams, Irwin Shaw, Arthur Miller. NYU 52.

3027 Geier, Woodrow A. Images of Man in Five American Dramatists: A Theological Critique. Vanderbilt R 59.

3028 Glenn, Stanley L. Ludicrous Characterization in American Comedy from the Beginning until the Civil War. Stanford S 55.

3029 Halline, Allan G. Main Currents of Thought in American Drama. Wis 35.

3030 Hubbard, Eleanore E. Plays on the Old World Background of American History. Boston College 36.

3031 Kaufman, Alvin. Attitudes and Adjustments of the Soldier Toward War and the Military as Revealed in the American Drama, 1940-60. Stanford S 66.

3032 Labrenz, Ernest T., Jr. A Critical Analysis of the Negative Attitudes in Plays Exclusive of Musical Comedies Which Won the Pulitzer Prize between 1948 and 1957. So Cal 62.

3033 Leonard, James. An Analysis of Representative Modern American War Plays. Cornell.

3034 Mangum, Valerie B. American Attitudes towards War as Reflected in American Drama, 1773-1946. Tex 47.

3035 Moe, Christian H. From History to Drama: A Study of the Influence of the

Pageant, the Outdoor Epic Drama, and the Historical Stage Play upon the Dramatization of Three American Historical Figures. Cornell S 58.

3036 O'Meara, Edward F. Some Influences of the Adoption of International Copyright on the American Drama. Notre Dame 40.

3037 Porter, Thomas E. Mythic Elements in Modern American Drama. NC 65.

3038 Roach, Josh P. A Study of Some Unpublished American Dramas. Denver 55.

3039 Robinson, Alice M. The Developing Ideas of Individual Freedom and National Unity as Reflected in American Plays, 1772-1819. Stanford 65.

3040 Salisbury, Harold. A Critical Evaluation of Dramatic Censorship in the United States. So Cal.

3041 Savage, George M., Jr. Regionalism in the American Drama. Wash 35.

3042 Sievers, Wieder D. An Analysis of the Influence of Freudian Psychology on American Drama, 1909-1939. So Cal 52.

3043 Smallwood, Clyde. Elements of the Existentialist Philosophy in Representative Modern American Drama. Denver.

3044 Soper, Paul L. Aesthetics and the Modern Theatre. Cornell S 41.

3045 Wiley, Charles G. A Study of the American Woman as She Is Presented in the American Drama of the Nineteen-Twenties. NM 57.

3046 Wismer, Lawrence H. Changing Concepts of Death in American Drama. 1885-1960. Stanford 63.
See also 2874.

MODES, STRUCTURE, TECHNIQUE

3047 Barer, Bertram. A Rhetorical Analysis of the American Presentational Social Theatre of the Thirties. Minn S 60.

3048 Burton, May E. A Study of Music as an Integral Part of the Spoken Drama in the American Professional Theatre: 1930-1955. Fla 57.

3049 Collins, John D. A Rhetorical Analysis of American Abolitionist Plays. Iowa S.

3050 Gild, David. Symbolism in American Drama. Yale.

3051 Ingle, Patricia. Departures from Realism on the New York Stage, 1919-1930. Ark 65.

3052 Keller, Alvin. The Correlation of Form to Content in the Social Drama of America, 1929-1945. Stanford.

3053 Lewis, Frank. Dramaturgical Analysis of Selected Contemporary British and American Courtroom Dramas. Mich State.

3054 Link, Gloria M. The Function of Comedy in the Denouement of Modern Mixed Genre Plays. Wis S 65.

3055 Manfull, Helen A. The New Realism (A Study of American Dramatic Realism, 1918-1929). Minn D 61.

3056 Moody, Richard. Romanticism in American Drama and the Theatre from the Beginning to 1900. Cornell 42.

3057 Mowry, Vera L. Satire in American Drama. Pittsburgh 50.

3058 Redfern, Richard K. The Study of Act-Structure in Drama. Cornell 51.

3059 Reed, Perley I. The Realistic Presentation of American Characters in Native Plays Prior to 1870. Ohio State 16.

3060 Smiley, Sam M. The Structure of Didactic Drama as Represented in American Plays of the Depression Era. Ind.

3061 Staub, August W. The Subjective Perspective: Aspects of Point of View in Modern Drama. La S 60.

3062 Templeton, Joan. Expressionism in British and American Drama. Ore.

3063 Thompson, David W. The Rise of Realism in American Drama and Theatre. Cornell 47.

3064 Turner, Darwin T. Techniques of and Critical Reactions towards American Non-Representational Drama on New York Professional Stages, 1920-1930. Chicago 56.

3065 Valgemae, Mardi. Expressionism in American Drama. UCLA 64.

3066 Willoughby, Pearl V. The Achievements of Modern Dramaturgy, British and American. Va 23.

PLAY TYPES AND DRAMATIC FORMS

3067 Andrews, Mary Lee. Modern Poetic Drama in America (1900-1942). NYU 43.

3068 Broussard, Louis. The Modern Allegorical Play in America. NYU 63.

3069 Bucks, Dorothy S. The American Drama of Ideas from 1890 to 1929.
      Northwestern 44.

3070 Carson, Herbert L. Modern Tragedy and Its Origins in Domestic Tragedy: A Study
      of Selected English and American Domestic Tragedies from Elizabethan to Modern
      Times. Minn S 59.

3071 Carter, Ralph P. American Romanticism and the "Romantic" Play in the First Half
      of the Nineteenth Century. Ind.

3072 Crooker, Earl T. The American Musical Play. Pa 57.

3073 Dawson, Mary E. The Idea of Tragedy in the Contemporary American Theatre.
      Iowa 44.

3074 Dierolf, Claude E. The Pageant Drama and American Pageantry. Pa 53.

3075 Dusenbury, Delwin B. A Study of Comedy in the American Theatre Represented in
      the Productions of Native Comedy in New York City from 1900 to 1920. Minn 47.

3076 Frank, Arnim P. Das Hörspiel: Vergleichende Beschreibung und Analyse einer neuen
      Kunstform, durchgeführt an amerikanischen, deutschen, englischen und französischen
      Texten. Frankfurt 63 publ.

3077 Gerstenberger, Donna L. Formal Experiments in Modern Verse Drama. Okla 58.

3078 Girard, Clet A. The Equestrian Drama of the Nineteenth Century. La 39.

3079 Goff, Lewin A. The Popular Priced Melodrama in America, 1890-1910, with Its
      Origins and Development to 1920. Western Reserve S 48.

3080 Gould, Arthur J. The Idea of Tragedy in Modern American Drama. Mich 48.

3081 Haberman, LeRoy D. American Farce on Broadway, 1914-1950. Stanford S 59.

3082 Joseph, Barbara A. Patterns for Modern American Comedy since 1923. Western
      Reserve 53.

3083 Kingsley, William H. Happy Endings, Poetic Justice, and the Depth and Strength of
      Characterization in American Children's Drama: A Critical Analysis. Pittsburgh 64.

3084 Knutson, Wayne S. A Definition of Modern Tragedy. Denver 57.

3085 Leggette, L. Poe. Festival Drama. Columbia Teachers College E 57.

3086 McDermott, Douglas. The Living Newspaper as a Dramatic Form. Iowa S 63.

3087 McLeod, Stuart R. Problems of Poetry and Dramaturgy in Modern Verse Drama.
      Fla 60.

3088 Martin, Charles B. The Survivals of Medieval Religious Drama in New Mexico.
      Mo S 59.

3089 Nardin, James T. A Study in Popular American Farce, 1865-1914. Chicago 50.

3090 Patterson, Perry W. A Critical Study of Jazz-Vaudeville Drama (1923-1934) in the
      United States. Denver S 65.

3091 Reardon, John D. Verse Drama in America from 1765 to the Civil War: The End
      of a Tradition. Kan 57.

3092 Smith, George A. American Dramatic Comedy: 1900-1950; a Study of Reflected
      Climate of Opinion in Changing Historical Perspective. Pa 56.

3093 Snyder, Sherwood, III. The Toby Shows. Minn 66.

3094 Tinsley, James R. A Study of the Techniques of Modern American Farce. Pa 62.

3095 Tunberg, Jacqueline Duffie. British and American Verse Drama, 1900-1965: A
      Survey of Style, Subject Matter, and Technique. So Cal 65.

3096 von Szeliski, John J. Pessimism and the Tragic Vision: A Study of Tragedy in the
      Modern American Theatre. Minn D 62.

3097 Wadleigh, Paul C. American Farce in the Nineteenth Century: Its Structure and
      Form. Ind S.

3098 West, William. A Critical Examination of Poetic Drama in English, 1930-1950.
      Stanford.
      See also 3874.

PLAYWRITING, PLAYWRIGHTS, DRAMATIZATION

3099 Busfield, Roger M., Jr. From Idea to Dialogue: An Analysis of the Playwriting Process as Derived from the Non-Dramatic Writings of a Selected Group of Successful Dramatists, 1899-1950. Fla State 54.

3100 Callaway, Marian H. A Comparative Study of the Development of Skills in Plot Construction by a Group of Living American Dramatists. Iowa S 41.

3101 Crain, Harold C. Characterization in the Plays of Modern Dramatists: Techniques and Practices. Iowa S 47.

3102 Ellett, Mel. Principles and Methods of Plotting in American Realistic Serious Drama, 1879 to 1950. Stanford S.

3103 Elliston, Stephen F. Dramatic and Narrative Art: Studies of Dramatizations on the New York Stage, 1919-1958. Ill 59.

3104 Ferguson, Phyllis M. Women Dramatists in the American Theatre, 1901-1940. Pittsburgh 57.

3105 Fowler, Frank. Modern American Dramatization. Columbia S 53.

3106 Hagan, Robert L. The Influence of the Well-Made Play upon American Playwriting. Western Reserve 50.

3107 Hogstrom, Harold R. American Playwrights' Attitudes toward War, 1919-1941. Syracuse.

3108 Johnson, Albert E. American Dramatizations of American Literary Materials from 1850-1900. Cornell 48.

3109 Loney, Glenn M. Dramatizations of American Novels, 1900-1917. Stanford 54.

3110 McIlrath, Patricia A. Typification in the Characterization of Contemporary American Drama: With an Analysis of Stereotype. Stanford 51.

3111 Miranne, Joseph J., Jr. An Investigation of the Nature of Short Story Adaptation in Dramatic Presentations for the Broadway Theater from 1930 to 1960. NYU E 62.

3112 Napiecinski, Thomas H. The Dramatization of the American Serious Novel, 1926-1952. Wis S 59.

3113 Teufel, William C. The Playwright in the United States Prior to the Act of 1909. Mich 60.

3114 Vardac, Alexander N. From Garrick to Griffith: Transition from Stage to Screen. Yale S 41.

REGIONAL STUDIES–Midwest

3115 Andrus, Thomas O. A History of the Legitimate Theatre in St. Paul, Minnesota, from 1918 to 1939. Minn D 61.

3116 Behringer, Clara M. A History of the Theatre in Ann Arbor, Michigan, from Its Beginnings to 1904. Mich FA 51.

3117 Brown, Irving M. The Indigenous Theatre in Cleveland, Ohio. Ohio State S.

3118 Dix, William S., Jr. The Theatre in Cleveland, Ohio, 1854-1875. Chicago FA 46.

3119 Donahoe, Ned. Theaters in Central Illinois, 1850-1900. Ill S 53.

3120 Dryden, Wilma J. Chicago Theatre as Reflected in the Newspapers, 1900 through 1904. Ill S 61.

3121 Dukore, Bernard. Maurice Browne and the Chicago Little Theatre. Ill S 58.

3122 Dunlap, James F. Queen City Stages: Professional Dramatic Activity in Cincinnati, 1837-1861. Ohio State S 54.

3123 Gafford, Lucile. History of the St. Charles Theater. Chicago 30.

3124 Gaiser, Gerhard W. The History of the Cleveland Theater from the Beginning until 1854. Iowa S 53.

3125 Grandstaff, Russell J. A History of the Professional Theatre in Cincinnati, 1861-1886. Mich 63.

3126 Grossman, Audley M., Jr. The Professional Legitimate Theater in Minneapolis from 1890 to 1910. Minn S 57.

3127 Hammack, James A. Pope's Theatre and St. Louis Theatrical History: 1879-1895. Iowa S 54.

3128 Herbstruth, Grant M.   Benedict DeBar and the Grand Opera House in St. Louis, Missouri, from 1855-1879. Iowa S 54.

3129 Johnson, Theodore C.   A History of the First Olympic Theatre of St. Louis, Missouri, from 1866-1879. Iowa S 58.

3130 Knaub, Richard K.   The History of English's Opera House and the English Theatre. Ind D 62.

3131 Lane, Paul E.   A History of the Professional Theatre in Lafayette, Indiana, from 1925-1950. Purdue.

3132 Ludwig, Jay. McVicker's Theatre, 1875-1896. Ill S 58.

3133 McDavitt, Elaine E.   A History of the Theatre in Detroit, Michigan, from Its Beginnings to 1862. Mich FA 47.

3134 O'Shea, Joseph J.   A History of the Theatre in the City of Milwaukee, 1848-1950. Northwestern.

3135 Peterson, William A.   A History of the Professional Theatre of Detroit, Michigan, September 13, 1875 to July 3, 1886. Fla State S 59.

3136 Rietz, Louise J.   History of the Theater of Kansas City, Missouri, from the Beginnings until 1900. Iowa S 39.

3137 Rydahl, Eugene E.   A History of the Legitimate Theater in East Saginaw, Michigan, from 1860 to 1884. Iowa S 58.

3138 Schick, Joseph S.   Cultural Beginnings and the Rise of the Theatre, German and American, in Eastern Iowa (Davenport), 1836-1863. Chicago 38.

3139 Silver, Reuben.   A History of the Karamu Theatre of Karamu House, 1915-1960. Ohio State D 61.

3140 Stolzenbach, Norma F.   The History of the Theatre in Toledo, Ohio, from Its Beginnings until 1893. Mich 54.

3141 Sturtevant, Catherine.   A Study of the Dramatic Productions of Two Decades in Chicago: 1847-57 and 1897-1907. Chicago 31.

3142 Thompson, Isabel C.   Amateur Theatricals in St. Louis, Missouri, 1875-1890. Iowa S 54.

3143 Utz, Kathryn E.   Columbus, Ohio, Theatre, Seasons 1840-41 to 1860-61.   Ohio State 52.

3144 Whiting, Frank M.   A History of the Theatre in St. Paul, Minnesota, from Its Beginning to 1890. Minn S 41.

3145 Wilt, Napier. History of the Chicago Theatre from 1847 to 1857. Chicago 23.

3146 Woods, Donald Z.   A History of the Theater in Minneapolis, Minnesota, from the Beginning to 1883. Minn FA 51.

3147 Youngerman, Henry C.   Theatrical Activities: Madison, Wisconsin, 1836-1907. Wis S 40.

REGIONAL STUDIES—Northeast

3148 Bonawitz, Dorothy M.   The History of the Boston Stage from the Beginning to 1810. Pa State 36.

3149 Borgers, Edward W.   A History of Dramatic Production in Princeton, New Jersey. NYU FA 50.

3150 Coder, William D.   A History of the Philadelphia Theater, 1856 to 1878. Pa 36.

3151 Fletcher, Edward G. History of the Pittsburgh Stage to 1855. Harvard 31.

3152 Gardner, Dorothea B. History of the Nixon Theater, Pittsburgh, Pennsylvania. Pittsburgh 59.

3153 James, Reese D.   Old Drury of Philadelphia: A History of the Philadelphia Theater, 1800-1835, Including a Facsimile Reprint of the Diary of William Burke Wood. Pa 32.

3154 Jennings, John H.   A History of the New Theater, New York, 1909-11.   Stanford S 53.

3155 Jones, Cecil D.   The Policies and Practices of Wallack's Theatre, 1852 to 1888. Ill S 59.

3156 Lewis, Stanley T. The New York Theatre: Its Background and Architectural Development: 1750-1853. Ohio State FA 54.

3157 Lifson, David S. The History of the Yiddish Art Theater Movement in New York from 1918 to 1940. NYU D 63.

3158 Lowrie, James A. A History of the Pittsburgh Stage, 1861-1891. Pittsburgh 43.

3159 McKenzie, Ruth H. Organization, Production, and Management at the Chestnut Street Theatre, Philadelphia, from 1791 to 1820. Stanford S 52.

3160 Marshall, Thomas F. A History of the Philadelphia Theatre, 1878-1890. Pa 41.

3161 Meconnahey, Joseph H. The History of the Philadelphia Theater from 1900-1910. Pa 37.

3162 Michael, Mary R. A History of the Professional Theatre in Boston from the Beginning to 1816. Radcliffe 41.

3163 Morse, William N. Contributions to the History of the New England Stage in the Eighteenth Century, with Special Reference to Boston and Portsmouth. Harvard 36.

3164 Neeson, Jack M. The Devil in Delaware: A Study of Theatre in New Castle County. Western Reserve 59.

3165 Pollock, Thomas C. The History of the Philadelphia Theater in the Eighteenth Century. Pa 30.

3166 Porter, Jack. A History of the Phoenix Theatre, New York City, 1953 to 1961. Denver D 62.

3167 Potts, Edgar L. The History of the Philadelphia Theater, 1890-1900. Pa 32.

3168 Reardon, William R. Banned in Boston: A Study of Theatrical Censorship in Boston from 1630 to 1950. Stanford S 53.

3169 Seiger, Marvin L. A History of the Yiddish Theatre in New York City to 1892. Ind S 60.

3170 Shank, Theodore. The Bowery Theater, 1826-1836. Stanford S 56.

3171 Wentz, John C. The Hedgerow Theatre: An Historical Study. Pa 54.

3172 Wilson, Arthur H. A History of the Philadelphia Theater, 1835-1855. Pa 31.

3173 Woodruff, John R. The Theatrical Venture in Boston. Cornell FA 49.

REGIONAL STUDIES–South

3174 Arnold, John C. A History of the Lexington [Ky.] Theater from 1887 to 1900. Ky S 56.

3175 Bradford, Clinton W. The Non-Professional Theater in Louisiana. La S 52.

3176 Bristow, Eugene K. Look Out for Saturday Night: A Social History of Professional Variety Theatre in Memphis, Tennessee, 1859-1880. Iowa S 57.

3177 Brown, Edward D. History of the Shreveport Little Theatre, Shreveport, Louisiana, 1922 to 1956. Denver S 58.

3178 Crum, Mabel T. The History of the Lexington [Ky.] Theater from the Beginning to 1860. Ky 56.

3179 Dart, Peter. A History of Legitimate Theatre in Dallas from 1856 to 1960. Iowa.

3180 Davis, Jackson. A History of Professional Theater in Dallas, Texas, 1920-1930. La D 62.

3181 Estes, Maxie C. A Century of Theatre Activity in the Capital City of Florida: An Historical Study of Theatrical Entertainment in Tallahassee, Florida, from 1857 to 1957. Fla State D 62.

3182 Faulkner, Seldon. The New Memphis Theater of Memphis, Tennessee, from 1859 to 1880. Iowa S 57.

3183 Free, Joseph M. The Theatre of Southwestern Mississippi to 1840. Iowa S 41.

3184 Hadley, Richard H. The Theatre in Lynchburg, Virginia, from Its Beginnings in 1822 to the Outbreak of the Civil War. Mich FA 47.

3185 Hill, West T. A Study of the Macauley's Theatre in Louisville, Kentucky, 1873-1880. Iowa S 54.

3186 Langworth, Helen. The Theater in the Frontier Cities of Lexington, Kentucky, and Cincinnati, Ohio, 1797-1835. Iowa S 53.

3187　Maiden, Lewis S.　A Chronicle of the Theater in Nashville, Tennessee, 1876-1900. Vanderbilt S 55.

3188　Pryor, William L.　An Examination of the Southern Milieu in Representative Plays by Southern Dramatists, 1923-1956.　Fla State 59.

3189　Ritter, Charles C.　The Theatre in Memphis, Tennessee, from Its Beginning to 1859. Iowa 56.

3190　Roppolo, Joseph P.　A History of the English Language Theater in New Orleans, 1845-1861.　Tulane 50.

3191　Shockley, Martin S.　A History of the Theater in Richmond, Virginia.　NC 38.

3192　Smither, Nelle K.　A History of the English Theatre at New Orleans, 1806-1842. Pa 41.

3193　Tedford, Harold C.　The Professional Theatre in Arkansas Outside of Little Rock from Its Beginning to 1889.　La.

3194　Watson, Charles S.　Early Dramatic Writing in the South:　Virginia and South Carolina Plays, 1798-1830.　Vanderbilt 66.

3195　Yocum, Jack H.　A History of the Theatre in Houston, 1836-1954.　Wis S 55.

REGIONAL STUDIES—West

3196　Bell, William C.　A History of the Denver Theater during the Post-Pioneer Period (1881-1901).　Northwestern S 41.

3197　Brady, Donald.　A History of the Professional Theatre in El Paso, Texas: 1880-1905. Tulane.

3198　Brown, Firman H., Jr.　A History of Theater in Montana.　Wis D 63.

3199　DeChaine, Faber B.　Colorado Mountain Theatre:　A History of Theatrical Festivals at Central City, Colorado, from 1932 to 1960.　Minn 63.

3200　Earnest, Sue W.　An Historical Study of the Growth of the Theatre in Southern California.　So Cal FA 47.

3201　Fenton, Frank L.　The San Francisco Theater, 1849-1859.　Stanford S 42.

3202　Gern, Jesse W.　Colorado Mountain Theatre:　History of the Theatre at Central City, 1859-1885 (Volumes One and Two).　Ohio State S 60.

3203　Hume, Charles V.　The Sacramento Theatre, 1849-1885.　Stanford S 55.

3204　Kline, Hebron C.　A History of the Denver Theatre during the Depression Era, 1929-1941.　Denver T 63.

3205　Krumm, Walter C.　The San Francisco Stage, 1869-1879.　Stanford D 61.

3206　Levy, Edwin L.　Elitch's Gardens, Denver, Colorado:　A History of the Oldest Summer Theatre in the United States (1890-1941).　Columbia S 60.

3207　McCrossan, Sister Joseph M.　The Role of the Church and the Folk in the Development of the Early Drama in New Mexico.　Pa RL 45.

3208　McElhaney, John S.　A History of the San Francisco Theatre, 1880-1890.　Stanford S.

3209　Miller, William C.　An Historical Study of Theatrical Entertainment in Virginia City, Nevada.　So Cal FA 47.

3210　Nichols, Dean G.　Pioneer Theatres of Denver, Colorado.　Mich 38.

3211　Schilling, Lester L.　The History of the Theater in Portland, Oregon, 1846-1959. Wis S 61.

3212　Stine, Lawrence C.　A History of Theatrical Activities in Deadwood, South Dakota, 1876-1890.　Iowa D 62.

3213　Vaughn, Jack.　A History of the Hawaiian Theatre.　Denver.

3214　Winters, Earle.　A History of Theatrical Activities in Denver, 1901 to 1921. Denver S 57.

SOCIAL AND POLITICAL ASPECTS

3215　Bahou, Victor S.　The Political Drama in America since 1930.　Syracuse PS 60.

3216　Elfenbein, Josef A.　American Drama, 1782-1812, as an Index to Socio-Political Thought.　NYU 52.

3217 Engar, Keith M. Political Satire in Selected American Plays of the Twentieth Century. Minn 52.
3218 Foster, Jacob F. The Development of Social Criticism in the Broadway Theatre during the Inter-war Period, 1919-1939. NYU 43.
3219 Harper, Robert D. Economic and Political Attitudes in American Drama, 1865-1900. Chicago 50.
3220 Himelstein, Morgan Y. Social Drama and the Communist Party in America, 1929-1941. Columbia 58.
3221 Lees, Charles L. An Introductory Study of the American People of the Eighteenth Century through Their Drama and Theatrical History. Wis 34.
3222 Modisette, Eldon L. Changing Political Thought in the American Drama, 1919-1951. Minn PS 54.
3223 Muir, Donald. The Song that Stings: An Analysis of Political Satire in American Musical Theatre, 1929-1941. Stanford.
3224 Nannes, Casper H. Politics in the American Drama, as Revealed by Plays Produced on the New York Stage, 1890-1945. Pa 49.
3225 Newell, Grace M. The Treatment of Social Issues in American Comedy, 1920-1942. Northwestern 48.
3226 Peteler, Patricia M. The Social and Symbolic Drama of the English-Language Theatre, 1929-1949. Utah S 61.
3227 Rabkin, Gerald E. Drama and Political Commitment: The Impact of Politics on American Drama of the 1930's. Ohio State 61.
3228 Russell, Helen. Social Satire as Depicted by American Women Playwrights. Denver S 58.
3229 Salem, James M. Revolution in Manners and Morals: The Treatment of Adultery in American Drama between the Wars. La 65.
3230 Schaffer, Pauline Wright. The Position of Women in Society as Reflected in Serious American Drama, 1890-1928. Stanford S 65.
3231 Sherr, Paul C. Political Satire in the American Musical Theatre of the 1930's. Pa 65.
3232 Streitberg, Dietmar. Untersuchungen zur literarischen Gestaltung der Sozialkritik im modernen amerikanischen Drama. Hamburg.
3233 Turner, Willis L. City Low-Life on the American Stage to 1900. Ill S 56.
3234 Waugh, Jennie. Das Theater als Spiegel der amerikanischen Demokratie. Berlin 36.
3235 Wittler, Clarence J. Some Social Trends in W.P.A. Drama. Catholic Soc 39.
See also 2854.

THEATER HISTORY−General

3236 Alden, Barbara. Differences in the Conception of Othello's Character as Seen in the Performances of Three Important Nineteenth-Century Actors on the American Stage: Edwin Forrest, Edwin Booth, Tommaso Salvini. Chicago 50.
3237 Ashby, Clifford C. Realistic Acting and the Advent of the Group in America: 1889-1922. Stanford S 63.
3238 Bailey, Mark. Lawrence Barrett, 1838-1891. Michigan S 42.
3239 Boardman, Abigail C. A Study of Revivals of Plays in the New York City (Broadway) Theatres from 1925 to 1940. Wis S 44.
3240 Collier, Gaylan. A Historical Survey of Six Dialects in the American Theatre. Denver S 57.
3241 Cowan, Robert A. Off-Broadway: A History, 1915-1962. Purdue D 62.
3242 Croman, Charlotte. Edwin Booth's *Hamlet:* An Investigation and Analysis of the Career-Long Interpretation of *Hamlet* by Edwin Booth, Including the Staging of the Play, and the Reaction of the Critical Audience Relating to the Development of the Role. NYU D 63.
3243 Driver, Leota S. Fanny Kemble Butler. Vanderbilt 31.
3244 Eysselinck, Walther. Theatricalism on the Twentieth-Century American Stage. Yale FA.
3245 Gale Cedric. Shakespeare on the American Stage in the Eighteenth Century. NYU 45.

3246 Gasper, Raymond D. A Study of the Group Theatre and Its Contributions to Theatrical Production in America. Ohio State S 55.

3247 Golden, Joseph. The Position and Character of Theater-in-the-Round in the United States. Ill S 54.

3248 Grimsted, David. A Mirror for Nature: American Theater, 1800-1850. UCB H 63.

3249 Henneke, Ben G. The Playgoer in America (1752-1952). Ill S 57.

3250 Highlander, James L. Daniel Frohman and the Lyceum Theatre. Ill S 60.

3251 Hodge, Francis R. Yankee Theater, 1825-1850. Cornell 48.

3252 Hyams, Frances I. A Brief History of the American Theatre, with Especial Reference to the Eighteenth Century, Supplemented by Collections toward a Bibliography before 1800. Radcliffe 16.

3253 Kelly, Michael F. The Reaction of the Catholic Church to the Commercial Theatre in New York City, 1900 to 1958. Iowa S 59.

3254 Kenvin, Roger L. Theme and Attitude in the American Musical Theatre. Yale FA 61.

3255 Kussrow, Van Carl, Jr. On with the Show: A Study of Public Arguments in Favor of Theatre in America during the Eighteenth Century. Ind S 59.

3256 Lippman, Monroe. The History of the Theatrical Syndicate: Its Effect upon the Theatre in America. Mich 37.

3257 Maloff, Saul. The New Theater Movement in America. Iowa S 53.

3258 Manser, Ruth B. The Influence of the American Actress on the Development of the American Theater from 1835 to 1935. NYU 38.

3259 Mates, Julian. The American Musical Stage before 1800. Columbia S 59.

3260 Naeseth, Henriette C. Sardou on the American Stage. Chicago 31.

3261 Parrott, Frederick J. The Mid-Nineteenth Century American Theater, 1840-1860: A Survey of Theatre Production, Comment, and Opinion. Cornell FA 48.

3262 Poggi, E. J. The American Theater: An Economic Study: 1870-1931. Columbia 65.

3263 Rankin, Hugh F. The Colonial Theatre: Its History and Operations. NC H 60.

3264 Robinson, Marie J. Revivals on the New York Stage, 1930-1950, with a Statistical Survey of Their Performances from 1750-1950 (Volumes I and II). Northwestern S 60.

3265 Robinson, Marion P. College Theatres of Tomorrow. Wis FA 45.

3266 Ryan, Patrick M., Jr. Albert Marshall Palmer, Producer: A Study of Management, Dramaturgy, and Stagecraft in the American Theatre, 1872 to 1896. Yale S 59.

3267 Sarlos, Robert. The Provincetown Players: Experiments in Style. Yale 65.

3268 Schaal, David G. Rehearsal-Direction Practices and Actor-Director Relationships in the American Theatre from the Hallams to Actor's Equity. Ill S 56.

3269 Schubert, Leland. The Realistic Tendency in the Theatre. Cornell FA 38.

3270 Shiffler, Harrold C. The Opposition of the Presbyterian Church in the United States of America to the Theater in America, 1750-1871. Iowa S 53.

3271 Springer, Roland A. Problems of Higher Education in the Broadway Drama: A Critical Analysis of the Broadway Plays of 1920-1950, in Order to Discover Their Handling of the Problems of Higher Education. NYU S 57.

3272 Stiver, Harry E., Jr. Charles Frohman and the Empire Theatre Stock Company. Ill S 60.

3273 Stolp, Dorothy E. Mrs. John Drew, American Actress-Manager, 1820-1897. La S 53.

3274 Swinney, Donald J. Production in the Wallack Theatres, 1852-1888. Ind D 62.

3275 Tillinghast, John K. Guthrie McClintic, Director. Ind 64.

3276 Walsh, Charles R. Shakespeare on the Colonial Stage. Fordham 48.

3277 Weston, Pearl O. Pageantry in the United States. Duquesne 34.

3278 White, Natalie E. Shakespeare on the New York Stage, 1891-1941. Yale FA 46.

3279 Vilhauer, William W. The Provincetown Playhouse as a Playwright's Theatre. Iowa S.

3280 Wilson, Garff B. American Styles and Theories of Acting from Edwin Forrest to David Belasco. Cornell S 40.

3281 Zimmerman, Leland L. The Federal Theater: An Evaluation and Comparison with Foreign National Theaters. Wis 56.
See also 2866, 2874, 4091, 4095, 4097, 4110, 4117, 4119, 4130, 4131, 4133, 4134, 4139, 4219, 4228.

ECONOMIC STUDIES

3282 Brennan, Lawrence D. The Concept of Business Ethics Reflected in America's
Literary Awakening, 1820-1835. NYU 51.
3283 Engelhart, Carl W. The Reaction against Industrialism in American Literature,
1800-1860. Minn 52.
3284 Flory, Claude R. Economic Criticism in American Fiction, 1792-1900. Pa 35.
3285 Hollenbach, John W. A Study of Economic Individualism in the American Novel,
1865-1888. Wis 41.
3286 Koerner, James D. The Triumph of the Dinosaurs: A Study of the Politico-Economic
Novel of Protest in America, 1888-1906. Wash (St. Louis) 52.
3287 Lovell, John, Jr. Champions of the Workers in American Literature of the Forties.
UCB 38.
3288 McCall, Raymond G. Attitudes toward Wealth in the Fiction of Theodore Dreiser,
Edith Wharton, and F. Scott Fitzgerald. Wis 57.
3289 Penrod, John A. American Literature and the Great Depression. Pa 54.
3290 Rose, Lisle A. A Descriptive Catalogue of Economic and Politico-Economic Fiction
in the United States, 1902-1909. Chicago 36.
3291 Souders, Robert L. The Successful American Business Man, 1865-1900: A Discrepancy
between Image and Reality. Iowa 58.
3292 Taylor, Walter F. Economic Unrest in American Fiction, 1880-1901. NC 30.
3293 Yocum, John H. An Analysis of the Influence of the Depression upon American
Literature, 1929-1938. Ottawa 38.
*See also 268, 760, 994, 995, 2535, 2942, 3262, 3320, 3330, 3402, 3404, 3413, 3420,
3431, 3443, 3456, 3464, 3976, 4067, 4069.*

EDUCATION AND SCHOLARSHIP

3294 Atwater, Elizabeth A. A History of Classical Scholarship in America. Pittsburgh C 38.
3295 Bertrand, Arthur L. The Religious Motive in the Development of Education in
Colonial Western Massachusetts. Conn E 65.
3296 Bibbs, Evelyn. Anthologies of American Literature, 1787-1964. Columbia 65.
3297 Boyd, Holland L. English Grammar in American Schools from 1850 to 1890.
Peabody E 35.
3298 Bullock, Thomas K. Schools and Schooling in Eighteenth Century Virginia. Duke
E 61.
3299 Dunmire, Burt L. The Development of American Literature Textbooks Used in the
United States from 1870 to 1952. Pittsburgh 54.
3300 Eddins, Doris K. A Critical Evaluation of a Selected List of Children's Literature
[1925-1951]. Mich State 56.
3301 Fawcett, Vera E. English Grammar in American Schools. Peabody 48.
3302 Fowler, Herbert E. Criticism of Education in Twentieth Century American Novels.
NYU E 32.
3303 Gilles, Claire L. Materials on Education in Selected Women's Magazines, 1890-1899,
1930-1939, and 1947-1956. Pa E 62.
3304 Hepler, John C. The Educational Content of Some National Literary Periodicals,
1850-1900. Peabody E 44.
3305 Hughes, Raymond G. An Analysis of the Fourth, Fifth, and Sixth McGuffey Readers.
Pittsburgh 43.
3306 Lewis, John S., Jr. The History of Instruction in American Literature in Colleges and
Universities of the United States, 1827-1939. NYU E 41.
3307 Lyman, Rollo L. English Grammar in American Schools before 1850. Chicago 17.
3308 Perrin, Porter G. The Teaching of Rhetoric in the American Colleges before 1750.
Chicago 36.
3309 Plover, Catherine L. The American Primer. Fordham E 36.

3310 Polson, Ruth E.   American Literature in New York State's Public Schools. Cornell 51.
3311 Schneider, Donald O.   Education in Colonial American Colleges, 1750-1770, and the Occupations and Political Offices of Their Alumni.   Peabody E 65.
3312 Sloane, William.   English and American Children's Books of the Seventeenth Century: An Annotated Check-list, together with the First Printed Catalogue of Children's Books.   Columbia 53.
3313 Tyler, Priscilla.   Grammars of the English Language to 1850:   With Special Emphasis on School Grammars Used in America.   Western Reserve 54.
      See also 47, 666, 784, 791, 982, 1017, 2367, 2368, 2518, 2594, 2669, 2850, 3271, 3339, 3400, 3409, 3459, 3506, 4051, 4052.

FICTION

GENERAL–Character Types and Themes

3314 Beck, Betty S.   The Fallible Narrator in Nineteenth-Century American Fiction. Okla 63.
3315 Blaine, Harold A.   The Frontiersman in American Prose Fiction, 1800-1860.   Western Reserve 36.
3316 Durham, Philip C.   The Objective Treatment of the "Hard-boiled Hero" in American Fiction: A Study of the Frontier Background of Modern American Literature. Northwestern 49.
3317 Edmondson, Elsie.   The Writer as Hero in Important American Fiction since Howells (Howells, James, Norris, London, Farrell, Cabell).   Mich 54.
3318 Fink, Sister Mary Joanna.   The Concept of the Artist and Creative Genius in American Naturalistic Fiction.   Notre Dame 65.
3319 Fletcher, Marie.   The Southern Heroine in the Fiction of Representative Southern Women Writers, 1850-1960.   La 63.
3320 Halsey, Van R. C.   The Portrait of the Businessman in Twentieth Century American Fiction.   Pa A 56.
3321 Harris, Isabelle W.   The Southern Mountaineer in American Fiction, 1824-1910. Duke 48.
3322 Harrison, Marion C.   Social Types in Southern Prose Fiction.   Va 21.
3323 Hinz, John P.   Restless Heir: The Boy in American Fiction.   Columbia 59.
3324 Kennedy, Sister Mary.   The Frontier Heroine in Middlewestern Fiction.   Ill.
3325 Kimber, Thomas.   The Treatment of the Quaker as a Character in American Fiction, 1825-1925.   So Cal 54.
3326 Lawrence, Elwood P.   The Immigrant in American Fiction, 1890-1910.   Western Reserve 44.
3327 Lindgren, Charlotte H.   The Common Seaman in Nineteenth Century American Fiction. Boston 61.
3328 Lumpkin, Ben G.   Diversity in the Characters Portrayed in Southern Regional Short Stories of the Nineteenth Century.   NC 44.
3329 Lynde, Richard D.   The Confidence Man in Nineteenth Century American Fiction. Stanford.
3330 Lynn, Kenneth S.   The Theme of Success in American Fiction, 1897-1925.   Harvard A 54.
3331 Makosky, Donald.   The Portrayal of Women in Wide-Circulation Magazine Short Stories 1905-1955.   Pa 66.
3332 Marovitz, Sanford E.   The Treatment of Outlaws and Villains in Selected Western Fiction from the Days of Cooper to the Present.   Duke.
3333 Martin, Cleo.   Physical Poverty as Treated in American Fiction, 1865-1917.   Iowa A.
3334 Mason, Walter S., Jr.   The People of Florida as Portrayed in American Fiction. Peabody 48.

3335 Melito, Rev. Ignatius M. Themes of Adolescence: Studies in American Fiction of Adolescence. Denver 65.

3336 Nievoll, Wilhelmine. Die Darstellung des Kindes in modernen englischen und amerikanischen Romanen und Erzählungen (seit 1930). Graz 51.

3337 Penrod, John H. Character Types and Humorous Devices in the Old Southwest Yarns. Peabody 52.

3338 Rans, G. The Origin and History of the Idea of Corruption in American Writing, and Its Expression in James Fenimore Cooper, Edgar Allan Poe, and Ralph Waldo Emerson. Leeds 63-64.

3339 Trabue, Ann M. An Analysis of Guidance Procedure Reflected in Student-Teacher Relationships Portrayed in Selected Popular Fiction. NC E 62.

3340 Willer, William H. Native Themes in American Short Prose Fiction, 1770-1835. Minn 44.

3341 Williams, Cratis D. The Southern Mountaineer in Fact and Fiction. NYU 61. *See also 3609.*

GENERAL—Special Topics, Gothicism.

3342 Ahearn, Mary L. The Rhetoric of Work and Vocation in Some Popular Northern Writings Before 1860. Brown 65.

3343 Albright, Daniel C. An Account of the Narrative Technique from Poe to James. Chicago 56.

3344 Babbitt, Samuel F. American Fiction and Historical Knowledge: The Uses of Imaginative Writing as a Source of Historical Insight. Yale 66.

3345 Berger, Harold L. Anti-Utopian Fiction of the Mid-Twentieth Century. Tenn.

3346 Bickham, Robert S. The Origins and Importance of the Initiation Story in Twentieth Century British and American Fiction. NM 61.

3347 Church, Elizabeth. The Gothic Romance: Its Origins and Development. Radcliffe 12.

3348 Ciancio, Ralph A. The Grotesque in Modern American Fiction: An Existential Theory. Pittsburgh 64.

3349 Davis, David B. Attitudes Towards Homicide in American Fiction, 1798-1860: A Study in Intellectual History. Harvard A 56.

3350 Deane, Paul C. Children's Fiction in America since 1900: A Study of Books in Series. Harvard A 66.

3351 DeClark, William E. The Relationship between Periodical Fiction and the Rise of Realism in the United States. NYU 52.

3352 Dooley, David J. The Impact of Satire on Fiction: Studies in Norman Douglas, Sinclair Lewis, Aldous Huxley, Evelyn Waugh, and George Orwell. Iowa 55.

3353 Emmons, Winfred S. The Materials and Methods of American Horror Fiction in the Nineteenth Century. La 52.

3355 Gianakos, Perry E. "The Yanko-Spanko War": Our War with Spain in American Fiction. NYU H 61.

3356 Gilley, Billy H. Social Trends as Reflected in American Fiction, 1870-1901. Ga H 66.

3357 Greet, Thomas Y. The Child's Eye: A Study of American Fiction Written from the Child's Point of View, Leading from *Huckleberry Finn* and *What Maisie Knew.* Wis.

3358 Hardman, Marion P. Terror in American Prose Fiction prior to 1835. Minn 39.

3359 Hedges, Elaine R. Attitudes toward City and Country in Works of Fiction, 1870 to 1890. Harvard.

3360 Hoffman, Frederick J. Freudianism: A Study of Influences and Reactions, Especially as Revealed in the Fiction of James Joyce, D. H. Lawrence, Sherwood Anderson, and Waldo Frank. Ohio State 42.

3361 Isani, Mukhtar A. The Oriental Tale in America through 1865: A Study in American Fiction. Princeton 62.

3362 Jancke, Anne. Studies in the Element of the Grotesque in Modern American Fiction. Helsinki.

3363 Kaul, Ajodhi N. The Image of Actual Society and Ideal Community in Nineteenth Century American Fiction. Yale 62.

3364 Kierzek, John M. American Historical Fiction after 1860. Minn 26.
3365 Lawson, Lewis A. The Grotesque in Recent Southern Fiction. Wis 64.
3366 Leland, Lowell P. Theories of Fiction in America, 1789-1870. Ohio State 40.
3367 Levine, Paul. Post-World War II American Fiction. Harvard.
3368 Mooney, Joan. American Detective Story. Minn.
3369 Palmer, Osmond E. Some Aspects of the Attitude toward Fiction in America to 1870 and a Bit Beyond. Chicago 53.
3370 Powers, William. The Narrative Concept and the American Consciousness. Ill 66.
3371 Redden, Sister M. Mauritia. The Gothic Fiction in the American Magazines, 1765-1800. Catholic 39.
3372 Rude, Roland V. A Consideration of Jung's Concept of the Self as an Aid to the Understanding of Character in Prose Fiction. Northwestern 60.
3373 Schmitt, Peter. The Virgin Land in the Twentieth Century: The Wilderness Romance in Popular Fiction, 1900-1929: A Study in Transcendental Idealism in an Age of Disillusionment. Minn.
3374 Schmitz, Neil. Politics and the West in American Fiction of the Gilded Age. Stanford.
3375 Sharma, Mohan L. The Functional Preface in American Fiction. Ohio State 65.
3376 Solomon, H. Eric. Studies in Nineteenth-Century War Fiction. Harvard 58.
3377 Spatz, Jonas. Hollywood in Fiction: Some Versions of the American Myth. Ind 64.
3378 Treguboff, Zoe L. A Study of the Social Criticism in Popular Fiction: A Content Analysis of Science Fiction. UCLA 55.
3379 Valencia, Willa. The Picaresque Tradition in Modern British Fiction and Modern American Fiction. Ill.
3380 Wheeler, Effie Jane. Narrative Art in the Prose Fiction of Eighteenth-Century American Magazines. Mich 42.
      See also 1869, 2149, 2183, 2871, 2875, 2918, 3284, 3290, 3292, 3516, 3609, 4108, 4112, 4143, 4144, 4371, 4384, 4391, 4413, 4467, 4479, 4484, 4491, 4492, 4493, 4498, 4501, 4504, 4505, 4509, 4522, 4532, 4555.

GENERAL–Studies in Realism and Naturalism

3381 Åhnebrink, Lars. The Beginnings of Naturalism in American Fiction: A Study of the Works of Hamlin Garland, Stephen Crane, and Frank Norris with Special Reference to Some European Influences, 1891-1903. Uppsala 50 publ.
3382 Arnavon, Daniel J. Le Roman réaliste et naturaliste aux États-Unis (1887-1917). Paris 50.
3383 Baker, James R. Studies in the Realistic Novel. Denver 55.
3384 Chambers, Robert W. The Influence of Magazine Journalists on the Rise of Realism in America, 1870-1890. Tex 64.
3385 Doderer, Hans. Studien zur Theorie und Technik des neurealistischen amerikanischen Romans. Marburg 56.
3386 Edwards, Herbert J. The American Controversy over English Realism in Fiction. Ohio State 29.
3387 Figg, Robert M. The Effect of Naturalism upon Form in the American Novel from 1893 to 1925. NC 65.
3388 Labrie, Rodrigue E. American Naturalism: A View from Within. Pa State 64.
3389 Lenehan, William T. Techniques and Themes in Early English and American Naturalistic Novels. Okla 64.
3390 Ransom, Ellene. Utopus Discovers America, or Critical Realism in the American Utopian Novel, 1798-1900. Vanderbilt 47.
3391 Runyan, Harry J. The Backgrounds and Origins of Realism in the American Novel, 1850-1880. Wis 49.
3392 Walcutt, Charles C. Naturalism in the American Novel. Mich 38.
3393 Wilson, Benjamin H. Quiet Realism: Women Writers in the William Dean Howells Tradition. NC 66.

3394 Wyman, Margaret. Women in the American Realistic Novel, 1860-1893: Literary Reflection of Social Fact. Radcliffe A 50.
See also 340, 487, 538, 544, 1040, 1353, 1549, 1578, 1764, 2004, 3318, 3351, 4022.

NOVEL—Character Types, Themes

3395 Bailey, Dale S. Slavery in the Novels of Brazil and the United States: A Comparison. Ind 61.
3396 Baumbach, Jonathan. The Theme of Guilt and Redemption in the Post-Second-World-War American Novel. Stanford 61.
3397 Belok, Michael V. The College Professor in the Novel, 1940-1957. So Cal E 58.
3398 Bluefarb, Samuel. The Escape Motif in the Modern American Novel: Mark Twain to Carson McCullers. NM 66.
3399 Bolger, Stephen. The Irish Immigrant in the American Novel, 1830-1860. Pa.
3400 Briggs, Frances M. The Changing Concept of the Public School Teacher as Portrayed in American Novels: 1900-1960. NC E 62.
3401 Bruce, Charles T. Major Literary Concepts of the Soldier as Illustrated in Certain American War Novels. Tex Tech 60.
3402 Cassady, Edward E. The Business Man in the American Novel: 1865-1903. UCB 39.
3403 Childers, Helen W. American Novels about Adolescence, 1917-1953. Peabody 58.
3404 Clarke, Gordon W. The Changing Conception of the Businessman in the American Novel, 1865-1940. Ill 49.
3405 Du Breuil, Alice J. The Novel of Democracy in America: A Contribution to the Study of the Progress of Democratic Ideas in the American Novel. Johns Hopkins 22.
3406 England, Kenneth. The Decline of the Southern Gentleman Character as He Is Illustrated in Certain Novels by Present-Day Southern Novelists. Vanderbilt 57.
3407 Fernberg, Babeth G. Treatment of Jewish Character in the Twentieth-Century Novel (1900-1940) in France, Germany, England, and United States. Stanford 44.
3408 Ferrell, Wilfred A. Portrait of the Politician in the American Novel: 1870-1910. Tex 59.
3409 Gober, Ruth B. The American Novelist Interprets the Student of Higher Education. Okla E 56.
3410 Grise, George. The People of Kentucky as Pictured by American Novelists. Peabody 50.
3411 Gurcke, Günther. Die Französin im Spiegel des modernen englischen und amerikanischen Romans. Greifswald 34.
3412 Hakac, John R. The Juvenile Hero as a Literary Device in Selected American Novels. Tex 63.
3413 Harden, Edgar F. The Image of the American in the English Novel: 1860-1900. A Study of the Two Dominant Types: The Businessman and the Heiress. Harvard 60.
3414 Harper, Howard M. Concepts of Human Destiny in Five American Novelists: Bellow, Salinger, Mailer, Baldwin, Updike. Pa State 64.
3415 Hirsch, David. The Intellectual in the American Novel, 1792-1860: A Study in the Search for Reality and Form. Ohio State 61.
3416 Kane, Patricia L. Legal Fictions: The Lawyer in the American Novel. Minn 61.
3417 Karolides, Nicholas J. The Image of the Pioneer in the American Novel, 1900-1950. NYU E 63.
3418 McElroy, John H. Images of the Seventeenth-Century Puritan in American Novels, 1823-1860. Duke 66.
3419 Madson, Arthur L. The Scapegoat Story in the American Novel. Okla 66.
3420 Mayberry, George B. Industrialism and the Industrial Worker in the American Novel, 1814-1890. Harvard A 42.
3421 Merchant, Frank. Theme of Prospecting and Mining for Gold and Silver in the American Novel. Denver 52.
3422 Middleton, Walter. The Young Man from the Provinces: Variations on a Theme in the American Novel. Columbia.

3423 Miller, Raymond A., Jr. Representative Tragic Heroines in the Work of Brown, Hawthorne, Howells, James, and Dreiser. Wis 57.
3424 Mueller, Walter E. Protestant Ministers in Modern American Novels, 1927-1958: The Search for a Role. Neb 61.
3425 Myrbo, Calvin L. An Analysis of the Character of the Clergyman in Novels for Adolescents. (Volumes One and Two.) Minn 64.
3426 Niemeyer, Gisela. Die Frau in gesellschaftskritischen amerikanischen Romanen zwischen den beiden Weltkriegen. Kiel 49.
3427 Noeldechen, Lotte. Kindergestalten im amerikanischen Roman. Berlin 36.
3428 Peterson, Levi S. The Ambivalence of Alienation: The Debate over Frontier Freedom in the Quality Western Novel of the Twentieth Century. Utah 65.
3429 Pomeranz, Regina E. The Search for Self in the Adolescent Protagonist in the Contemporary American Novel: A Method of Approach for the College Teacher of Literature. Columbia 66.
3430 Preuss, Marianne. Europäer im Spiegel amerikanischer Romane der neueren Zeit. Freiburg 53.
3431 Robinson, Francis C. The Wealthy Class in the American Novel, 1870-1930. Stanford 52.
3432 Rundle, Marjorie A. The Concept of the Lady in the American Novel, 1850-1900. Cincinnati 56.
3433 Shuck, Emerson S. Clergymen in Representative American Novels, 1830-1930: A Study in Attitudes toward Religion. Wis 43.
3434 Shulman, Irving. The Juvenile Delinquent in the American Novel. UCLA.
3436 Steinberg, Abraham H. Jewish Character in the American Novel to 1900. NYU 55.
3437 Walters, Dorothy J. The Theme of Destructive Innocence in the Modern Novel: Greene, James, Cary, Porter, Okla 60.
3438 Witham, W. Tasker. The Forge of Life: Problems of Adolescents in American Novels, 1920-1958. Ill 61.
      See also 4099, 4111, 4135.

NOVEL–Types of Novel

3439 Barnett, James H. Divorce and the American Divorce Novel. Pa Soc 39.
3440 Bertram, Ray M. The Novel of America's Past: A Study of Five American Historical Novelists, 1925-1950 (James Boyd, Esther Forbes, Kenneth Roberts, Walter D. Edmonds, Howard Fast). Mich 53.
3441 Blackburn, Alexander L. The Picaresque Novel: A Literary Idea, 1554-1954. Cambridge 63.
3442 Bludworth, Rosa L. A Study of the Biblical Novel in America, 1940-1949, with a Survey of the Biblical Novel in General in the Nineteenth and Twentieth Centuries. Tex 55.
3443 Bowman, John S. The Proletarian Novel in America. Pa State 39.
3444 Brown, Herbert R. The Sentimental Novel in America, 1789-1860. Columbia 40.
3445 Burns, Stuart L. The Novel of Adolescence in America: 1940-1963. Wis 64.
3446 Dickens, William B. A Guide to the American Political Novel, 1865-1910. Mich 53.
3447 Frank, John F. The Twentieth-Century American Novel of Manners: O'Hara, Marquand etc. Pa.
3448 Grahame, Roberta M. A Study of the Cross-section Novel Written in English since 1915 Minn 40.
3449 Greenberg, Alvin D. The Novel of Disintegration: A Study of a World View in Contemporary Fiction. Wash 64.
3450 Groman, George L. The American Political Novel and Its Reflection of Emerging Progressivism: A Study of Representative Political Fiction, 1891-1915. NYU 63.
3451 Johnson, Jean O. The American Political Novel in the Nineteenth Century. Boston 58
3452 Johnson, Robert E. The American Political Novel, 1792-1950, a Survey. UCLA 56.
3453 Jones, Joel M. Everyman's Usable Past. The American Historical Novel. NM 66.

3454 Kerr, Elizabeth M. The Twentieth Century Sequence Novel. Minn 42.
3455 Kirkpatrick, Jean R. The Temperance Novel in the United States. Pa.
3456 Ledbetter, Kenneth L. The Idea of a Proletarian Novel in America, 1927-1939. Ill 63.
3457 Leisy, Ernest E. The American Historical Novel before 1860. Ill 23.
3458 Liedel, Donald E. The Antislavery Novel, 1836-1861. Mich H 61.
3459 Lyons, John O. The Novel of Academic Life in America. Fla 60.
3460 Millgate, M. H. The American Novel of Society. Leeds 59-60.
3461 Nicholl, Grier. The Christian Social Novel in America, 1865-1918. Minn 64.
3462 Parrington, Vernon L., Jr. The Utopian Novel in America. Brown 43.
3463 Pilkington, William T. A Survey of the Southwestern Novel since 1920. Tex Christian.
3464 Rideout, Walter B. The Proletarian Novel in the United States: A Literary History and a Critique. Harvard 50.
3465 Ross, Eugene G. The American Novel of Fantasy. Va 49.
3466 See, Carolyn P. The Hollywood Novel: An Historical and Critical Study. UCLA 63.
3467 Shurter, Robert L. The Utopian Novel in America, 1865-1900. Western Reserve 36.
3468 Smith, David R. Origins of the International Novel: Studies in Transatlantic Fiction, 1812 to 1865. Claremont 60.
3469 Wright, Robert G. The Christian Social Novel in America, 1865-1900. Geo Wash.
3470 Yarnall, John N. Romance *à la mode*, 1896-1906. Pittsburgh 38.
See also 1795, 2629, 3471, 3475, 3476, 3498.

NOVEL–Special Studies

3471 Arden, Eugene. The New York Novel: A Study in Urban Fiction. Ohio State 53.
3472 Batson, E. Beatrice. The Treatment of American History in the American Novel, 1890-1910. Peabody 56.
3473 Beck, Robert R. The "Picturesque Wrong" in Novels about Political Problems. Minn.
3474 Bewley, E. A. M. Form in the Classic American Novel. Cambridge 56-57.
3475 Burrows, Robert N. The Image of Urban Life as It Is Reflected in the New York City Novel, 1920-1930. Pa 59.
3475a Enzer, Hyman A. The American First Novelist: A Study of Commitment and the Literary Career. NYU 63.
3476 Everett, Ruth Elizabeth. The Brooklyn Novel and the Brooklyn Myth: Source Materials for Teaching the Urban Novel. Columbia 66.
3477 Foster, Ruel E. Freudian Influences in the American Novel. Vanderbilt 41.
3478 Hall, Ernest J. The Satirical Element in the American Novel. Pa 22.
3479 Haugh, Robert F. Sentimentalism in the American Proletarian Novel. Mich 48.
3480 Heagarty, Mary Alice. Aesthetic Distance in the Techniques of the Novel. Ill 64.
3481 Hertel, Robert R. The Decline of the Paperbound Novel in America, 1890-1910. Ill LS 58.
3482 Hinchcliffe, A. P. Symbolism in the American Novel, 1850-1950: An Examination of the Findings of Recent Literary Critics in Respect of the Novels of Hawthorne, Melville, James, Hemingway, and Faulkner. Manchester 62-63.
3483 Kaltenbacher, Therese. Frauenfragen im amerikanischen Frauenroman. Berlin 36 publ.
3484 Lippert, Ralph. The Role of the Family in the Modern Novel from Howells to Wouk. Wis.
3485 Mills, Nicolaus. English "Novel" and American "Romance": A Comparative Study. Brown 66.
3486 Morris, Ann R. A Study of Rhythm in the Novel. Fla State 61.
3487 Ross, Maude C. Moral Values of the American Woman as Presented in Three Major American Authors [Hawthorne, James, Faulkner]. Tex 64.
3488 St. John, William E. The Conception of the Novel as Presented by the Leading English and American Novelists since 1800. So Cal 36.
3489 Schneider, Robert W. Man and the Progressive Novelists. Minn H 59.

3490　Starr, Nathan C.　The Sea in the English Novel from Defoe to Melville.　Harvard 18.
See also 2871, 3704, 3753, 3864, 4076, 4098, 4450, 4457, 4460, 4502, 4527, 4627.

NOVEL–Special Studies, After 1900

3491　Barsness, John A.　The Breaking of the Myth:　A Study of Cultural Implications in the Development of the Western Novel in the Twentieth Century.　Minn.

3492　Beja, Morris.　Evanescent Moments:　The Epiphany in the Modern Novel. Cornell 63.

3493　Bogart, Max.　A Study of Certain Legally Banned Novels in the United States, 1900-1950.　NYU 56.

3494　Carpenter, Thomas P.　The Material of Abnormal Psychology in Some Contemporary English and American Novels.　Stanford 47.

3495　Collins, Robert G.　Four Critical Interpretations in the Modern Novel.　Denver 61.

3496　Cooperman, Stanley R.　Expectation and Impact in the Post-World War I Novel of Protest.　Ind 62.

3497　Franchere, Hoyt C.　A Study of Tragedy and the Tragic Character in the Recent American Novel.　Wash 50.

3498　Gelfant, Blanche H.　The American City Novel, 1900-1940:　A Study of the Literary Treatment of the City in Dreiser, Dos Passos and Farrell.　Wis 51.

3499　Gröger, Erika.　Die Widerspiegelung der atomproblematik im englisch-amerikanischen Roman, 1946-1962.　Leipzig 64.

3500　Higgins, Claire M.　A Study of Metaphor and Simile in the American Literary Novel and the American Popular Novel, 1911-1940.　NYU E 54.

3501　Hockey, Dorothy.　The Good and the Beautiful:　A Study of Best-Selling Novels in America, 1895-1920.　Western Reserve 47.

3501a　Honeywell, J. Arthur.　An Enquiry into the Nature of Plot in the Twentieth-Century Novel.　Chicago 64.

3502　Howell, John M.　The Waste Land Tradition in the American Novel.　Tulane 63.

3503　Klein, Marcus N.　The Novel in America in the 1950's:　An Introduction to a Thematic Study.　Columbia 62.

3504　Kruse, Horst H.　Die Romane der "Flaming Youth":　Ein Beitrag zur Interpretation des amerikanischen Romans von 1920-1930.　Kiel 62 publ.

3505　Lee, Lynn.　The Serious Novel as Popular American Literature, 1920-1930; 1950-1960. Minn.

3506　Lee, Robert C.　Portrayal of the College in Modern American Novels, 1932-1942. Peabody E 44.

3507　Lehan, Richard D.　Existentialism and the Modern American Novel.　Wis 59.

3508　Leopold, Robert E.　The Contemporary Novel and Its Condensation.　Columbia 63.

3509　Levitt, Morton P.　From a New Point of View: Studies in the Contemporary Novel. Pa State 65.

3510　Linebarger, Genevieve C.　The Federal Government in the American Novel, 1900-1950. Md 53.

3511　Mohrmann, Hermann.　Kultur-und Gesellschaftsprobleme des amerikanischen Romanes der Nachkriegszeit (1920-1927).　Giessen 34 publ.

3512　Rice, Joe Allen.　Flash of Darkness:　Black Humor in the Contemporary American Novel.　Fla State.

3513　Shapiro, Stephen A.　The Ambivalent Animal:　Man in the Contemporary British and American Novel.　Wash 65.

3514　Stamm, Hans J.　Die sozialkritischen Strömungen im modernen amerikanischen Roman (1920-1950).　Freiburg 55.

3515　Stanford, Raney B.　The Tradition of Heroism and the Modern Novel.　Columbia 65.
See also 2870, 3109, 3112, 4102, 4115, 4461, 4573, 4584.

NOVEL–Special Studies, Before 1900

3516　Accetta, Michael A.　Gothic Elements in the Early American Novel, 1775-1825. Pittsburgh 54.

3517 Bell, Vereen M. Character and Point of View in Representative Victorian Novels. Duke 59.

3518 Crego, Robert F. The Spirit of Individualism as Reflected in the American Novel of the 1840's. NYU 50.

3519 Dunlap, George A. The City in the American Novel, 1789-1900. Pa 34.

3520 Finch, Eugene D. The Beginnings of the American Novel, 1789-1798. Yale 32.

3521 Gulbenkian, Vahe R. The Slum Movement in English and American Fiction, 1880-1900: A Chapter in the History of the Modern Novel. Western Reserve 51.

3522 Harrison, James G. American Newspaper Journalism as Described in American Novels of the Nineteenth Century. NC 45.

3523 Hoffmann, Charles G. The Development toward the Short Novel Form in American Literature, with Special Reference to Hawthorne, Melville and James. Wis 52.

3524 Howard, Charles E. Romantic Love in Major American Novels, 1789-1860. Vanderbilt 59.

3525 Hunt, Theodore. Le Roman américain, 1830-1850. Paris 37 publ.

3526 Hurley, Leonard B. The American Novel, 1830-1850: Its Reflections of Contemporary Religious Conditions, with a Bibliography of Fiction. NC 32.

3527 Kramer, Maurice I. The Fable of Endurance: A Study of the American Novel between Hawthorne and Howells. Harvard 58.

3528 Loshe, Lillie D. The Early American Novel (1789 to 1830). Columbia 07.

3529 Martin, Terence J. The Emergence of the Novel in America: A Study in the Cultural History of an Art Form. Ohio State 54.

3530 Meyer, Kenneth. Social Class and Family Structure: Attitudes Revealed by the Earliest American Novels, 1789-1815. Minn.

3531 Nelson, Arnold G. Class and Status in the American Novel, 1789-1850. Minn 53.

3532 Reninger, Harry W. The Theory and Practice of the American Novel, 1867-1903. Mich 39.

3533 Schirone, Charles. The Spirit of Aristocracy as Reflected in the American Novel of the 1830's. NYU E 55.

3534 Suderman, Elmer F. Religion in the American Novel: 1870-1900. Kan 61.
See also 3285, 3286, 4459, 4475, 4550.

NOVEL—War Novels

3535 Billings, Robert S. Attitudes of American War Novels, 1917-23 and 1942-48, toward the Enemy, the Army and the Purpose of the War. Iowa 52.

3536 Connor, James R. Pen and Sword: World War I Novels in America, 1916-1941. Wis H 61.

3537 Gräf, Karl. Die Gestalt des Generals im amerikanischen R_man über den 2. Weltkrieg: Ein Beitrag zur literaturwissenschaftlichen Betrachtung des zeitgenössischen amerikanischen Romans. Jena 59.

3538 Klotz, Marvin. The Imitation of War, 1800-1900: Realism in the American War Novel. NYU 59.

3539 Luchting, Wolfgang A. Das Erlebnis des Krieges im amerikanischen Roman über den Zweiten Weltkrieg. Munich 56.

3540 Marsh, John L. A Circle of Meaning: American Novelists Face the Military Necessity. Pa 59.

3541 Oldsey, Bernard S. Aspects of Combat in the Novel, 1900-1950. Pa State 55.

3542 Posman, Harry. The American Citizen-Soldier: A Sociological Analysis of War Novels. Columbia 57.

3543 Schuster, Richard. American Civil War Novels to 1880. Columbia 61.

3544 Spicehandler, Daniel. The American War Novel. Columbia 60.

3545 Waldmeier, Joseph J. Ideological Aspects of the American Novels of World War II. Mich State 59.

3546 Weber, John S. The American War Novel Dealing with the Revolutionary and Civil Wars. Wis 48.
See also 2870, 3396, 3401, 4072.

SHORT STORY

3547 de Araujo, Victor. The Short Story of Fantasy: Henry James, H. G. Wells, and E. M. Forster. Wash 65.

3548 Deubach, Vila A. A Survey of Social Conscience Short Stories in American Magazines, 1830-1930. Colo 49.

3549 Freywald, Carin. Symbole und ihre Funktion in der modernen amerikanischen *short story*. Hamburg.

3550 Karlson, Robert. Criticism of the American Short Story, 1885-1919. Geo Wash.

3551 Lieberman, Elias. The American Short Story. NYU 11.

3552 Marler, Robert F. The Development of the American Short Story, 1849-1861. Geo Wash.

3553 Moore, Jack B. Native Elements in American Magazine Short Fiction, 1741-1800. NC 63.

3554 Peck, Ellen. The American Short Story from Crane to Anderson. Stanford.

3555 Rhode, Robert D. The Functions of Setting in the American Short Story of Local Color, 1865-1900. Tex 40.

3556 Roch, John H. The American Short Story, 1865-1885. Columbia 58.

3557 Speck, Ernest B. The American Short Story, 1930-1940: A Study in Form and Content. Tex 59.

3558 Waldbrecht, Ernestine M. Untersuchungen über die amerikanische Short Story: Einflüsse und Strömungen zwischen den beiden Weltkriegen. Vienna 49.

3559 Wirzberger, Karl-Heinz. Die Entwicklung der amerikanischen *Short-Story* Aufstieg und Formauflösung einer Literaturgattung. Berlin (H) 51.

3560 Wright, Austin M. The Changing American Short Story, 1919-1931. Chicago 59.
See also 3111, 3328, 3340, 4463, 4480, 4497, 4522, 4541.

FINE ARTS

3561 Green, Samuel M. An Introduction to the History of American Illustration from Its Beginning in the Late 17th Century until 1850. Harvard FA 44.

3562 Hulme, Francis P. A History of Music-Imagery in European Literature with Special Emphasis on Nineteenth and Twentieth Century English, American, and French Literature. Minn 47.

3563 Kelley, Abner W. Music and Literature in the American Romantic Movement. NC 29.

3564 Kienitz, John F. The Generation of the 1850's, 1860's, and 1870's in the Fine Arts of the United States in Relation to Parallel Phases of American Culture. Wis FA 38.

3565 Kwiat, Joseph J. The Revolt in American Painting and Literature, 1890-1915: A Study in Cultural and Intellectual Relationships. Minn A 50.

3566 Simoni, John P. Art Critics and Criticism in Nineteenth Century America. Ohio State FA 52.

3567 Skidmore, Marie E. The American Emblem Book and Its Symbolism. Ohio State FA 4

3568 Smith, Hugh. The Literary Manifestation of a Liberal Romanticism in American Jazz. NM 55.

3569 Williamson, Jerry M. The Transitional Period between Romanticism and Realism in the American Arts. Fla State 63.

3570 Wood, Harry E., Jr. The Accepted American Meanings of Color as Shown in Literature, Folklore, and Art. Ohio State FA 41.
See also 330, 789, 2612, 2658, 2667, 2920, 3048, 3996, 4307, 4314, 4435.

FOLKLORE

3571 Abrahams, Roger D. Negro Folklore from South Philadelphia: A Collection and Analysis. Pa 61.

3572   Atterbury, Louie W.   Folklore of the Lower Snake River Valley: A Regional Study. Denver 61.

3573   Baughman, Ernest W.   A Comparative Study of the Folktales of England and North America.   Ind 53.

3574   Bluestein, Eugene.   The Background and Sources of an American Folksong Tradition. Minn 60.

3575   Boswell, George W.   Reciprocal Influences of Text and Tune in the Southern Traditional Ballad.   Peabody 50.

3576   Botkin, Benjamin A.   The American Play-Party Song.   Neb 31.

3577   Browne, Earl W.   Variant Forms of English and Scottish Popular Ballads in America. So Cal 61.

3578   Browne, Ray B.   Alabama Folk Songs.   UCLA 56.

3579   Buckley, Bruce R.   Frankie and Her Men: A Study of the Interrelationships of Popular and Folk Traditions.   Ind 62.

3580   Campa, Arthur L.   Spanish Folk-Poetry in New Mexico.   Columbia RL 46.

3581   Charles, Norman.   Values in Twentieth-Century American Popular Songs.   Pa 58.

3582   Claudel, Calvin A.   A Study of Louisiana French Folktales in Avoyelles Parish. NC RL 48.

3583   Coffin, Tristram P.   A Handbook of the Traditional Ballad in North America.   Pa 49.

3584   Combs, Josiah H.   Folk-Songs du midi des États-Unis.   Paris 25 publ.

3585   Cook, Harold.   Shaker Music: A Manifestation of American Folk Culture.   Western Reserve Mu 47.

3586   Cox, J. H.   Folk-Songs of the South.   Harvard 24.

3587   Dundes, Alan.   The Morphology of North American Indian Folktales.   Ind 62.

3588   Dworzak, Hilda.   Beitrage zur neuen englisch-amerikanischen Tier-geschichte. Vienna 30.

3589   Gower, Herschel.   Traditional Scottish Ballads in the United States.   Vanderbilt 57.

3590   Greenway, John.   American Folksongs of Social and Economic Protest.   Pa 51.

3591   Halpert, Herbert N.   Folktales and Legends from the New Jersey Pines: A Collection and a Study.   Ind 48.

3592   Haywood, Charles.   Bibliography of the American Folklore and Folk Song. Columbia 51.

3593   Hudson, Arthur P.   Folk-Songs of Mississippi and Their Background: A Study, with Texts.   NC 30.

3594   Jansen, William H.   Abraham "Oregon" Smith: Pioneer, Folk Hero, and Tale-Teller. Ind 49.

3595   Kinne, Frances B.   A Comparative Study of British Traditional Ballads and American Indigenous Ballads.   Frankfurt 57.

3596   Laws, George M., Jr.   Native American Balladry: A Descriptive Study and a Bibliographical Syllabus of the Ballads Sung in the United States.   Pa 49.

3597   Le Mon, Melvin.   Pennsylvania Anthracite Miners' Folk-Songs.   Rochester Mu 42.

3598   Macmillan, C. J.   The Folk Songs of Canada.   Harvard 09.

3599   Mangold, Ruth Maria.   Die Motivwelt der amerikanischen Volksballade.   Freiburg 64.

3600   Mintz, Jerome R.   The Legends of the Hasidim: A Study of Folklore and Culture. Ind 61.

3601   Montgomery, Guy.   Studies in Primitive Folksong.   UCB 20.

3602   Morris, Alton C.   Folksongs of Florida and Their Cultural Background.   NC 41.

3603   Owens, William A.   Texas Folk-Songs.   Iowa 41.

3604   Richmond, Winthrop E.   Place Names in the English and Scottish Popular Ballads and Their American Variants.   Ohio State 47.

3605   Roberts, Leonard W.   Eastern Kentucky Folktales: A Collection and a Study.   Ky 53.

3605a Turner, Frederick W., III.   Badmen, Black and White: The Continuity of American Folk Traditions.   UCLA 65.

3606   Westerhoff, Gerhard.   Christlich-religiöse Züge in den englisch-schottischen Volksballaden und ihren nordamerikanischen Fassungen.   Bonn 42.

3607 Wilgus, Donald K. A History of Anglo-American Ballad Scholarship since 1898. Ohio State 54.
See also 315, 358, 457a, 1226, 1238, 2455, 2725, 3570, 4106, 4448, 4473.

FOREIGN RELATIONSHIPS

GENERAL

3608 Bradbury, M.S. American Literary Expatriates in Europe since 1865. Manchester 63-64.
3609 Wegelin, Christof A. The Concept of Europe in American Fiction from Irving to Hawthorne. Johns Hopkins 47.
See also 2818, 2934, 3430, 3468, 3795, 4058, 4383, 4610.

ENGLISH–General

3610 Baum, Bernard. The Baconian Mind in Early Nineteenth Century America. Mich 42.
3611 Bryant, William A. Conceptions of America and the Americans by the English Romantic Poets: 1790-1850. Vanderbilt 41.
3612 Coleman, Ernest C. The Influence of the Addisonian Essay in America before 1810. Ill 36.
3613 Falk, Robert P. Representative American Criticism of Shakespeare, 1830-1885. Wis ?
3614 Hirsch, Lester. English Opinions of America in Revolt: A Study of the Pamphlets fro 1773 to 1790. NYU 53.
3615 Hook, Andrew D. Literary and Cultural Relations between Scotland and America, 1763-1830. Princeton 60.
3616 Johnson, Louise H. America in the Thought of the Leading British Men of Letters: 1830-1890. Wis 43.
3617 Jones, Joseph J. British Literary Men's Opinions about America, 1750-1832. Stanford 34.
3618 Kincheloe, H. G. British Periodical Criticism of American Literature, 1851-1870. Duke 48.
3619 Lathem, E. C. English Verse and Literary Prose Published in America Before 1776. Oxford 60-61.
3620 Panten, Günther. Die Amerikanismen im "Manchester Guardian Weekly" (1948-1954): Ein Beitrag zur Funktion der englischen Zeitung in den amerikanisch-britischen Sprachbeziehungen der Gegenwart. Mainz 58 publ.
3621 Pfeffer, Karl Heinz. England im Urteil der amerikanischen Literatur vor dem Bürgerkrieg. Berlin 31 publ.
3622 Pierce, Ella J. Appreciation of the Elizabethans during the New England Renaissance (1830-1880). Cornell 36.
3623 Schwegel, Douglas M. The Use of American Motifs by British Poets of the Romantic Period. Minn 60.
3624 Shain, Charles E. A British Image of America: A Survey of America and the Americans as They Appeared in the English Novel, 1830-1890. Princeton 49.
3625 Spiller, Robert E. The American in England during the First Half Century of Independence. Pa 24.
3626 Steen, Ivan D. The British Traveler and the American City, 1850-1860. NYU 63.
3627 Talbot, N. C. English Reactions to American Literature: A Study in the Periodicals, 1870-1887. Leeds 62-63.
3628 Ullreich, Josefine. Urteile bedeutender englischer Schriftsteller über die Vereinigten Staaten von Nordamerika in der ersten Hälfte des 19. Jahrhundert. Vienna 50.
3629 Wheeler, Paul M. America through British Eyes: A Study of the Attitude of *The Edinburgh Review* toward the United States of America from 1802 until 1861. Johns Hopkins 30.
See also 329, 388, 811, 1193, 1357, 1755, 2352, 2857, 2860, 3413, 3849, 4604, 4607, 4614, 4618.

ENGLISH–Individual Authors and America

3630 Bailey, Dorothy D. American Literary Criticism of George Meredith, 1860-1917. Wis 50.

3631 Betsky, Sarah Z. America, American Literature and D. H. Lawrence: A Study in Reciprocity. NYU 54.

3632 Blois, Raymond E. The American Reputation and Influence of William Blake. Boston 41.

3633 Braly, Earl B. The Reputation of David Hume in America. Tex 55.

3634 Brengle, Richard L. Very Knowing Americans. Jonathan Swift and America: His Reputation and Influence, 1720-1860. Columbia 62.

3635 Byrd, Milton. The Vogue of Edmund Burke in America to 1830. Wis 53.

3636 Cate, Hollis L. The Literary Reception of George Eliot's Novels in America (1858-1882). Ga 62.

3637 Coyle, William T. The Reputation of Anthony Trollope in the United States, 1858-1920. Western Reserve 48.

3638 Dykes, Eva Beatrice. Pope and His Influence in America from 1715 to 1850. Radcliffe 20.

3639 Earle, Osborne. The Reputation and Influence of William Godwin in America. Harvard 38.

3640 Eidson, John O. Tennyson in America: His Reputation and Influence from 1827 to 1858. Duke 41.

3641 Epps, Jennie Lee. The Influence of John Milton on the Five Major New England Poets. SC 29.

3642 Gladish, Robert W. Elizabeth Barrett Browning and America, 1838-1861: A Study of Her American Friendships and of Her Publication and Reputation in America. Chicago A.

3643 Goetze, Margret. Thomas Carlyle im Lichte der nordamerikanischen Kritik. Mainz 51.

3644 Green, Martin B. The Reputation of D. H. Lawrence in America. Mich 57.

3645 Greer, Louise. Browning in America: A Study of Browning Criticism and of Browning's Reputation in the United States, 1839-1890. Va 40.

3646 Heventhal, Charles R. Robert Burton's *Anatomy of Melancholy:* Notes on Its History and Popularity in America. Columbia 65.

3647 Hyder, Clyde W. Swinburne's Reputation in England and America. Harvard 30.

3648 Keough, Lawrence. The Critical Reception of G. Bernard Shaw's Plays in America: 1894-1950. So Cal.

3649 Krug, Werner. Lord Byron als dichterische Gestalt in England, Frankreich, Deutschland und Amerika. Giessen 32 publ.

3650 Lang, Daniel R. Dr. Samuel Johnson in America: A Study of His Reputation, 1750-1812. Ill 39.

3651 Lefkowitz, Allan B. Matthew Arnold's Other Countrymen: The Reputation of Matthew Arnold in America from 1853 to 1870. Boston 64.

3652 Leonard, W. E. Byron and Byronism in America. Columbia 05.

3653 Link, Seymour. Matthew Arnold's "Sweetness and Light" in America, 1848-1938. Peabody 39.

3654 McCormick, James P. Robert Browning's Reputation in the Nineteenth Century in England and America. Northwestern 37.

3655 Martin, Dexter. D. H. Lawrence and America. Pa.

3656 Nelson, Rowland W. The Reputation of Lord Chesterfield in Great Britain and America, 1730-1936. Northwestern 38.

3657 Newton, Annabel. Wordsworth in Early American Criticism. Mich 27.

3658 Orians, George H. The Influence of Walter Scott upon America and American Literature before 1860. Ill 26.

3659 Pfeiffer, Karl G. Periodical Criticism of Walter Savage Landor by His English and American Contemporaries. NC 39.

3660 Powell, Desmond S. Criticism of Byron in France, Germany, and America. Cornell 27.

3661 Power, Julia A. Shelley in America in the Nineteenth Century. Neb 38.

3662 Pringle, Kenneth R. The American Tours of William Makepeace Thackeray, 1852-1853, 1855-1856. Western Reserve 34.

3663 Raleigh, John H. The Growth of a Tradition: Arnold in America, 1865-1901 and the Aftermath. Princeton 48.

3664 Riggs, Roy A. The Vogue of Robert Louis Stevenson In America, 1880-1900. Ohio State 54.

3665 Schneider, Duane B. Sydney Smith's Reputation in America to 1900. Colo 65.

3666 Seat, William R. Harriet Martineau in America. Ind 57.

3667 Sibley, Agnes. Alexander Pope's Prestige in America, 1725-1835. Columbia 49.

3668 Smith, David E. John Bunyan in America: A Critical Inquiry. Minn 62.

3669 Stein, Roger R. Art and Morality: Impact of John Ruskin's Thought in America. Harvard 60.

3670 Stryker, Philip D. Anthony Trollope in the United States. Northwestern 48.

3671 Tedlock, E. W., Jr. D. H. Lawrence and America: A Biographical and Critical Study of the Influence of the United States and Mexico on the Thought and Writing of D. H. Lawrence. So Cal 51.

3672 Watters, Reginald E. The Vogue and Influence of Samuel Richardson in America: A Study of Cultural Conventions, 1742-1825. Wis 41.

3673 Whitmer, Anne B. American Reaction to the Literary Criticism of Samuel Taylor Coleridge, 1830-1860. Ohio State 39.

3674 Widger, Howard D. Thomas Carlyle in America: His Reputation and Influence. Ill 4(

3675 Williamson, Ward. An Analytical History of American Criticism of the Works of Sean O'Casey, 1924-1958. Iowa 62.

3676 Wilson, Jack H. George Eliot in America, Her Vogue and Influence, 1858-1900. NC 65.

3677 Winslow, Donald J. Thomas Hardy: His British and American Critics. Boston 42.

3678 Winther, Sophus K. The Literary Reputation of Matthew Arnold in England and America. Wash 27.

3679 Yoder, Richard A. The Influence of Coleridge in America, 1817-1836. Pa 64.

3680 Zanger, Jules. Captain Frederick Marryat's *Diary in America:* A Critical Edition. Wash (St. Louis) 54.

3681 Zimmerman, Lester F. Some Aspects of Milton's American Reputation to 1900. Wis 49.
See also 1484, 1486, 1751, 1824, 1837, 1845, 1872, 1887, 1892, 1899, 2193, 2203, 2139, 2164, 2648, 2652, 2876, 4597.

FRENCH–General

3682 Arnavon, Daniel J. Les Lettres américaines devant la critique française (1887-1917). Paris 50.

3683 Brown, Esther E. The French Revolution and the American Man of Letters. Mo 48.

3684 Chazin, Maurice. French Culture as Reflected in *The Atlantic Monthly,* 1857-1900. Johns Hopkins RL 29.

3685 Copans, Simon J. French Opinion of American Democracy, 1852-1860. Brown RL

3686 Fäy, Bernard. Bibliographie critique des ouvrages français relatifs aux États-Unis, 1770-1800. Paris 24 publ.

3687 Gibson, Delbert L. The United States as Seen in the Leading French Literary Periodicals, 1900-1930. Wis RL 39.

3688 Halperin, Maurice. Le Roman de Tristan et Iseut dans la littérature anglo-américaine au XIXe et au XXe siècle. Paris 31 publ.

3689 Jaffe, Adrian H. French Literature in American Periodicals, 1741-1800. NYU RL 5(

3690 Jones, Malcolm B. French Literature and American Criticism, 1870-1900. Harvard RL 36.

3691 Joyaux, Georges M. French Thought in American Magazines, 1800-1848. Mich State 51.

3692 Kalfayan, Armen. The United States of America and the Post-War Literature of France. Iowa RL 32.

3693 Koch, Jay K. The Reception and Influence of Modern American Poetry in France, 1918-1950. Columbia 59.

3694   Lacy, Helen M.   French Lyric Poetry in English and American Translations: A Bibliography. Peabody RL 34.
3695   Lapp, John C.   The New World in French Poetry of the Renaissance. Cornell RL 42.
3696   Lewis, H. Michael.   Les Derniers jugements des écrivains français sur la civilisation américaine. Poitiers 31.
3697   Lloyd, Everett T.   The Evolution of the Attitude in the United States toward Emile Zola. NYU RL 46.
3698   McBride, John deWitt, Jr.   America in the French Mind during the Bourbon Restoration. Syracuse 54.
3699   McCarthy, Thomas J.   American Premiere Criticism of Selected Contemporary French Plays Produced on the New York Stage, 1946-1960. So Cal 65.
3700   McGee, Sidney-Lamont.   La Littérature américaine dans la *Revue des Deux-Mondes* (1831-1900). Montpellier 27 publ.
3701   Mantz, Harold E.   French Criticism of American Literature before 1850. Columbia RL 17.
3702   Mathes, John C.   The New York Theatre Critics' Standards: Their Evaluation of French Drama, 1945-1961. Mich 65.
3703   Mickelson, Joel C.   Attitudes of Americans in France toward Contemporary French Political Life, 1860-1914. Pa 56.
3704   Moriarty, Jane V.   The American Novel in France. Wis 54.
3705   Orr, John B.   Images of America in the Contemporary French Novel, 1920-1955. Minn.
3706   Rabinovitz, Albert L.   The Criticism of French Novels in American Magazines, 1830-1860. Harvard RL 41.
3707   Rémond, René.   Les États-Unis devant l'opinion française. Paris 62 publ.
3708   Shepherd, James L.   L'Amérique du Nord dans la littérature française (1830-1840). Paris 53.
3709   Smith, Anne W.   Criticism of American Life and Letters in the *Revue Encyclopédique.* Northwestern RL 43.
3710   Swigart, Beulah Hope.   The Americas as Revealed in the *Encyclopédie.* Ill RL 40.
3711   Taupin, René.   L'Interprétation américaine de la poésie française contemporaine (essai de bibliographie). Paris 30.
3712   Tennis, LeGrand.   Frenchmen in Colonial Virginia. Va 41.
3713   Tinker, Edward L.   Les Écrits de langue française en Louisiana au XIXe siècle: Essais biographiques et bibliographiques. Paris 33 publ.
       See also 1480, 1482, 1530, 1583, 2128, 2140, 2176, 2187, 2192, 2450, 2799, 3411, 4602, 4606, 4615, 4620, 4621.

FRENCH—Individual Authors and America

3714   Adelhöfer, Inge.   Die Interpretation englischen und amerikanischen Geistes in André Maurois Werk. Berlin (F) 61.
3715   Barr, Mary-Margaret H.   Voltaire in America, 1744-1800. Columbia RL 40.
3716   Canter, Jacob.   The Literary Reputation of Baudelaire in England and America, 1857-1934. Harvard RL 40.
3717   Cohen, Rubin.   Balzac in the United States during the Nineteenth Century. Columbia RL 50.
3718   Giamatti, Valentine J.   Le Chevalier de Chambray in America, 1778-1783. Harvard RL 40.
3719   Griffith, Benjamin.   Balzac aux États-Unis. Paris 31 publ.
3720   Hall, Bita May.   Critical Opinion of Romain Rolland in the United States. Columbia RL 52.
3721   Herring, Margaret T.   America in the Works of Victor Hugo. Pa RL 38.
3722   Jackson, Ernest A.   The Critical Reception of Gustave Flaubert in the United States, 1860-1960. Mich 62.
3723   McEwen, Marjorie R.   Anatole France in the United States. Columbia RL 45.
3724   Marshall, James F.   Stendahl and America. Ill RL 48.

3725 Rosselet, Jeanne. A Contribution to the Study of Victor Hugo in the United States. Radcliffe 30.

3726 Salvan, Albert J. Zola aux États-Unis. Columbia RL 43.

3727 Spurlin, Paul M. Montesquieu and American Opinion, 1760-1801. Johns Hopkins RL 36.

3728 Swain, Jeraldine N. L. The Critical Reception of Albert Camus in the United States, 1946-1964. So Cal.

3729 Tougas, Gerard R. Marcel Proust: Aspects of Anglo-American Criticism. Stanford RL 54.

See also 1561, 1563, 2129, 2131, 2153, 2160, 2180, 2182, 2190, 2220, 2622, 2684, 2695, 2699.

GERMAN AND CENTRAL EUROPEAN–General

3730 Ballinger, Sara E. The Reception of the American Novel in German Periodicals, 1945-1957. Ind 59.

3731 Colwell, James L. The American Expatriate Experience in Berlin, 1920-1933. Yale.

3732 Condoyannis, George E. German American Fiction from 1850 to 1914. Columbia G 53.

3733 Crispin, Robert L. The Currency and Reception of German Short Prose Fiction in England and America as Reflected in the Periodicals, 1790-1840. Pa State G 55.

3735 Desczyk, Gerhard. Amerika in der Phantasie deutscher Dichter. Leipzig 23.

3736 Dietel, Günther. Studien zur Aufnahme und Beurteilung der deutschen Literatur in Amerika, 1919-1939. Jena 52.

3737 Dobert, Eitel W. Die Schriften der deutsch-amerikanischen Achtungvierziger. Md G 54.

3738 Ehle, Ralph V. America Reflected in Two German Periodicals: *Die Deutsche Rundschau* and *Die Neue Rundschau*, 1900-1928. Johns Hopkins 33.

3739 Eisele, Susanne. Das Deutschlandbild in der amerikanischen Literatur des zweiten Weltkrieges. Erlangen 61.

3740 Feller, Max K. Die Aufnahme amerikanischer Literatur in der deutschsprachigen Schweiz. Berlin (H) 49.

3741 Fink, Hermann. Der Einflusz des amerikanischen Englisch auf die deutsche Werbesprache der Gegenwart. Mainz.

3742 Frese, Hans. Das deutsche Buch in Amerika: Übersetzungen der Jahre 1918-1935. Marburg 37 publ.

3743 Kolbeck, Sister M. Orestes. American Opinion on the *Kulturkampf*, 1871-1882. Catholic H 42.

3744 Leitel, Erich. Die Aufnahme der amerikanischen Literatur in Deutschland: Übersetzungen der Jahre 1914-1944: Mit einer Bibliographie. Jena 58.

3745 Locher, Kaspar T. The Reception of American Literature in German Literary Histories in the Nineteenth Century. Chicago 50.

3746 Meyer, Klaus-Jürgen. Die deutsche Rezeption der amerikanischen Jazz-Sprache (Fachsprache und Slang). Mainz.

3747 Möhl, Gertrud. Die Aufnahme amerikanischer Literatur in der deutsch-sprachigen Schweiz während der Jahre 1945-1950. Zürich.

3748 Mueller, Bertha. American Criticism of Recent German Literature. Wis G 36.

3749 Mürbe, Hans J. The American Image of Germany Set Forth in Nineteenth-Century Travel Books. Ohio State 64.

3750 Pickl, Norbert. Amerikanische Interpretation des europäischen Totalitarismus. Munich.

3751 Scherer, George A. C. The German National Mind and Character in Representative American Periodicals, 1933-1939. Iowa G 44.

3752 Schroeder, Samuel. Amerika in der deutschen Dichtung von 1850-1890. Heidelberg 36.

3753 Springer, Anne M. The American Novel in Germany: A Study of the Critical Reception of Eight American Novelists between the Two World Wars. Pa 59.

3754 Timpe, Eugene F.   The Reception of American Literature in Germany, 1861-1871. So Cal 61.

3755 Van de Luyster, Nelson.   Emigration to America as Reflected in the German Novel of the Nineteenth Century: Especially in the Fiction of Bitzius, Laube, Gutzkow, Auerbach, Freytag, Storm, Keller, Spielhagen, Hayse, Raabe.   NC G 42.

3756 Vollmer, Clement.   The American Novel in Germany, 1871-1913.   Pa G 15.

3757 Wacker, Helga.   Untersuchungen zur Gestalt der deutschen Schriftsprache beim Deutschtum der Vereinigten Staaten, Kanadas und Australiens sowie Südafrikas, Palästinas und Südamerikas: Auf Grund der Sprache der überseeischen deutschen Zeitungen.   Tübingen 56.

3758 Weyl, Shalom.   North-America (Canada and the United States) in German Literature (1918-1945).   Toronto G 52.
       See also 324, 372, 813, 1490, 1742, 1878, 1943, 2201, 2451, 2471, 2524, 2849, 4361, 4382, 4591, 4598.

GERMAN AND CENTRAL EUROPEAN–Individual Authors and America

3759 Ashby, Nanette.   The Sealsfield Controversy: A Study of Publication Conditions Affecting the Reception in America of the Works of Charles Sealsfield.   Stanford 39.

3760 Aufderheide, Elfriede.   Das Amerikaerlebnis in den Romanen von Charles Sealsfield. Göttingen 46.

3761 Baker, Thomas S.   Lenau and Young Germany in America.   Johns Hopkins G 95.

3762 Born, Jürgen.   Die Aufnahme und der Einflusz Franz Kafkas in Amerika.   Berlin (F).

3763 Cappel, Edith.   The Reception of Gerhart Hauptmann in the United States.   Columbia G 52.

3764 Cartwright, Françoise D.   Amerikanische Gedanken in den literarischen Werken Maeterlincks.   Berlin 35 publ.

3765 Dallmann, William P.   Spirit of America as Interpreted in the Works of Charles Sealsfield.   Wash (St. Louis) G 35.

3766 Djordjewitsch, Milosch.   Charles Sealsfields Auffassung des Amerikanertums und seine literarhistorische Stellung.   Munich 30 publ.

3767 Drimmer, Melvin.   Nietzsche in American Thought, 1895-1925.   Rochester H 65.

3768 Faust, Albert B.   Charles Sealsfield: Materials for a Biography: A Study of His Style: His Influence upon American Literature.   Johns Hopkins G 92.

3769 Foster, Milton P.   The Reception of Max Nordau's Degeneration in England and America.   Mich 54.

3770 Frey, Erich A.   Amerika in den Werken Thomas Manns.   So Cal G 63.

3771 Graewert, Theodor.   Otto Ruppius und der Amerikaroman im 19. Jahrhundert. Jena 35 publ.

3772 Hale, Nathan.   The Americanization of Sigmund Freud: The Popularization of Freud in America, 1909-1933.   UCB.

3773 Hecken, Dorothea.   Das Grillparzerbild im anglo-amerikanischen Ausland, mir einer Studie über den deutschen literarischen Einflusz in Amerika.   Berlin 44.

3774 Hermsdorf, Klaus.   Franz Kafkas Romanfragment "Der Verschollene" ("Amerika"). Berlin (H) 59.

3775 Heydt, Alfred von der.   Friederich Bodenstedt in Amerika und sein Buch Vom Atlantischen zum Stillen Ozean.   Cornell G 48.

3776 Kauffmann, LeRoy C.   The Influence of Friedrich Nietzsche on American Literature. Pa 63.

3777 Klein, Manfred.   Goethe and the Genteel Tradition in America.   Boston 61.

3778 Landa, Bjarne E.   The American Scene in Friedrich Gerstächer's Works of Fiction. Minn G 52.

3779 Matlaw, Myron.   Some Kotzebue Plays in England and America: The Stranger and Pizarro.   Chicago G 54.

3780 Roswell, May M.   Bertolt Brecht's Plays in America.   Md 61.

3781 Sachs, Henry B.   Heine in America.   Pa G 06.

3782 Schmidt, Max L.   Amerikanismen bei Charles Sealsfield.   Bonn 37 publ.

3783   Weck, Frederick W.   Jean Paul Friedrich Richter's Relation to American Literature. Mich G 16.

3784   Weiss, Gerhard.   Die aufnahme Heinrich Heines in Grossbritannien und den Vereinigter Staaten von Amerika (1828 bis 1856):   Eine Studie sur Rezeption des Menschen und Prosakünstlers.   Mainz 55.

3785   Zylstra, Henry.   E. T. A. Hoffmann in England and America.   Harvard 40.
See also 826, 1034, 2144, 2174, 2470, 2685, 2687, 2691, 2722, 2738, 2745, 2809, 2900.

ITALIAN

3786   Baker, Paul R.   The American in Italy, 1800-1860.   Harvard 60.

3787   Bollinger, Evangeline G.   Dante's *Divine Comedy* in English and American Criticism since 1910.   Mich 51.

3788   Capponi, Guido.   Italy and Italians in Early American Periodicals (1741-1830).   Wis 5

3789   Green, Rose B.   The Evolution of Italian-American Fiction as a Document of the Interaction of Two Cultures.   Pa A 62.

3791   Mathews, J. Chesley.   Dante and Major American Writers.   UCB 38.

3792   Smith, Lawrence.   The Literary and Political Use of American Literature by Italian Writers in the 1930's and 40's.   Harvard.

3793   White, Robert L.   Some Passionate Pilgrims: The Image of Italy in American Romanticism.   Minn 59.
See also 1403, 1727, 2449a, 4622.

MISCELLANEOUS

3794   Baker, Ray P.   History of English Canadian Literature to the Confederation: Its Relation to the Literature of Great Britain and of the United States.   Harvard 16.

3795   Cürten, Ulrich.   Das europäische Amerikabuch seit 1945.   Freiburg.

3796   Gauthier, J. D.   Le Canada français et le roman américain.   Laval 49.

3797   Levine, Samuel H.   Changing Concepts of Palestine in American Literature to 1867. NYU 53.

3798   Magee, William H.   Trends in the English Canadian Novel in the Twentieth Century. Toronto 50.

3799   Neidle, Cecyle S.   The Foreign-Born View America: A Study of Autobiographies Written by Immigrants to the United States.   NYU 62.

3800   Schramm, Richard.   The Image of India in Selected American Literary Periodicals: 1870-1900.   Duke 64.

ORIENTAL

3801   Cecil, L. Moffitt, Jr.   Our Japanese Romance: The Myth of Japan in America, 1853-1905.   Vanderbilt 47.

3802   Chu, Limin.   The Images of China and the Chinese in the *Overland Monthly,* 1868-1875, 1883-1935.   Duke 66.

3803   Foster, John B.   China and the Chinese in American Literature, 1850-1950.   Ill 53.

3804   Gardner, John.   The Image of the Chinese in America, 1885-1915.   Pa.

3805   Miner, Earl R.   The Japanese Influence on English and American Literature, 1850-1950.   Minn 55.

3806   Morales, Alfredo T.   The Influence of American Literature on Filippino Democracy. Mich 46.

3807   Winters, Lee E., Jr.   The Relationship of Chinese Poetry to British and American Poetry of the Twentieth Century.   UCB 56.
See also 225a, 814, 968, 1255, 1840, 2497, 2513, 2515, 2534, 2688, 2690, 3800, 3979, 4355, 4587, 4603.

RUSSIAN

3808   Brown, Deming.   American Authors in Soviet Russia, 1917-1941.   Columbia Slavic 51

3809   DeMarr, Mary J.   In a Strange Land: Contributions to American Literature by
Russian and Russian-Jewish Immigrants.   Ill 63.
3810   Fiske, John C.   American Classics in Soviet Criticism.   Harvard 54.
3811   Gettmann, Royal A.   Turgenev in England and America.   Ill 37.
3812   Lefevre, Carl A.   Gogol's First Century in England and America (1841-1941).   Minn 44.
3813   Meister, Charles W.   English and American Criticism of Chekhov.   Chicago 49.
3814   Smith, J. Allan.   Tolstoy's Fiction in England and America.   Ill Slavic 39.
3815   Whitt, Joseph.   The Psychological Criticism of Dostoevsky: 1875-1951, A Study of
British, American, and Chief European Critics.   Temple 53.

SCANDINAVIAN AND DUTCH

3816   Andersen, Annette.   Ibsen in America.   Iowa 31.
3817   Anderson, Carl.   The Swedish Reception of Sinclair Lewis and His Contemporaries.
Pa 54.
3818   Borgwardt, Elisabeth.   Das skandinavische Element im amerikanischen Roman.
Greifswald 37.
3819   Larson, Esther E.   Swedish Commentators on the American Scene, 1638 to 1865.
NYU H 58.
3820   Lieder, P. R.   Scandinavian Influence on English and American Literature, 1815-1850.
Harvard 15.
3821   Moyne, Ernest J.   Studies in Cultural Relations between Finland and America.
Harvard 48.
3822   Oppewall, Peter.   The Critical Reception of American Fiction in the Netherlands,
1900-1953.   Mich 61.
3823   Paulson, Arthur C.   The Norwegian-American Reaction to Ibsen and Bjørnson,
1850-1900.   Iowa 33.
3824   Rapp, Esther E.   Strindberg's Reception in England and America.   Colo 40.
3825   Skårdal, Dorothy B.   Double Heritage: Scandinavian Immigrant Experience Through
Literary Sources.   Harvard A 63.
3826   Ter Maat, Cornelius J.   Three Novelists and a Community: A Study of American
Novelists with Dutch Calvinist Origins.   Mich E 63.
3827   Thorson, Gerald H.   America Is Not Norway: The Story of the Norwegian-
American Novel.   Columbia 57.
3828   Thune, Ensaf.   Main Currents of Ibsen Interpretation in England and America.
Wash 62.
3829   White, George L., Jr.   Scandinavian Themes in American Fiction.   Pa 35.
See also 1729, 2057, 2078, 2305.

SPANISH AND LATIN AMERICAN

3830   Berry, Thomas E.   A History of the Recent Translations of the American Novel
into Spanish.   Pittsburgh 49.
3831   Borrowdale, Howard O.   Mexican Mirage: A Study of the Belletristic Literature
Based upon the Maximilian Empire in Mexico, 1864-1867.   So Cal 45.
3832   Cobb, Carl W.   Translations from English and American Poetry in Colombia.   Tulane 61.
3833   Corbitt, Roberta D.   This Colossal Theater: The United States Interpreted by José
Martí.   Ky RL 55.
3834   Daniel, Elizabeth R.   Spanish-American Travelers in the United States before 1900:
A Study in Inter-American Literary Relations.   NC RL 59.
3835   De Onis, José M.   The United States as Seen by Spanish-American Writers (1776-1890).
Columbia RL 52.
3836   Espinosa, José E.   Americanism in Argentine Literature: A Commentary on Critical
Opinion.   Cornell RL 34.
3837   Ferguson, J. DeLancey.   American Literature in Spain.   Columbia 16.
3838   Fraker, Charles F.   The Development of Modernism in Spanish-American Poetry.
Harvard 31.

3839 Herrick, George H. American and Spanish-American Literature in California and Central American Higher Education. So Cal E 60.
3840 Kolker, Sister M. Delphine. Spanish Legends in English and American Literature: 1800-1860. Catholic 53.
3841 Manchester, Paul T. A Bibliography and Critique of the Spanish Translations from the Poetry of the United States. Peabody 27.
3842 Muste, John M. The Spanish Civil War in the Literature of the United States and Great Britain. Wis 60.
3843 Nepper, Dorothy N. Sarmiento in the United States. Bryn Mawr RL 44.
3844 Robinson, Cecil. Mexico and the Hispanic Southwest in American Literature. Columbia 60.
3845 Stimson, Frederick S. Spanish Themes iń Early American Literature: Novels Drama, and Verse, 1770-1830. Mich 52.
3846 Walls, Aileen. Cultural Image of the United States: North American Novelists and South American Reviews. Ill 62.
3847 Zardoya, Maria Concepcion. España en la poesia americana. Ill 52.
See also 1741, 2148, 2674.

HUMOR AND SATIRE

3848 Berger, Arthur A. Li'l Abner: An American Satire. Minn 65.
3849 Enkvist, Nils E. American Humor in England. Helsinki 53 publ.
3850 Glietenburg, Ilse. Die Comics, Wesen und Wirkung. Munich 56.
3851 Hausdorff, Don M. Depression Laughter: Magazine Humor and American Society, 1929-33. Minn 63.
3852 Heiser, Merrill. Representative Early American Satirists. Wis 48.
3853 Horner, George F. A History of American Humor to 1765. NC 38.
3854 Ives, Edward D. The Satirical Song Tradition in Maine and the Maritime Provinces of Canada, with Particular Reference to Larry Gorman. Ind 62.
3855 Kellogg, Thelma L. Early American Social Satire before 1800, with Especial Reference to Social Satire in the Early American Almanac. Radcliffe 29.
3856 Kitch, John C. Dark Laughter: A Study of the Pessimistic Tradition in American Humor. Northwestern 64.
3857 Steadman, Mark S., Jr. American Humor: 1920-1955. Fla State 63.
3858 Tandy, Jennette. The Crackerbox Philosophers. Columbia 25.
See also 1696, 2019, 2303, 2365, 2374, 2510, 2511, 2762, 2801, 3057, 3081, 3082, 3089, 3092, 3094, 3097, 3352, 3478, 3512, 3985, 3991, 4030, 4280, 4360, 4369, 4500, 4608.

INDIANS

3859 Behen, Dorothy M. The Captivity Story in American Literature, 1577-1826: An Examination of Written Reports in English, Authentic and Fictitious, of the Experiences of White Men Captured by the Indians North of Mexico. Chicago 52.
3860 Bissell, B. H. The American Indian in English Literature of the Eighteenth Century. Yale 23.
3861 Buntin, Arthur R. The Indian in American Literature, 1680-1760. Wash H 61.
3862 Daugherty, George H., Jr. North American Indian Literature. Chicago 25.
3863 Day, A. Grove. Types of North American Indian Poetry in English Translation. Stanford 44.
3864 Jones, G. Elwood, Jr. The American Indian in the American Novel (1875-1950). NYU 58.
3865 Jones, Henry B. The Death Song of the "Noble Savage": A Study in the Idealization of the American Indian. Chicago 24.

3866 Kenny, Hamill T. The Origin and Meaning of the Indian Place-Names of Maryland. Md 51.

3867 Leechman, Douglas. The "Red Indian" of Literature: A Study in the Perpetuation of Error. Ottawa 41.

3868 Morgan, Paul. The Treatment of the Indian in Southwestern Literature since 1915: A Study in Primitivism. Tex 54.

3869 Paige, Harry W. The Songs of the Teton Sioux. SUNY (Albany).

3870 Pearce, Roy H. The Indian and the American Mind, 1775-1800: A Study in the History and Impact of Primitivistic Ideas. Johns Hopkins 45.

3871 Russell, J. Almus. The Indian in American Literature. Cornell 29.

3872 Schulz, Franz. Der nordamerikanische Indianer und seine Welt in den Werken von Ernest Hemingway und Oliver La Farge. Mainz 65 publ.

3873 Seale, Lea L. Indian Place-Names in Mississippi. La 39.

3874 Sitton, Fred. The Indian Play in American Drama, 1750-1900. Northwestern D 62.

3875 Thompson, Stith. European Borrowings and Parallels in North American Indian Tales. Harvard 14.

3876 Walton, Eda L. Navajo Poetry: Its Content and Form. UCB 21.

3877 Wasserman, Maurice M. The American Indian as Seen by the Seventeenth Century Chroniclers. Pa 54.

3878 Weiler, Thea. Der Indianer in der nordamerikanischen Literatur. Munich 24.

LANGUAGE

GENERAL

3879 Abbott, Orville L. A Study of the Verb Forms and Verb Uses in Certain American Writings of the Seventeenth Century. Mich State 54.

3880 Anthony, Edward M., Jr. Test Frames for Structures with *up* in the Modern American English. Mich 54.

3881 Balla, Leonore. Entwicklungstendenzen im amerikanischen Wortegebrauch der Gegenwart nachgewiesen an einigen Tageszeitungen und Wochenschriften. Marburg 48.

3882 Bentley, Harold W. A Dictionary of Spanish Terms in English, with Special Reference to the American Southwest. Columbia 32.

3883 Beyer, Erich. Studien zur amerikanischen Sportsprache unter besonderer Berücksichtigung des Baseballspieles und seines Wortschatzes. Marburg 48.

3884 Brauburger, Herbert. Studien zu den amerikanischen Neologismen des 17. und 18. Jahrhunderts, unter besonderer Berücksichtigung des englischen Sprachmaterials. Cologne 54.

3885 Bridgman, Richard. The Stylization of Vernacular Elements in American Fiction, 1880-1925. UCB 60.

3886 Burkett, Eva M. A Study of American Dictionaries of the English Language before 1861. Peabody 36.

3887 Carr, Elizabeth B. Trends in Word Compounding in American Speech. La 54.

3888 Criswell, Elijah H. Lewis and Clark: Linguistic Pioneers. Mo 37.

3889 Curtis, Roy G. An Investigation of Some of the Structures of Independent Utterances in Modern American English. Mich 48.

3890 Davis, Alva L. A Word Atlas of the Great Lakes Region. Mich 49.

3891 Drake, Glendon. Prescriptive Linguistics in America since 1825. Mich.

3892 Eyestone, Maxine A. Tests and Treatment of Compound Substantives in Modern American English with Special Emphasis on Stress and Intonation Patterns. Mich State 54.

3893 Frank, Erika Olga. Modern American Language in the Service of Present Day Advertisement: A Survey of Linguistic Means Available for the Psychology of Selling. Vienna 47.

3894 Frings, Manfred S. Studien zur Frage der Archaismen im amerikanischen Englisch. Cologne 53.

3895 Gläser, Rosemarie. Entwicklungstendenzen im politischen Wortschatz der englisch-amerikanischen Gegenwartssprache. Leipzig 62.
3896 Gold, Robert S. A Lexicon of Jazz Slang. NYU 61.
3897 Gustafson, Walter W. The Swedish Language in the United States. NYU 29.
3898 Herlinghaus, Karlwilhelm. Baseball: eine wortgeschichtliche Untersuchung. Kiel.
3899 Hietsch, Otto. G. I. Slang: An Analysis of United States Army Slang of World War II. Vienna 48.
3900 Hülsbergen, Helmut. Studien zu den amerikanischen Neologismen des 19. Jahrhunderts. Cologne 57.
3901 Hunter, Edwin R. The American Colloquial Idiom, 1830-1860. Chicago 25.
3902 Keaton, Anna L. Americanisms in Early American Newspapers. Chicago 33.
3903 McJimsey, George D. Topographic Terms in Virginia. Columbia 39.
3904 McMullen, Edwin W. English Topographic Terms in Florida, 1563-1874. Columbia 5(
3905 Mathews, Mitford McL. Notes and Comments Made by British Travelers and Observers upon American English, 1770-1850. Harvard 36.
3906 Monson, Samuel C. Representative American Phonetic Alphabets. Columbia 54.
3907 Mount, Robert F. Mid-Nineteenth Century New England Literary Dialect: A Study of Five Authors. Columbia S 64.
3908 Neumann, J. H. American Pronunciation According to Noah Webster. Columbia 24.
3909 Nichols, Edward J. An Historical Dictionary of Baseball Terminology. Pa State 39.
3910 Orbeck, Anders. Early English Pronunciation in the United States. Columbia 25.
3911 Paulovsky, Louis H. Das Eindringen und die Aufnahme von Amerikanismen in das britische Alltagsenglisch der Gegenwart. Vienna 43.
3912 Raffler, Walburga M. von. Studies in Italian-English Bilingualism. Ind 54.
3913 Reusch, Joseph. Die alten syntaktischen Reste im modernen Slang. Münster 94.
3914 Rühmekorb, Walter. Wortbildende Kräfte in der heutigen anglo-amerikanischen Presse und Umgangssprache und im Slang. Kiel 54.
3915 Shewmake, Edwin F. English Pronunciation in Virginia. Va 20.
3916 Sleator, Mary D. Phonology and Morphology of an American English Dialect. Ind 57.
3917 Sobotka, Rudolf. Die englische Sprache in den Schlagzeilen der anglo-amerikanischen periodischen Presse. Vienna 51.
3918 Steger, Stewart A. American Dictionaries. Va 13.
3919 Stone, Ruth M. Studien über den deutschen Einflusz auf amerikanische Englisch. Marburg 34 publ.
3920 Traver, Alice A. The Modificational Patterns of the Substantive Head Construction in Present-Day American English. Mich 45.
3921 Trittschuh, Travis E. The Semantics of Political Cartoon and Slogan in America, 1876-1884. Ohio State 53.
3922 Tyler, Priscilla. Grammars of the English Language to 1850: With Special Emphasis o School Grammars Used in America. Four Studies. Western Reserve 63.
3923 Ulherr, Hans. Der Gebrauch des Anredepronomens der zweiten Person Singular in der englischen Sprache Nordamerikas (von den Anfängen der Kolonialzeit bis um 1800). Erlangen 56.
3924 Wächtler, Kurt. Studien zum informellen Wortschatz, zur Headline-Syntax und zum betont informellen Stil in amerikanischen Tageszeitungen und Wochenschriften. Marburg 51.
3925 Weldner, Heinrich. Die Durchdringung des britischen Englisch mit amerikanischen Spracheigentümlichkeiten. Jena 49.
3926 Williams, Hazel B. A Semantic Study of Some Current, Pejoratively Regarded Symbols Involving Negroes in the United States. NYU 53.
See also 576, 1273, 1284, 1692, 2829, 3620, 3741.

REGIONAL AND ETHNIC DIALECTS

3927 Arnold, David B. Linguistic Variation in a New England Community. Harvard L 62.

3928   Bloch, Bernard.   The Treatment of Middle English Final and Preconsonantal R in the Present-Day Speech of New England.   Brown 35.
3929   Caffee, Nathaniel M.   A Phonological Study of the Speech of a Homogeneous Group in Charlottesville, Va.   Va 34.
3930   Carson, William P.   Literary Dialect of the Southern Highlander.   Columbia 26.
3931   Dearden, E. Jeannette.   Dialect Areas of the South Atlantic States as Determined by Variations in Vocabulary.   Brown 43.
3932   De Camp, David.   The Pronunciation of English in San Francisco.   UCB 54.
3933   Duke, Francis J.   A Phonetic Study of Italo-American Speech in Richmond, Va.   Va 38.
3934   Emerson, Oliver F.   The Ithaca Dialect: A Study of Present English.   Cornell 91.
3935   Farrison, William E.   The Phonology of the Illiterate Negro Dialect of Guilford County, North Carolina.   Ohio State 37.
3936   Frank, Yakira H.   The Speech of New York City.   Mich 49.
3937   Frey, John W.   The German Dialect of Eastern York County, Pennsylvania.   Ill G 42.
3938   Gilbert, Glenn G.   The German Dialect Spoken in Kendall and Gillespie Counties, Texas.   Harvard L 63.
3939   Hall, Joseph S.   The Phonetics of Great Smoky Mountain Speech.   Columbia S 41.
3940   Hawkins, Jane D.   The Speech of the Hudson River Valley.   Brown 41.
3941   Heflin, Woodford A.   Characteristic Features of New Mexico English between 1805 and 1890.   Chicago 41.
3942   Idol, Harriett R.   A Strobophotographic Study of Southern Intonation.   La 37.
3943   Kilpatrick, Rachel S. H.   The Speech of Rhode Island: The Stressed Vowels and Diphthongs.   Brown 37.
3944   Lawrence, Vivian S.   Dialect Mixture in Three New England Pronunciation Patterns: Vowels and Consonants.   Columbia 60.
3945   Lucke, Jessie R.   A Study of the Virginia Dialect and Its Origin in English.   Va 49.
3946   Lynn, Klonda.   A Phonetic Analysis of the English Spoken by Mexican Children in the Elementary Schools of Arizona.   La 40.
3947   McMillan, James B.   Phonology of the Standard English of East Central Alabama.   Chicago 46.
3948   Norman, Arthur M. Z.   A Southeast Texas Dialect Study.   Tex 55.
3949   Pardoe, T. Earl.   A Historical and Phonetic Study of Negro Dialect.   La 37.
3949a Pederson, Lee A.   The Pronunciation of English in Metropolitan Chicago.   Chicago 64.
3950   Potter, Edward E.   The Dialect of Northwestern Ohio: A Study of a Transition Area.   Mich 55.
3951   Reed, Carroll E.   The Pennsylvania German Dialect Spoken in the Counties of Lehigh and Berks: Phonology and Morphology.   Brown 41.
3952   Seifert, Lester W. J.   The Pennsylvania German Dialect Spoken in the Counties of Lehigh and Berks: Vocabulary.   Brown 41.
3953   Shoemaker, Alfred L.   Studies on the Pennsylvania German Dialect of the Amish Community in Arthur, Illinois.   Ill G 40.
3954   Simpson, Claude M., Jr.   The English Speech of Early Rhode Island, 1636-1700.   Harvard 36.
3955   Stanley, Oma.   The Speech of East Texas.   Columbia 36.
3956   Tidwell, James N.   The Literary Representation of the Phonology of the Southern Dialect.   Ohio State 48.
3957   Trager, Edith Crowell.   The Kiowa Language: A Grammatical Study.   Pa 60.
3958   Williamson, Juanita V.   A Phonological and Morphological Study of the Speech of the Negro of Memphis, Tennessee.   Mich 61.
        See also 1748, 1752.

LIBRARIES AND READING

3959   Cantrell, Clyde H.   The Reading Habits of Ante-Bellum Southerners.   Ill LS 60.

3960 Carrier, Esther J. Fiction in Public Libraries of the United States, 1876-1900. Mich LS 60.
3961 Finkler, Norman. History of the Philadelphia Free Library, 1925-1955. Pa A.
3962 Grimm, Dorothy. A History of the Library Company of Philadelphia, 1731-1835. Pa A 55.
3963 Houlette, William D. Plantation and Parish Libraries in the Old South. Iowa H 33.
3964 Keep, A. B. The Library in Colonial New York. Columbia 09.
3965 Kraus, Joe W. Book Collections of Five Colonial College Libraires: A Subject Analysis. Ill LS 60.
3966 Lincoln, Sister Mary E. The Cultural Significance of the Minneapolis Public Library. Minn LS 58.
3967 Parham, Paul. Malcolm Glenn Wyer and the Development of American Libraries in the West. Denver.
3968 Powell, Benjamin E. The Development of Libraries in Southern State Universities to 1920. Chicago LS 47.
3969 Ranz, James. The History of the Printed Book Catalogue in the United States. Ill LS 60.
3970 Robinson, Ruth W. Four Community Subscription Libraries in Colonial Pennsylvania: Darby, Hatboro, Lancaster and Newtown, 1743-1790. Pa 52.
3971 Shores, Louis. Origins of the American College Library, 1638-1800. Peabody E 34.
3972 Spain, Frances L. Libraries of South Carolina: Their Origins and Early History, 1700-1830. Chicago LS 45.
3973 Thierbach, Hans. Die Bedeutung der öffenlichen Bibliotheken für die amerikanische Volksbildung. Berlin 41.

LITERARY HISTORY

CHARACTER TYPES

3974 Cady, Edwin H. The Concept of the Gentleman in Representative American Authors. Wis 43.
3975 Cawelti, John G. A History of Self-Made Manhood: The Ideal of the Self-Made Man in Nineteenth Century America. Iowa A 60.
3976 Cross, Marimae. The Image of the Capitalist in Literature and Politics, 1890-1912. Minn.
3977 DeBakey, Lois E. The Physician-Scientist as Character in Nineteenth-Century American Literature. Tulane 63.
3978 Ewens, Sister Ruth. The Nun in American Literature and Life: Variations on the International Theme. Minn.
3979 Fenn, William P. Ah Sin and His Brethren in American Literature. Iowa 32.
3980 Goldstone, Richard H. The Pariah in Modern American and British Literature: An Illustration of a Method for Teachers of Literature. Columbia 60.
3981 Hays, Peter L. The Maimed Figure: An Ancient Archetype in Modern Literature. Ohio State 65.
3982 Hoar, Victor M. The Confidence Man in American Literature. Ill 65.
3983 Leach, Joseph. The Establishment of the Texan Tradition: The Origins of a Sectional Character Type before 1860. Yale A 48.
3984 Mattingly, Caroline. The American Gentleman in Theory and Practice, 1830-1860. Wash 40.
3985 Meriwether, Frank T. The Rogue in the Humor of the Old Southwest. La 52.
3987 Rapp, Maria. Jeanne d'Arc in der englischen und amerikanischen Literatur. Tübingen 35.
3988 Sipple, Margaret N. The Mysterious Stranger in American Literature. Wis.
3989 Steckmesser, Kent L. The Hero of the American West in History and Legend. Chicago 60.
3990 Talbert, Joy K. John Brown in American Literature. Kan 41.

3991 Williams, Arthur R. The Irishman in American Humor: From 1647 to the Present. Cornell 49.
3992 Zipes, Jack D. Studies of the Romantic Hero in German and American Literature. Columbia 65.
See also 3423.

SPECIAL TOPICS—After 1900

3993 Comegys, Robert G. The Agrarian and Rural Tradition as Reflected in National Periodical Literature: 1919-1929. Stanford 58.
3994 Critoph, Gerald E. The American Literary Reaction to World War I. Pa 57.
3995 Ditsky, John M. Nostalgia for the Land in the Works of Four Twentieth Century American Writers. NYU.
3996 Frantz, Donald H. Search for Significant Form, 1905-1915: An Evaluation of the Symbols of Tradition and Revolt in American Literature, Painting, and Music. So Cal R 60.
3997 Guttman, Allen. The Wound in the Heart: American Responses to and Interpretations of the Spanish Civil War. Minn A 61.
3998 Harnack, Mildred F. Die Entwicklung der amerikanischen Literatur der Gegenwart in einigen Hauptvertretern des Romans und der Kurzgeschichte. Giessen 41.
3999 Hilfer, Anthony C. The Revolt from the Village in American Literature: 1915-1930. NC 63.
4000 Johnson, Oakley C. Literary Allusions and References in Contemporary American Literature. Mich 28.
4001 Lee, Charles. The Book-of-the-Month Club: The Story of a Publishing Institution. Pa 55.
4002 Linick, Anthony. A History of the American Literary *Avant-Garde* Since World War II. UCLA H 65.
4003 Lokke, Virgil. The Literary Image of Hollywood. Iowa A 55.
4004 Minkoff, Paul. The Transformation of the Radical Intellectuals of the 1930's. NYU.
4005 Orth, Michael. A History of the Formation, Growth, and Maturity of the Literary and Artistic Colony at Carmel, California. NM.
4006 Richwine, Keith N. The New Art and the New Freedom: A History of Bohemian Groups in America, 1910-1918. Pa A.
4007 Schafer, Charles H. The Causes of War in American Popular and Professional Literature, 1910-1920. Md 55.
4008 Stewart, John L. The Fugitive-Agrarian Writers: A History and a Criticism. Ohio State 48.
4009 Stuckey, William J. A Critical History of the Pulitzer Prize Novels, 1917-1947. Wash (St. Louis) 59.
4010 Susman, Warren I. Pilgrimage to Paris: The Background of American Expatriation, 1920-1934. Wis H 58.
4011 Warren, Frank A. The Social and Intellectual Thought of American Liberals in the 1930's . Brown.
4012 Weight, Glenn S. The Humanist Controversy in American Literature: 1900-1932. Pa State 56.
4013 West, B. June. Attitudes toward American Women as Reflected in American Literature between the Two World Wars. Denver 54.
4014 Wouters, Alfrédie F. M. America in Literature, 1920-1940. Cornell 50.

SPECIAL TOPICS—Before 1900

4015 Almy, Robert F. The Role of the Club in American Literary History, 1700-1812. Harvard 35.
4016 Baker, William D., Jr. The Influence of Mesmerism in Nineteenth-Century American Literature. Northwestern 50.
4017 Briggs, F. Allen. Didactic Literature in America, 1825-1850. Ind 53.

4018 Carroll, Isabel. Social and Historical Background of American Maritime Literature, 1780-1830. Harvard 60.

4019 Cary, Richard. The Genteel Tradition in America, 1850-1875: With Selections from Unpublished Letters of Bayard Taylor, Edmund Clarence Stedman, Richard Henry Stoddard, and Thomas Bailey Aldrich. Cornell 52.

4021 Dolan, Anne M. The Literary Salon in New York, 1830-1860. Columbia 57.

4022 Dunbar, John R. The Reception of European Literary Naturalism in the United States: 1870-1900. Harvard A 47.

4023 Garlitz, Barbara. The Cult of Childhood in Nineteenth-Century England and America. Radcliffe 59.

4024 Harris, John W., Jr. The Glorification of American Types in American Literature from 1775 to 1825. NC 28.

4025 Hassold, Ernest C. A History of the Histories of American Literature before the Civil War. Chicago 32.

4026 Hazard, Lucy L. The Frontier in American Literature. UCB 25.

4027 Jones, Robert C. The Attack on Pretension: America, 1850-1900. Tex 58.

4028 Keeler, Clinton C. The Grass Roots of Utopia: A Study of the Literature of the Agrarian Revolt in America, 1880-1902. Minn 54.

4029 Kiefer, Sister Monica. A History of the Changing Status of the American Child in the Colonial and Early National Periods as Revealed in Juvenile Literature. Pa H 43.

4030 Linneman, William R. American Life as Reflected in Illustrated Humor Magazines: 1877-1900. Ill 60.

4031 McCarthy, Stephen A. America in the 1800's: A Bibliographical Study of Intellectual and Cultural Development. Chicago LS 41.

4032 Morse, Dorothea B. Study of Juvenile Writings of Eight American Authors of the Second Half of the Nineteenth Century. Ill 52.

4033 Nichol, John W. American Literature and Social Crisis, 1837-1842. Ohio State 54.

4034 Parrish, Stephen M. Currents of the Nineties in Boston and London: Fred Holland Day, Louise Imogen Guiney, and Their Circle. Harvard 54.

4035 Philbrick, Norman D. Democracy and Social Comedy in America from 1800 to 1833. Cornell 49.

4036 Piercy, Josephine K. Studies in Literary Types in Seventeeth-Century America, with Particular Emphasis upon the Beginnings of the Essay, 1607-1710. Yale 37.

4038 Ross, Danforth R. The Genteel Tradition: Its Characteristics and Its Origins. Minn 54

4039 Rushing, Jane Gilmore. House Symbolism in the Work of Five New England Romanticists. Tex Tech 57.

4040 Thomson, Woodruff C. The Spanish-American War in American Literature. Utah 62.

4041 Tomsich, John M. The Genteel Tradition in America. Wis H 63.

4042 Turner, John M., Jr. The Response of Major American Writers to Darwinism, 1859-1910. Harvard 56.

4043 Welker, Robert. Birds in Nineteenth-Century America: A Cultural Study. Harvard A 53.

4044 Wild, Henry D. Democratic Idealism in American Literature from Penn to Whitman. Chicago 24.

4045 Wilson, Raymond J. The Idea of the Community in the Thought of Late Nineteenth Century Intellectual Leaders. Wis.

4046 Wishy, Bernard W. Images of the American Child in the Nineteenth Century. Columbia H 58.

SPECIAL TOPICS–Undated

4047 Betts, William W., Jr. The Faust Tradition in American Literature. Pa State 54.

4048 Buckley, Frank. Trends in American Primitivism. Minn H 39.

4049 Eichinger, Johann. The American Bestseller. Vienna 51.

4050 Engel, Bernard F. Historians of American Literature since 1870. UCB 57.

4051 Foster, Richard A. The School in American Literature. Columbia (Teachers College) 30.

4052   Greenberg, Abraham H.   The Ethnocentric Attitudes of Some Jewish-American Writers: Educational Implications.   Yeshiva 56.

4053   Gremmels, James C.   The Small Town in American History and Literature.   Denver.

4054   Guest, Charles B.   The Position of Women as Considered by Representative American Authors since 1800.   Wis 43.

4055   Heeney, Sister St. Agnes.   The Cathedral in Four Major New England Authors: A Study in Symbolical Inspiration.   Pa 57.

4056   Herron, Ima H.   The Small Town in American Literature.   Duke 35.

4057   Hughes, Helen McGill.   The Human-Interest Story: A Study of Popular Literature.   Chicago Soc 38.

4058   Lewin, David.   The Literary Expatriate as a Social Critic of America.   NYU 53.

4059   Martin, Edward A.   Debunking and Debunkers.   Columbia 62.

4060   Muller, Hans.   Social Stratification in Magazine Fiction and Its Relation to the Socio-Economic Status of Its Readers.   Chicago LS 42.

4061   Prasad, Thakar G.   The Mask of Liberty.   Denver 65.

4062   Rooney, Charles J., Jr.   Utopian Literature as a Reflection of the Social Forces in America: 1865-1917.   Geo Wash.

4063   Schwartz, Sister M. Florentine.   School Life in American Prose.   Niagara 45.

4064   Trachtenberg, Alan.   Brooklyn Bridge: Fact and Symbol, 1869-1930:   A Study of an American Monument.   Minn 62.

4065   West, John O.   To Die Like a Man: The "Good" Outlaw Tradition in the American Southwest.   Tex 64.

THEMES

4066   Baldwin, Donald N.   The Wilderness Concept.   Denver.

4067   Clark, James J.   The Theme of Success in American Literature, 1914-1929.   NYU 58.

4068   Eisinger, Chester E.   The Freehold Concept in American Letters, 1607-1800.   Mich 46.

4069   Griswold, A. Whitney.   The Theme of Success in American Literature of the Last Quarter of the Nineteenth Century.   Yale PS 33.

4070   Langer, Lawrence L.   The Vital Tension: Developments of the Moral and Material Imagination in Post-Civil War America.   Harvard 61.

4071   Nash, Roderick W.   Wilderness and the American Mind.   Wis H 65.

4072   Phipps, Frank.   The Image of War in America, 1891-1917:   A Study of a Literary Theme and Its Cultural Origins and Analogies.   Ohio State 54.

4073   Walker, Robert G.   Censure of Majority Rule as a Theme in American Literature, 1787-1853.   Mich 42.

4074   Weathers, Winston W.   The Broken Word: The Theme of Communication Failure in Twentieth-Century Literature.   Okla 64.

LITERARY NATIONALISM

4075   Birnbaum, Henry.   American Literary Nationalism after the War of 1812:   1815-1825.   Geo Wash 54.

4076   Campbell, Charles A., Jr.   "The Great American Novel":   A Study in Literary Nationalism, 1870-1900.   Minn 52.

4077   Chmaj, Betty.   The Double Attraction: A History of the National Artistic Will, 1890-1917.   Mich H 61.

4078   Coberly, James H.   The Growth of Nationalism in American Literature, 1800 to 1815.   Geo Wash 50.

4079   Cole, Charles W.   The Beginnings of Literary Nationalism in America, 1775-1800.   Geo Wash 39.

4080   McConnaughey, David A.   Nationalism and American Letters, 1865-1900.   Cornell 50.

4081   Maddox, Notley S.   Phases of Literary Nationalism in America, 1855-1900.   Ohio State 40.

4082   Phillips, Annie R.   Expressions of Cultural Nationalism in Early American Magazines, 1741-1789.   Brown 53.
4083   Potter, Hugh M., III.   The "Romantic Nationalists" of the 1920's.   Minn 65.
4084   Stahr, William E.   Literary Nationalism in America, 1826-1835.   Geo Wash.
4085   Tracy, Thomas J.   The American Attitude toward American Literature during the Years 1800-1812.   St . John's (Brooklyn) 41.
See also 2108, 4250.

LYCEUM

4086   Graham, Mary W.   The Lyceum in Ohio from 1840 to 1860.   Ohio State S 51.
4087   Greef, Robert J.   Public Lectures in New York, 1851-1878:   A Cultural Index of the Times.   Chicago 41.
4088   Mead, Carl D., Jr.   Eastern Lecturers in Ohio, 1850-1870.   Ohio State S 47.
4089   Weaver, Richard L., II.   The Lyceum Movement in Michigan, 1800-1850.   Ind.
4090   White, K. C. R.   The Lyceum in America.   Harvard 18.

NEGRO

4091   Archer, Leonard C.   The National Association for the Advancement of Colored People and the American Theatre: A Study of Relationships and Influence.   Ohio State S 59.
4092   Barton, Rebecca C.   Race Consciousness and American Negro Literature.   Greifswald 34 publ.
4093   Bartsch, Ernst.   Das Negerproblem im Spiegel des zeitgenössischen amerikanischen Romans.   Leipzig 53.
4094   Barz, Hermine.   The Development of the Poetry of the Negro in North America.   Mainz 51.
4095   Belcher, Fannin S., Jr.   The Place of the Negro in the Evolution of the American Theatre, 1767-1940.   Yale FA 46.
4096   Blue, Ila J.   A Study of Literary Criticism by Some Negro Writers, 1900-1955.   Mich 60.
4097   Bond, Frederick W.   The Direct and Indirect Contribution Which the American Negro Has Made to Drama and the Legitimate Stage, with the Underlying Conditions Responsible.   NYU 39.
4098   Bone, Robert A.   A History of the Negro Novel from the Civil War to World War II.   Yale 55.
4099   Byrd, James W.   The Portrayal of White Character by Negro Novelists, 1900-1950.   Peabody 54.
4100   Cronholm, Anna-Christie (Kube).   Die nordamerikanische Sklavenfrage im deutschen Schrifttum des 19. Jahrhunderts.   Berlin (F) 58.
4101   Erno, Richard B.   The Image of the Negro in Ante-Bellum Southern Diaries.   Minn 61.
4102   Farrell, Harold A.   Theme and Variation: A Critical Evaluation of the Negro Novel, 1919-1947.   Ohio State 49.
4103   Fenderson, Lewis H.   Development of the Negro Press: 1827-1948.   Pittsburgh 49.
4104   Feuser, Willfried.   Das Verhältnis von Individuum und sozialer Umwelt in der Darstellung amerikanischer Negerschriftsteller 1930-1959.   Freiburg 60 publ.
4105   Ford, Nick A.   The Negro Author's Use of Propaganda in Imaginative Literature.   Iowa 45.
4106   Galvin, Emma C. B.   The Lore of the Negro in Central New York State.   Cornell 43.
4107   Gilbert, Robert B.   The Negro in Southern Fiction and Social Studies, 1920-1950.   Vanderbilt 53.
4108   Gloster, Hugh M.   American Negro Fiction from Charles W. Chestnutt to Richard Wright.   NYU 43.

4109   Goldman, Hannah Stern.   American Slavery and Russian Serfdom: A Study in Fictional Parallels.   Columbia 55.

4110   Hicklin, Fannie Frazier.   The American Negro Playwright, 1920-1964.   Wis S 65.

4111   Ives, Chauncey B.   Development in the Fictional Themes of Negro Authors.   NC 57.

4112   Jackson, George B.   Of Irony in Negro Fiction: A Critical Study.   Mich 53.

4113   Jackson, Margaret Y.   An Investigation of Biographies and Autobiographies of American Slaves Published between 1840 and 1860:   Based upon the Cornell Special Slavery Collection.   Cornell 54.

4114   James, Stuart B.   Race Relations in Literature and Sociology.   Wash 60.

4115   Johnson, Beulah V.   The Treatment of the Negro Woman as a Major Character in American Novels, 1900-1950.   NYU 55.

4116   Lash, John S.   The Academic Status of the Literature of the American Negro: A Description and Analysis of Curriculum Inclusions and Teaching Practices.   Mich E 46.

4117   Lawson, Hilda J.   The Negro in American Drama.   Ill 39.

4118   Ley, Margaret.   Spirituals: Ein Beitrag zur Analyse der religiösen Liedschöpfung bei den nordamerikanischen Negern in der Zeit der Sklaverei.   Munich 54.

4119   Linnehan, Edward G.   We Wear the Mask: Life and Character of the Negro in American Drama.   Pa A 49.

4120   Loggins, Vernon.   The Negro Author: His Development in America.   Columbia 31.

4121   Lombard, Lee R.   Contemporary Negro Writers of New York: An Inquiry into Their Social Attitudes.   NYU E 49.

4122   Mason, Julian D., Jr.   The Critical Reception of American Negro Authors in American Magazines, 1800-1885.   NC 62.

4123   Mauk, Marielies.   Der Kampf um die Neger-Emanzipation in der englisch-amerikanischen Literatur.   Freiburg 36 publ.

4124   Mays, Benjamin E.   The Idea of God in Contemporary Negro Literature.   Chicago R 35.

4125   Moore, William L.   The Literature of the American Negro prior to 1865:   An Anthology and a History.   NYU E 42.

4126   Nelson, John H.   The Negro Character in American Literature.   Cornell 23.

4127   Nichols, Charles H.   A Study of the Slave Narrative.   Brown 49.

4128   Nilon, Charles.   The Treatment of Negro Characters by Representative American Novelists: Cooper, Melville, Tourgée, Glasgow, Faulkner.   Wis 52.

4129   Oliver, Clinton F.   The Name and Nature of American Negro Literature: An Interpretative Study in Genre and Ideas.   Harvard A 65.

4130   Pembrook, Carrie D.   Negro Drama through the Ages: An Anthology.   NYU 47.

4131   Poag, Thomas E.   The Negro in Drama and the Theater.   Cornell 43.

4132   Pride, Armistead S.   A Register and History of Negro Newspapers in the United States, 1827-1950.   Northwestern 50.

4133   Sandle, Floyd L.   A History of the Development of the Educational Theatre in Negro Colleges and Universities, 1911-1959.   La 59.

4134   Sherman, Alfonso.   The Diversity of Treatment of the Negro Character in American Drama Prior to 1860.   Ind S 64.

4135   Smith, Helena M.   Negro Characterization in the American Novel: A Historical Survey of Work by White Authors.   Pa State 59.

4136   Starke, Catherine J.   Negro Stock Characters, Archetypes, and Individuals in American Literature: A Study for College Teachers.   Columbia 63.

4137   Starling, Marion W.   The Slave Narrative: Its Place in American Literary History.   NYU 46.

4138   Thomas, Ruth M.   Selected Readings by Negro Authors for the Young Adolescent.   NYU 46.

4139   Troesch, Helen D.   The Negro in English Dramatic Literature and on the Stage and a Bibliography of Plays with Negro Characters.   Western Reserve 40.

4140   Turner, Lorenzo D.   Anti-Slavery Sentiment in American Literature Prior to 1865.   Chicago 26.

4141 Wagner, Jean P. Thème raciaux et religieux chez les poètes américains noirs après P. L. Dunbar. Paris 57.
4142 Wiley, Electa C. A Study of the Noble Savage Myth in Characterizations of the Negro in Selected American Literary Works. Ark 64.
4143 Williams, Joseph. Conditions Assigned by Providence: Proslavery Sentiments in American Fiction Before the Civil War. Harvard 64.
4144 Woolridge, Nancy B. The Negro Preacher in American Fiction before 1900. Chicago 42.
4145 Wormley, Margaret J. The Negro in Southern Fiction, 1920-1940. Boston 48.
      See also 838, 893, 899, 918, 923, 1624, 2590, 3571, 3926, 3935, 3958.

NONFICTIONAL PROSE

4146 Benson, Mabel G. A Study of the Rhetorical Characteristics of the *Federalist*. Chicago 45.
4147 Bingham, Marjorie W. Twentieth-Century American Nature Writing: The Genre and Its Meaning. Minn.
4148 Bradford, Robert W. Journey into Nature: American Nature Writing, 1733-1860. Syracuse 57.
4149 Carlock, Mary S. I Celebrate Myself, and Sing Myself: Character-Types in Early American Autobiographies, 1840-1870. Columbia 58.
4150 Cederstrom, Moyle F. American Factual Voyage Narratives, 1815 to 1860. Wash 32.
4151 Coard, Robert. From Benjamin Franklin to Henry Adams: A Study of American Autobiography. Ill 52.
4152 Conway, Adaline M. The Essay in American Literature. NYU 11.
4153 Davidson, Harry C. The Immigrant Autobiography as a Document of Cultural Assimilation. Chicago 30.
4154 Frease, Forrest W. As I Remember: Aspects of American Life between the First World War and the Second World War as Recalled by Autobiographers. Pa A 52.
4155 Genthe, Charles V. World War I Personal Narratives in America, 1914-1918. Wash State.
4156 Haselton, Stephen J. The Fairest Mead: Biography in America before 1865. Columbia 59.
4157 Hicks, Philip M. The Development of the Natural History Essay in American Literature. Pa 23.
4158 Hiten, Stephen S. The Historical Background of the Election Sermon and a Rhetorical Analysis of Five Sermons Delivered in Massachusetts between 1754 and 1775. Mich S 6(
4159 Hobbs, Charles. The Southern Colonial Sermons: 1700-1763. Tenn.
4160 Hudson, Robert L. American Sermons: A Study in Purpose, Background, and Psychological Approach. Peabody 48.
4161 Kerr, Harry P. The Character of Political Sermons Preached at the Time of the America Revolution. Cornell S 62.
4162 McGehee, Judson D. The Nature Essay as a Literary Genre: An Intrinsic Study of the Works of Six English and American Nature Writers. Mich 58.
4163 Meserole, Harrison T. The American Familiar Essay, 1815-1835. Md 60.
4164 Miller, Ralph N. The Historians Discover America: A Study of American Historical Writing in the Eighteenth Century. Northwestern 46.
4165 Murphy, George D. The New Biographers of the 1920's and Their Revaluation of the American Tradition. Pa 64.
4166 Pettis, Louis W. Recent Approaches to Nature: Viewpoints of Selected American Non Fiction Nature Writers, 1945-1964. Peabody 65.
4167 Sawey, Orlan L. The Cowboy Autobiography. Tex 53.
4167a Sayre, Robert F. The Examined Self: Henry Adams and Henry Janes and American Autobiography. Yale 62.

4168   Shaffer, Arthur H.   The Shaping of a National Tradition: Historical Writing in America, 1783-1820.   UCLA H 66.
4169   Shea, Daniel B.   Spiritual Autobiography in Early America.   Stanford 66.
4170   Smith, William R.   American Historial Writing: 1783 to 1815.   Chicago.
4171   Van Tassel, David D.   Recording America's Past: American Historical Writing, 1607-1889.   Wis H 56.
4172   Webb, James W.   Biography in American Literature, 1800-1860.   NC 58.
   See also 2632, 3375, 3799, 4036, 4386, 4514, 4530.

PERIODICALS AND JOURNALISM

GENERAL STUDIES

4173   Allen, Charles A.   *The Advance Guard:*   A Chapter in the History of the American Little Magazine.   Iowa 42.
4174   Cairns, William B.   On the Development of American Literature, 1815-1833, with Especial Reference to Periodicals.   Wis 97.
4175   Chunn, Calvin E.   History of News Magazines.   Mo 50.
4176   Cook, Elizabeth C.   Literary Influences in Colonial Newspapers, 1704-1750.   Columbia 12.
4177   Del Porto, Joseph A.   A Study of American Anti-Slavery Journals.   Mich State 53.
4178   Downes, Alan J.   Optimism and Pessimism in American Magazines, 1850-1960.   Wash H 61.
4179   Doyle, Mildred D.   Sentimentalism in American Periodicals, 1741-1800.   NYU 41.
4180   Drucker, Darrell I.   The Genteel Rebellion: A Study of American Journalistic Impressionism in Terms of Its Audience.   Minn 56.
4181   Garwood, Irving.   American Periodicals from 1850 to 1860.   Chicago 22.
4182   Hove, Halder L.   The Norwegian Immigrant Press, 1870-1920.   Chicago.
4183   Johnson, Warren B.   The Content of American Colonial Newspapers Relative to International Affairs, 1704-1763.   Wash H 63.
4184   Kleber, Brooks E.   The Colonial Newspaper and the Emergence of an American Community.   Pa H 57.
4185   Kobre, Sidney.   The Development of the Colonial Newspaper.   Columbia Soc 44.
4186   Lewis, Benjamin M.   A History and Bibliography of American Magazines, 1800-1810.   Mich LS 56.
4187   Lyon, Betty L.   A History of Children's Secular Magazines Published in the United States from 1789-1899.   Johns Hopkins E 42.
4188   McBride, Sarah E.   A Hundred Years of Women's Magazines.   Minn.
4189   Merrill, Goldie P.   The Development of American Secular Juvenile Magazines, a Study of the Educational Significance of Their Content.   Wash E 39.
4190   Mott, Frank L.   American Magazines, 1865-1880.   Columbia 28.
4191   Neil, J. Meredith.   Aesthetic Opinion in Early American Periodicals to 1815.   Wash State.
4192   Noel, Mary.   The Heyday of the Popular Story Weekly.   Columbia H 52.
4193   Phillips, George H.   An Analysis of 835 Articles in the Leading American Periodicals for the Period 1890-1914 to Determine What was Said About American Daily Newspapers.   Iowa J 62.
4194   Rein, Irmgard.   Amerikanische Goodwill-Zeitschriften.   Münster 42.
4195   Richardson, Lyon N.   A History of Early American Magazines, 1741-1789.   Columbia 31.
4196   Smith, Culver H.   The Washington Press in the Jacksonian Period.   Duke H 33.
   See also 2878, 2891, 2905, 2906, 3017, 3522, 3689, 4132, 4511, 4556.

INDIVIDUAL STUDIES

4197   Ames, William E.   A History of the *National Intelligencer*, 1800-1869.   Minn H 62.

4198 Bell, William J. A Historical Study of *The Kansas City Star* since the Death of William Rockhill Nelson, 1915-1949. Mo 49.

4199 Beyers, Coralie M. *The Dial,* 1916-1920: An Intellectual History. Utah.

4200 Bowen, Frances Jean. The *New Orleans Double Dealer,* 1921-1926: A Critical History. Vanderbilt 54.

4201 Bradshaw, Margaret A. A History of the *Bookman,* 1895-1933. NC.

4202 Brocki, Sister Mary D., C.S.S.F. A Study of *Cosmopolitan Magazine,* 1890-1900: Its Relation to the Literature of the Decade. Notre Dame 59.

4203 Bryer, Jackson R. "A Trial-Track for Racers": Margaret Anderson and the *Little Review.* Wis 64.

4204 Carter, John D. The San Francisco *Bulletin,* 1855-1865: A Study in the Beginnings of Pacific Coast Journalism. UCB H 41.

4205 Castles, William H., Jr. The *Virginia Gazette,* 1736-1766: Its Editors, Editorial Policies, and Literary Content. Tenn 62.

4206 Christin, Robert E., Jr. *McClure's Magazine,* 1893-1903: A Study of Popular Culture. Ohio State 58.

4207 Cohen, Hennig. The *South Carolina Gazette,* 1732-1775: Its History and Some Aspects of Its Cultural Content. Tulane 51.

4208 Cowan, Louise. *The Fugitive:* A Critical History. Vanderbilt 53.

4209 Craven, Robert K. The Place of Literature and the Arts in the Traditional Society: A Study of the *American Review.* Kan.

4210 Dean, Harold L. The *New England Courant,* 1721-1726: A Chapter in the History of American Culture. Brown 42.

4211 Dolmetsch, Carl R., Jr. A History of *The Smart Set* Magazine, 1914-1923. Chicago 57.

4212 Dowgray, John G. L., Jr. A History of Harper's Literary Magazines, 1850-1900. Wis H 56.

4213 Farrior, John E. A Study of the *North American Review:* The First Twenty Years. NC 54.

4214 Fonaroff, Benjamin S.N. *The New Republic* from 1919-1939: A Study of American Liberal Thought Between the Two World Wars. Minn A.

4215 Free, William J. *The Columbian Magazine* and American Literary Nationalism. NC 62.

4216 Fuller, Landon E. The *United States Magazine and Democratic Review,* 1837-1859: A Study of Its History, Contents, and Significance. NC 48.

4217 Gentry, Richard H. Liberalism and *The New Republic,* 1914-1960. Ill J 60.

4218 Gimmestad, Victor E. A History of the *Evangelical Review.* Wis 51.

4219 Gordon, George N. Theatrical Movements in the *Theatre Arts* Magazine from 1916 to 1948: A Description and Analysis. NYU S 57.

4220 Greenbaum, Leonard A. *The Hound & Horn:* Episodes in American Literary History, 1927-1934. Mich 63.

4221 Greene, Sue N. The Contribution of *The Monthly Anthology and Boston Review* to the Development of the Golden Age of American Letters. Mich State 64.

4222 Handley, John G. A History of *Theatre Arts Magazine:* 1916-1948. La S 60.

4223 Harrington, Richard P. *The Monthly Anthology and Boston Review,* 1803-1811: Literary Excellence as Interpreted by "A Society of Gentlemen." Tex 64.

4224 Hart, Jim A. An Historical Study of the *St. Louis Globe-Democrat,* 1852-1958. Mo J 59.

4225 Hauck, Richard B. The Literary Content of the New York *Spirit of the Times,* 1831-1856. Ill 65.

4226 Houghton, Donald E. *The New Yorker:* Exponent of a Cosmopolitan Elite. Minn H 55.

4227 John, Arthur W. A History of *Scribner's Monthly* and the *Century Illustrated Monthly Magazine,* 1870-1900. Harvard 51.

4228 Katter, Nafe E. *Theatre Arts* under the Direction of Edith J. Isaacs. Mich S 63.

4229 Klein, Walter. The *North American Review* and Abolitionism. NYU.

4230 Montesi, Albert J. The *Southern Review* (1935-1942): A History and Evaluation. Pa State 55.

4231 Leverette, William E. Science and Values: A Study of Edward L. Youman's *Popular Science Monthly,* 1872-1887. Vanderbilt H 63.

4232 Long, Edgar. *Russell's Magazine* as an Expression of Ante-Bellum South Carolina Culture. SC 32.

4233 Macdonald, Thomas J. *The Overland Monthly,* 1868-1898. Stanford.

4234 Magnus, Hans U. *Time:* Studie über die amerikanischen Nachrichtenmagazine. Berlin (F) 62.

4235 Mahan, Howard F. Joseph Gales, the *National Intelligencer,* and the War of 1812. Columbia H 58.

4236 Meersman, Roger L. An Analysis of *Theatre Magazine* in Relation to the American Theatre. Ill.

4237 Mitchell, Robert E. American Life as Reflected in the *Atlantic Monthly,* 1857-1881. Harvard 51.

4238 Mobley, Lawrence E. *The Golden Era Magazine,* 1852-1866. Mich State.

4239 Mosher, Frederic J. Chicago's "Saving Remnant": Francis Fisher Browne, William Morton Payne, and the *Dial* (1880-1892). Ill 50.

4240 Olsen, Norman. The *Forum* as a Magazine of Literary Comment: 1886-1907. Duke 63.

4241 Pearson, Justus R., Jr. *The Galaxy,* 1866-1878. Columbia 55.

4242 Pecek, Louis G. The Beadle Story Papers, 1870-1897: A Study of Popular Fiction. Ohio State 59.

4243 Prior, Granville T. A History of the Charleston *Mercury,* 1822-1852. Harvard H 47.

4244 Queenan, John. *The Portfolio:* A Study of the History and Significance of an Early American Magazine. Pa 54.

4245 Ragan, Fred D. The *New Republic:* Red Hysteria and Civil Liberties. Ga H 65.

4246 Rahn, Helmut. *The Atlantic Monthly:* Geschichte und Bedeutung einer Zeitschrift: 1857-1881. Frankfurt 61.

4247 Rieger, Wolfgang. *The Dial:* Monographie einer Zeitschrift. Bonn 54.

4248 Roadman, George H. The Life and Times of the Washington *Reporter,* 1808-1877. Pittsburgh H 57.

4249 Robbins, J. Albert, Jr. The History of *Graham's Magazine:* A Study in Periodical Publication. Pa 47.

4250 Sacks, Claire. The Seven Arts Critics: A Study of Cultural Nationalism in America, 1910-1930. Wis 55.

4251 Satterwhite, Joseph N. *Godey's Lady's Book* and Fiction: 1830-1850. Vanderbilt 54.

4252 Seaton, Esta K. The Changing Image of the American Woman in a Mass Periodical *(The Ladies' Home Journal,* 1890-1919). Minn.

4253 Smith, James E. One Hundred Years of the *Hartford Courant.* Harvard H 43.

4254 Spencer, Otha C. Twenty Years of *Life:* A Study of Time, Inc.'s, Picture Magazine and Its Contributions to Photo-Journalism. Mo J 57.

4255 Spivey, Herman E. *The Knickerbocker Magazine,* 1833-1865: A Study of Its History, Contents and Significance. NC 35.

4256 Sterne, Richard C. Political, Social, and Literary Criticism in the New York *Nation,* 1865-1881: A Study in Change of Mood. Harvard 57.

4257 Stewart, Paul R. *The Prairie Schooner:* A Little Magazine's First Twenty-five Years. Ill 54.

4258 Streeter, Robert E. Critical Thought in the *North American Review,* 1815-1865. Northwestern 43.

4259 Sylvester, Howard E. *The American Museum,* a Study of Prevailing Ideas in Late Eighteenth-Century America. Wash 54.

4260 Test, George A. The Vital Connection: A Study of the *New Republic* Magazine as a Literary Journal, 1914-1922. Pa 60.

4261 Tuppet, Mary M. A History of *The Southwest Review:* Toward An Understanding of Regionalism. Ill 66.

4262 Turner, Alice L. A Study of the Contents of *The Sewanee Review* with Historical Introduction. Peabody 31.

4263 Turner, Susan Jane. A Short History of *The Freeman,* a Magazine of the Early Twenties, with Particular Attention to the Literary Criticism. Columbia 56.
4264 Williams, Ellen B. The Early History of *Poetry: A Magazine of Verse.* Chicago.
4264a Wotherspoon, James R. The San Francisco *Argonaut,* 1877-1907. UCB 62.
    See also 1079, 1080, 1350a, 1367, 1704, 1927, 2635, 2655, 2893, 2907, 2913, 2921, 2924, 3684, 3802, 4315, 4322, 4378, 4537, 4576, 4590.

REGIONAL STUDIES

4265 Bentley, Imogene. Texas Literary and Educational Magazines: Their History and Educational Content. Peabody 41.
4266 Brantley, Raburn L. Georgia Journalism of the Civil War Period. Peabody 28.
4267 Cardwell, Guy A. Charleston Periodicals, 1795-1860: A Study in Literary Influences, with a Descriptive Check List of Seventy-five Magazines. NC 37.
4268 Doepke, Dale K. St. Louis Magazines before the Civil War, 1832-1860. Wash 63.
4269 Flanders, Bertram H. Georgia Literary Periodicals to 1865. Duke 42.
4270 Fowle, Priscilla H. Boston Daily Newspapers, 1830-1850. Radcliffe H 20.
4271 Groen, Henry J. A History of the German-American Newspapers of Cincinnati before 1860. Ohio State G 44.
4272 Hounchell, Saul. The Principal Literary Magazines of the Ohio Valley to 1840. Peabody 34.
4273 Kennedy, Chester B. Newspapers of the California Northern Mines, 1850-1860: A Record of Life, Letters and Culture. Stanford 50.
4274 Kruh, Reine. Un Siècle de Magazines Californiens, 1850-1950. Paris 62.
4275 Lyon, William H., Jr. The Pioneer Editor in Missouri. Mo H 58.
4276 McDougall, Robert L. A Study of Canadian Periodical Literature of the Nineteenth Century. Toronto 51.
4277 McLean, Francis E. Periodicals Published in the South before 1880. Va 28.
4278 Robinson, Elwyn B. The Public Press of Philadelphia during the Civil War. Western Reserve H 36.
4279 Rogers, Edward R. Four Southern Magazines. Va 02.
4280 Seigel, Don M. The Humor of the *New Yorker,* 1925-1940. Fla State.
4281 Stewart, Guy H. History and Bibliography of Middle Tennessee Newspapers, 1799-1876. Ill H 57.
4282 Terwilliger, W. Bird. A History of Literary Periodicals in Baltimore. Md 41.
    See also 4478.

PHILOSOPHY AND INTELLECTUAL HISTORY

4283 Bloomfield, Maxwell H., III. The American Mind as Reflected in Representative American Magazines, 1900-1914. Tulane H 62.
4284 Flood, Verle D. A Study in the Aesthetics of Taste in America: The Role of Common Sense Philosophy in the Literary Criticism of the Boston Anthologists. Iowa 59.
4285 Hux, Samuel H. American Myth and Existential Vision: The Indigenous Existentialism of Mailer, Bellow, Styron, and Ellison. Conn 65.
4285a Jaher, Frederic C. Doubters and Dissenters: A Study of Cataclysmic Thought in America, 1885-1918. Harvard 61.
4286 Manicas, Peter T. The Concept of the Individual in the Philosophies of William Graham Sumner, William James, Josiah Royce, and Lester Ward. / SUNY (Buffalo) P 63.
4287 Marcus, Richard. The Colonial Mind in New England. Colo.
4288 Skotheim, Robert A. American Historians and American Ideas: Histories of Ideas Between the 1870's and the 1950's. Wash H 62.
4289 Wilson, David. The Streaks of the Tulip: The Literary Aspects of Eighteenth Century American Natural Philosophy. Minn.
    See also 786, 812, 943, 990, 991, 1279, 1612, 1614, 1883, 1903, 2092, 2101, 2282, 2293, 2432, 2499, 2533, 2826, 2855, 2952, 2962, 3043, 3044, 3507, 3870, 4011, 4012, 4032, 4338, 4344, 4346, 4538, 4578, 4582, 4594, 4596.

POETRY

HISTORY AND INFLUENCES

4290 Allen, Gay W. A History of the Prosody of the Chief American Poets. Wis 34.

4291 Bailey, Frederick. The Historical Ballad: Its Tradition in Britain and America. Tenn 63.

4292 Bates, Mary D. Columbia's Bards: A Study of American Verse from 1783 through 1799. Brown 54.

4293 Bottorff, William K. An Edition of *American Poems, Selected and Original*, 1793. Brown 64.

4294 Bradshaw, Sidney E. On Southern Poetry prior to 1860. Va 00.

4295 Brown, Maurice F., Jr. Harvard Poetic Renaissance, 1885-1910. Harvard 58.

4296 Brown, William R. American Soldier Poets of the Second World War. Mich 65.

4297 Carlson, Eric W. The Expanding Range of Poetic Function in American Democracy. Boston 47.

4298 Cox, H. Morris, Jr. The Charleston Poetic Renascence, 1920-1930. Pa 58.

4299 Ewing, George W. Some Verse of the Temperance Movement. Tex 62.

4300 Fein, Richard J. Major American Poetry of World War II: A Critical Study. NYU 60.

4301 Foster, Stephen M. Ambiguous Gifts: The Impress of Science on Contemporary Anglo-American Poetry. Wash 65.

4302 Gillis, Everett A. American Prosody in the Eighteen-Nineties, with Special Reference to Magazine Verse. Tex 48.

4303 Gordon, Armistead C., Jr. Virginia Writers of Fugitive Verse. Va 21.

4304 Hart, James A. American Poetry of the First World War (1914 to 1920): A Survey and Checklist. Duke 65.

4305 Huddleston, Eugene L. Topographical Poetry in America, 1783-1812. Mich State 65.

4306 Kindilien, Carlin T. A Study of American Verse, 1890-1899, Based upon the Volumes from That Period Contained in the Harris Collection of American Poetry and Plays in the Brown University Library. Brown 53.

4307 Lenhart, Charmenz. The Influence of Music upon American Poetry. Ill 52.

4308 Loftus, Sister M. Charitas. The Democratic Movement in Modern American Poetry, 1912-1925. Fordham 36.

4309 McCormack, Jeanne E. The Pulitzer Prize Poems. Purdue.

4310 McMichael, James L. Rhetoric and the Skeptic's Void: A Study of the Influence of Nominalism on Some Aspects of Modern American Poetic Style. Stanford 66.

4311 Miner, Louie. Our Rude Forefathers: American Political Verse, 1783-1788. Columbia 37.

4312 Murphy, Marguerite P. The Free Verse Movement in England and America, 1908-1925. Radcliffe 48.

4313 Otis, William B. American Verse, 1625-1807: A History. NYU 08.

4314 Pollak, Georgiana H. The Influence of Music on American Poetry. NYU 50.

4315 Putzel, Max. American Verse in *Reedy's Mirror*. Yale 58.

4316 Raiziss, Sonia. The Relation of Certain Modern Poets to the Metaphysical Poets of the Seventeenth Century. Pa 44.

4317 Silverman, Kenneth E. Colonial American Poetry: An Anthology. Columbia 64.

4318 Steinmetz, Marion L. A History of American Poetry (1860-1869). Brown 57.

4319 Sugarman, Milton H. A Bibliography of a Collection of Anonymous Poetical Pamphlets of the Eighteenth Century in the Library of the University of Cincinnati. Cincinnati 53.

4320 Taupin, René. L'Influence du symbolisme français sur la poésie américaine (de 1910 à 1920). Paris 30.

4321 Waggoner, Hyatt H. Science and Modern American Poetry. Ohio State 42.
See also 2869, 2872, 2873, 3693, 4094.

THEORY, TECHNIQUE, CRITICISM

4322 Beary, Thomas J. Poetic Theory and Practice in the *New Masses* and *Spirit*, 1930-1939. NYU 51.

4323 Bigelow, Gordon. The Dominance of Rhetoric in American Poetry, 1775-1815. Johns Hopkins 50.
4324 Duffey, Bernard I. The Place of Poetry: Theories of Poetic Value in the Formalist Literary Criticism of England and the United States, 1908 to the Present. Ohio State 4
4325 Eckman, Frederick W. The Language of American Poetry, 1900-1910. Ohio State 5
4326 Fields, Kenneth W. The Rhetoric of Artifice in Modern American Poetry. Stanford.
4327 Graff, Gerald E. The Dramatic Theory of Poetry. Stanford 64.
4328 Hester, Marcus B. An Analysis of the Meaning of Poetic Metaphor. Vanderbilt P 64.
4329 Hoesch, Jörg. Vorstufen zur modernen objektiven Dichtung in England und Amerika. Freiburg.
4330 Kaplan, Robert B. An Analysis of Contemporary Poetic Structure, 1930-1955. So Cal 63.
4331 Krieger, Murray. Towards a Contemporary Apology for Poetry. Ohio State 52.
4331a Kuntz, Joseph M. Poetry Explication, 1950-1959: A Bibliographical Study of Interpretation of British and American Poems. Denver 61.
4332 Logan, John F. The Blue Guitar: A Semantic Study of Poetry. Tex P 62.
4333 Mayer, Elisabeth. Die Leistungen der Modernen Technik in der Dichtung Englands und der Vereinigten Staaten. Freiburg 38.
4334 O'Connor, William V. Sense and Sensibility in Modern Poetry. Chicago 48.
4335 Philbrick, Charles H., II. Theories of Rhythm in English and American Prosody from 1800 to 1950. Brown 53.
4336 Quinn, Sister Mary B. Metamorphosis in Modern American Poetry. Wis 52.
4337 Rackin, Phyllis R. Poetry without Paradox: The Limitations of the New Criticism on the Lyric. Ill 62.
4338 Tejera, Victorino. Philosophy and the Art of Poetry: A Survey of Some Contemporary Relations among Poetic Criticism, Philosophy, and Poetry. Columbia P 56.
4339 Theall, Donald F. Communication Theories in Modern Poetry: Yeats, Pound, Eliot, Joyce. Toronto 55.
4340 Woodward, Barbara C. Theories of Meaning in Poetry, 1915-1940: A Critical History. Mich 46.
4341 Wray, Judith E. Theories and Methods of Representative Contemporary Poets as Readers of Their Own Poetry. Wis S 61.
See also 2912, 2913.

TYPES AND THEMES

4342 Bridges, William E. The Family Circle in American Verse: The Rise and Fall of an Image. Brown 63.
4343 Brown, Harry M. The Christ Image: Concepts of Christ in Contemporary American Poetry. Western Reserve 55.
4344 Conner, Frederick W. Cosmic Optimism: A Study of the Interpretation of the Idea of Evolution by American Poets from Ralph Waldo Emerson to Edwin Arlington Robinson. Pa 44.
4345 Davenport, John S. The Ode in American Literature. NC 34.
4346 Dodge, Stewart C. The Use of Evolutionary Theory by American Poets: 1900-1950. Ill 58.
4347 Foster, John L. The Modern American Long Poem. Mich 61.
4348 Grant, Rena V. Environment in the Poetry of the West. UCB 42.
4349 Grigsby, Gordon K. The Modern Long Poem: Studies in Thematic Form. Wis 60.
4350 Harcourt, John B. Themes of American Verse, 1840-1849: A Survey of the Volumes from That Period Contained in the Harris Collection of American Poetry in Brown University. Brown 52.
4351 Hensen, Robert E. Sorry after a Godly Manner: A Study of the Puritan Funeral Elegy in New England, 1625-1722. UCLA 57.
4352 Kay, Arthur M. The Epic Intent and the American Dream: The Westering Theme in Modern American Narrative Poetry. Columbia 61.

4353 Keller, Karl. The Metaphysical Strain in Nineteenth Century American Poetry. Minn 64.
4354 Mills, Ralph J. The Development of Apocalyptic Vision in Five Modern Poets. Northwestern 63.
4355 North, William R. Chinese Themes in American Verse. Pa 34.
4356 Power, Sister Mary J. The Question of Belief as Evidenced by Certain Representative Contemporary Poets, 1900-1935. Fordham 36.
4357 Raizis, Marios B. The Prometheus Theme in British and American Poetry. NYU 66.
4358 Rivers, James. Physical Science in British and American Poetry, 1920-1950: Themes and Imagery. SC.
4359 Roller, Bert. Children in American Poetry, 1610-1900. Peabody 30.
4360 Roth, George L., Jr. Verse Satire and the New Republic, 1790-1820. Princeton 49.
4361 Schaumann, Herbert F. Fundamental Characteristics of German-American Lyrics. Cornell G 36.
4362 Schramm, Wilbur L. Studies in the Longer Narrative Poetry of America, 1775-1860. Iowa 32.
4363 Shankle, George E. Poetry of American Farm Life. Peabody 26.
4364 Sterner, Lewis G. The Sonnet in American Literature. Pa 30.
4365 Stone, Edith O. Democratic Values in Modern Narrative Poems. Mich 60.
4366 Voigt, G. P. The Religious and Ethical Elements in Major American Poets. SC 25.
4367 Walker, Robert H. Social Themes in Late Nineteenth Century American Verse: A Quantitative Study. Pa A 55.
4368 Werner, Dorothy L. The Idea of Union in American Verse. Pa 31.
      See also 2861, 3067, 3077, 3087, 3095, 3098, 3847, 4141.

POLITICS AND GOVERNMENT

4369 Anderson, Frank W., Jr. American Literary Political Satire, 1812-1850. NC 51.
4370 Auerbach, M. Morton. Conservatism and Its Contemporary American Advocates. Columbia PS 58.
4371 Baker, Donald G. Political Values in Popular Fiction: 1919-1959. Syracuse PS 61.
4372 Brubaker, Bill R. Political Appointments of American Literary Men. Ohio State.
4373 Chalmers, David M. The Social and Political Philosophy of the Muckrakers. Rochester H 55.
4374 Clark, Joseph E. The American Critique of the Democratic Idea, 1919-1929. Stanford H 58.
4375 Fäy, Bernard. L'Esprit révolutionnaire en France et aux États-Unis à la fin du XVIIIᵉ siècle. Paris 24 publ.
4376 Gregory, Donald L. The American Author as Political Office-Holder. Ohio State.
4377 Grenier, Judson A. The Origins and Nature of Progressive Muckraking. UCLA 65.
4378 Hanson, Michael J. The Progressive Movement as Seen in *McClure's Magazine:* 1893 to 1917. Wy 58.
4379 Harvey, Robert D. A Study of the Literary Techniques of "Muckraking" Journalism in Relation to Realistic Fiction. Chicago.
4381 Heimert, Alan. Romanticism and American Political Thought. Harvard PS.
4382 Kamman, William F. Socialism in German-American Literature. Pa 17.
4383 Lucker, Dorothy F. The American Interest in European Democracy: A Study of the Literary Reaction to the Revolutions of 1848. Tex 42.
4384 Lydenberg, John. Pre-Muckraking: A Study of Attitudes toward Politics as Revealed in American Fiction from 1870 through 1901. Harvard A 46.
4385 Marks, Barry. The Concept of Propaganda in Twentieth-Century America. Minn 58.
4386 Murdaugh, James E. Political Thought in the Early American Essay. Va 25.
4387 Regier, Cornelius. The Era of Muck-rakers. Iowa H 22.
4388 Rothweiler, Robert L. Ideology and Four Radical Novelists: The Response to Communism of Dreiser, Anderson, Dos Passos, and Farrell. Wash (St. Louis) PS 60.

4389 Sanders, David S. Pattern of Rejection: Three American Novelists and the Commun Literary Line, 1919-1949. UCLA 56.
4390 Smith, Maynard O. Principles of Republican Government in the *Federalist*. New School for Social Research PS 53.
4391 Thal-Larsen, Margaret W. Political and Economic Ideas in American Utopian Fiction, 1868-1914. UCB 41.
4392 Weaver, Irvin W. The Social Philosophy of *The Federalist*. Boston P 53.
      See also 71, 205, 212, 216, 339, 406, 985, 996, 1885, 1911, 2089, 2102, 2105, 2364, 2372, 2588, 2638, 2749, 2782, 2856, 2863, 2886, 2932, 3215, 3216, 3217, 3219, 3220, 3222, 3223, 3224, 3227, 3231, 3374, 3405, 3408, 3446, 3450, 3451, 3452, 3473, 3976, 4073, 4311, 4592.

PRINTING, PUBLISHING, CENSORSHIP

4393 Bishop, Wallace P. The Struggle for International Copyright in the United States. Boston H 59.
4394 Blum, Eleanor. Paperbound Books in the United States in 1955: A Survey of Content. Ill 59.
4395 Boyer, Paul B. The Vice-Society Movement and Book Censorship in America, 1873-1933. Harvard H 66.
4396 Clark, Rev. Aubert J. The Movement for International Copyright in Nineteenth-Century America. Cath H 61.
4397 Curry, William L. Comstockery: A Study in the Rise and Decline of a Watchdog Censorship. Columbia 57.
4398 Elbers, Gerald W. Censorship of American Literature, 1870-1935. Minn.
4399 Hewlett, Leroy. James Rivington, Loyalist Printer, Publisher, and Bookseller of the American Revolution, 1724-1802: A Biographical-Bibliographical Study. Mich LS 5
4400 Kaser, David E. Messrs. Carey and Lea of Philadelphia, 1822-1838. Mich LS 56.
4401 Kidder, Robert W. The Contribution of Daniel Fowle to New Hampshire Printing, 1756-1787. Ill LS 60.
4402 Larus, Joel. The Origin and Development of the 1891 International Copyright Law o the United States. Columbia PS 60.
4403 McCoy, Ralph E. Banned in Boston: The Development of Literary Censorship in Massachusetts. Ill 56.
4404 Merritt, LeRoy C. The United States Govenment as Publisher. Chicago LS 42.
4405 Norris, Joe L. Pioneer Marketing Associations of the American Book Trade, 1873-19 Chicago H 39.
4406 Russell, F. A. The History of Printing in Illinois since 1870. Ill H 15.
4407 Schick, Frank L. The Paperbound Book in America: The History of Paperbacks and Their European Antecedents. Mich LS 57.
4408 Schuyler, L. R. The Liberty of the Press in the American Colonies. NYU H 04.
4409 Starkey, Lawrence G. A Descriptive and Analytical Bibliography of the Cambridge, Massachusetts, Press from Its Beginnings to the Publication of Eliot's Indian Bible in 1663. Va 49.
4410 Sutton, Walter E. Cincinnati as a Publishing and Book Trade Center, 1796-1880. Ohio State H 46.

PSYCHOLOGY AND LITERATURE

4411 Kerr, Howard H. Spiritualism and Psychical Research in American Literature, 1850-1910. UCLA.
4412 Rudder, Helmut de. Die Wandlung des sozialen Selbstbewusstseins der amerikanische Intellektuellen von der Depression bis zur Gegenwart. Hamburg 57.
      See also 2895, 2896, 2910, 3042, 3360, 3370, 3477, 3494, 3772, 4016.

PURITANISM

4413 Brooks, Charles B. Puritanism in American Fiction, 1820-1870. Princeton 43.

4414 Davis, Tom. Typology in New England Puritanism. Mo.

4415 Dönt, Christiane E. Waren die Puritaner Neu-Englands geistesgeschichtlich bedeutungsvoller als man gemeinhin annimmt? Vienna 50.

4416 Fulcher, John R. Puritan Piety in Early New England: A Study in Spiritual Regeneration from the Antinomian Controversy to the Cambridge Synod of 1648 in the Massachusetts Bay Colony. Princeton R 63.

4417 Gilsdorf, Aletha J. The Puritan Apocalypse: New England Eschatology in the Seventeenth Century. Yale H 65.

4418 Goldman, Irvin. The Beginnings of Theories of Natural Ethics and Theology in Seventeenth Century America. Mich 38.

4419 Hornberger, Theodore R. American Puritanism and the Rise of the Scientific Mind. Mich 34.

4420 Hudson, Roy F. The Theory of Communication of Colonial New England Preachers, 1620-1670. Cornell S 54.

4421 Israel, Calvin. American Puritan Literary Theory: 1620-1728. UCD.

4422 Jackson, Elizabeth. Reaction against Puritanism in American Periodicals of the Eighteenth Century. Radcliffe 16.

4423 Levy, Babette M. Preaching in the First Half-Century of New England History. Columbia 42.

4424 Miller, Perry G. The Establishment of Orthodoxy in Massachusetts. Chicago 31.

4425 Mills, Barriss. Attitudes of Some Nineteenth Century American Writers toward Puritanism. Wis 42.

4426 Morgan, Edmund S. Religion and the Family in Seventeenth Century New England. Harvard A 42.

4427 Parkes, Henry B. New England and the Great Awakening: A Study in the Theory and Practice of New England Calvinism. Mich H 29.

4428 Perluck, Herbert A. Puritan Expression and the Decline of Piety. Brown 55.

4429 Pettit, Norman. The Image of the Heart in Early Puritanism: The Emergence in England and America of the Concept of Preparation for Grace. Yale 63.

4430 Terris, Walter F. The Right to Speak: Massachusetts, 1628-1685. Northwestern. H 62.

4431 Turner, Maxine. Revisions in the *Bay Psalm Book*. Auburn.

4432 Vitelli, James R. The Resurrection of the Puritan: A Study of an American Literary Symbol. Pa A 55.
See also 465, 1210, 1225, 1233, 1236, 1327, 1328, 1329, 1410, 1454, 1805, 2245, 2346, 2347, 2473, 2477, 2884, 3418, 4160, 4351, 4593.

REGIONALISM

GENERAL

4433 Haas, Jakob. Versuch einer Darstellung der Heimatliteratur in den Vereinigten Staaten von Nordamerika (einige typische Heimatschriftsteller aus verschiedenen Gegenden der Vereinigten Staaten). Bonn 35.

MIDDLE ATLANTIC

4434 Berbrich, Joan D. The Influence of Long Island on Three Major Writers. NYU 64.

4435 Callow, James T. Knickerbocker Writers among the Fine Arts: 1807-1855. Western Reserve.

4436 Ditter, Dorothy E. The Cultural Climate of the Centennial City, Philadelphia, 1875-1876. Pa H 47.

4437 Ehrlich, Heyward B. A Study of Literary Activity in New York City during the 1840-Decade. NYU 63.

4438 Eldridge, Herbert. Literary Ideals and Intentions in Philadelphia, 1783-1827.
Pa 61.

4440 Jackson, M. Katherine. Outlines of the Literary History of Colonial Pennsylvania.
Columbia 06.

4441 Lemay, J. A. Leo. A Literary History of Colonial Maryland. Pa 64.

4442 Moore, Henrietta. Early Literary Activity in New York. Columbia 04.

4443 O'Donnell, Thomas F. The Regional Fiction of Upstate New York. Syracuse 57.

4444 Robacker, Earl F. Changing Trends in the Nature of Literary Works by and about the
Pennsylvania Dutch. NYU 41.

4445 Scott, Eleanor B. Literary Tendencies and Activities in New York, 1789-1840.
Wis 25.

4446 Uhler, John E. Literary Taste and Culture in Baltimore. John Hopkins 27.

4447 Wheeler, Joseph T. Literary Culture in Colonial Maryland, 1700-1776. Brown H 39.

4448 Wyld, Lionel D. The Erie Canal in Folklore and Literature. Pa 59.
See also 3571, 3591, 3597.

MIDWEST

4449 Aaron, Daniel B. Cincinnati, 1818-1838: A Study of Attitudes in the Urban West
Harvard A 42.

4450 Agee, William H. Chicago in the Novel: The Alienated Individual in the New Americ
Minn.

4451 Atkeson, Mary M. A Study of the Local Literature of the Upper Ohio Valley, with
Especial Reference to the Pioneer and Indian Tale, 1820-1840. Ohio State 19.

4452 Clifton, Lucile. The Beginnings of Literary Culture in Columbus, Ohio, 1812-1840.
Ohio State 48.

4453 Dondore, Dorothy A. The Prairie and the Making of Middle America. Columbia 24.

4454 Duncan, Hugh D. Chicago as a Literary Center: Social Factors Influencing Chicago
Literary Institutions from 1885 to 1920. Chicago Soc 49.

4455 Ford, Margaret Patricia. The Cleveland Literary Scene, 1870-1900. Western
Reserve 57.

4456 Gillard, Kathleen I. Michigan as Recorded in Its Writings. Peabody 50.

4457 Grey, Lennox B. Chicago and the "Great American Novel." Chicago 35.

4458 Jacobs, Elijah L. A History of Missouri Literature, 1780-1930. So Cal 49.

4459 Ludtke, Roy P. The Image of the Land in Novels Portraying the Dakotas and
Minnesota between 1850 and 1900. Columbia (Teachers College) 55.

4460 Maillard, Denyse. L'Enfant américain dans le roman du Middle-West. Paris 35.

4461 Meyer, Roy W. The Middle-Western Farm Novel in the Twentieth-Century.
Iowa A 57.

4462 Miller, James M. The Genesis of Western Culture: The Upper Ohio Valley, 1800-
1825. Pa State 36.

4463 Radke, Merle L. Local-Color Fiction in Middle-Western Magazines, 1865-1900.
Northwestern 65.

4464 Rusk, R. L. The Literature of the Middle-Western Frontier. Columbia 24.

4465 Schneider, Sister Mary L. The Literary Functions of the Land in Pertinent Works of
Hamlin Garland, Willa Cather, Ole Rølvaag, and Other "Middle Border" Authors.
Notre Dame.

4466 Shumaker, Arthur W. A Literary History of Indiana, with Emphasis on the Imaginativ
Literature of the First Hundred Years, 1821-1921. Iowa 58.

4467 Spotts, Carleton B. The Development of Fiction on the Missouri Frontier (1830-
1860). Pa State 34.

4468 Taylor, Jean E. Main Currents of Regional Literature in the Lower Middle West from
1870 to 1927. Mo 28.

4469 Unglesby, Ina H. Kansas as Depicted in Literature from the Beginning to 1886. La 4
See also 3324.

NEW ENGLAND

4470 Birdsall, Richard D. The First Century of Berkshire Cultural History. Columbia H 54.

4471 Carmel, Sister Marie. La Littérature française de Nouvelle-Angleterre. Laval 45.

4472 Carroll, Richard S. Studies in the Background and Practice of Prose Style in New England, 1640-1750. Harvard 51.

4473 Dorson, Richard M. New England Popular Tales and Legends. Harvard A 43.

4474 Evans, Evan A., Jr. Literary References in New England Diaries, 1700-1730. Harvard 40.

4475 Jacobs, Briant S. The Novel in Ante-Bellum Boston. Iowa 44.

4475a Jobes, Katherine E. The Resolution of Solitude: A Study of Four Writers of the New England Decline. Yale 61.

4476 Jones, Easley S. The Decline of Introspection in New England Letters. Ill 18.

4477 Sears, Donald A. Portland, Maine, as a Cultural Center, 1800-1836. Harvard 52.

4477a Westbrook, Perry D. Acres of Flint: Writers of Rural New England, 1870-1900. Columbia 52.

4477b Widenmann, Helene. Neuengland in der erzählenden Literatur Amerikas. Berlin 35 publ.

4477c Wright, T. G. Aspects of Early Literary Culture in New England. Yale 17.

SOUTH

4478 Atchison, Ray M. Southern Literary Magazines, 1865-1887. Duke 56.

4479 Bamberg, Robert D. Plantation and Frontier: A View of Southern Fiction. Cornell 61.

4480 Beale, Robert C. The Development of the Short Story in the South. Va 10.

4481 Beasley, William M. The New South and Five Southern Novelists, 1920-1950. Vanderbilt 57.

4482 Blankenstein, Mark. The Southern Tradition in Minor Mississippi Writers since 1920. Ill 65.

4483 Bowes, Frederick P. The Intellectual Life of Early Charleston. Princeton H 41.

4484 Bush, Robert B. Louisiana Prose Fiction, 1870-1900. Iowa 57.

4485 Caulfield, Ruby V. A. The French Literature of Louisiana. Columbia RL 29.

4486 Clayton, Bruce L. Southern Critics of the New South, 1890-1914. Duke H 66.

4487 Collins, Carvel E. The Literary Tradition of the Southern Mountaineer, 1824-1900. Chicago 44.

4488 Davenport, Frances G. Cultural Life in Nashville on the Eve of the Civil War. Vanderbilt H 36.

4489 Davis, Frank B. The Literary Societies of Selected State Universities of the Lower South. La 49.

4490 Dillard, Irene. History of Literature in South Carolina. NC 24.

4491 Dillon, Sister Mary I. The Influence of the South on American Fiction, 1870-1921. Fordham 22.

4492 Duvall, Severn P., Jr. The Legend of the South and Southern Historical Fiction, 1820-1861. Princeton 55.

4493 Eaton, Richard B., Jr. Notions of Democracy in Southern Prose Fiction: 1828-1900. NC.

4494 Ellison, Rhoda C. Early Alabama Publications: A Study in Literary Interests, with a Check List of Alabama Imprints, 1807-1870. NC 45.

4495 Fishwick, Marshall W. Virginia, 1902-1941: A Cultural History. Yale A 49.

4496 Floan, Howard R. The South in Northern Eyes, 1831-1861: A Study of Ante-Bellum Attitudes toward the South among the Major Northern Men of Letters Who Were Actively Writing on the Eve of the Civil War. Columbia 54.

4497 Freeman, Bernice. Georgia Short Stories, Chiefly Contemporary. Columbia (Teachers College) 52.

4498 Gossett, Louise Y. Violence in Recent Southern Fiction. Duke 61.

4499 Griffin, Max L. The Relations with the South of Six Major Northern Writers, 1830-1861. NC 43.
4500 Hall, Wade H. A Study of Southern Humor: 1865-1913. Ill 61.
4501 Harrington, Catherine S. Southern Fiction and the Quest for Identity. Wash 63.
4502 Hartin, John S. The Southeastern United States in the Novel Through 1950: A Bibliographic Review. Mich 57.
4503 Hoole, William S. The Literary and Cultural Background of Charleston, 1830-1860. Duke 34.
4504 Hubbell, Jay B. Virginia Life in Fiction. Columbia 22.
4505 Johnson, J. G. Southern Fiction prior to 1860: An Attempt at a First-hand Bibliography. Va 09.
4506 Kane, Hope F. Colonial Promotion and Promotion Literature of Carolina, 1660-1700. Brown H 30.
4507 Kennerly, Sarah L. Confederate Juvenile Imprints: Children's Books and Periodicals Published in the Confederate States of America, 1861-1865. Mich LS 57.
4508 McIlwaine, Ardrey S. The Southern Poor-White: A Literary History. Chicago 37.
4509 McLaurin, Nancy D. A Study of the Southern Frontier in Prose Fiction Prior to 1860. SC 58.
4510 Miles, Guy S. Literary Beginnings in Nashville, 1815-1825. Vanderbilt 41.
4511 Moore, Rayburn S. Southern Writers and Northern Literary Magazines, 1865-1890. Duke 56.
4512 Newman, Carol M. Virginia Literature: A Catalogue of Authors. Va 03.
4513 Osterweis, Rollin G. Patterns of Romanticism in the Ante-Bellum South. Yale H 46.
4514 Owen, Mary C. The Rise of the Nineteenth-Century Southerner as Portrayed in Biographies. Peabody 48.
4515 Patrick, Walton R. Literature on the Louisiana Plantation Home prior to 1861: A Study of Literary Culture. La 37.
4516 Phipps, Paul. The Concept of Greek and Latin Classics in South Carolina, 1828-1860. Johns Hopkins 61.
4517 Purcell, James S., Jr. Literary Culture in North Carolina before 1820. Duke 50.
4518 Rion, Mary. Civilization on the Frontier: Literary Activity in Kentucky before 1830. Johns Hopkins 57.
4519 Robertson, Thomas L., Jr. The Unfolding Magnolia: A Literary History of Mississippi until 1876. Vanderbilt 60.
4520 Rock, Virginia J. The Making and Meaning of *I'll Take My Stand:* A Study in Utopian-Conservatism, 1925-1939. Minn 61.
4521 Shapiro, Henry D. The "Mountain Whites" in the American Imagination: The Discovery of Appalachia, 1870-1920. Rutgers.
4522 Skaggs, Merrill A. The Plain-Folk Tradition in Southern Local-Color Fiction. Duke 6
4523 Weaver, Richard M. The Confederate South, 1865-1910: A Study in the Survival of a Mind and a Culture. La 43.
4523a Whittington, Joseph R. The Regional Novel of the South: The Dilemma of Innocence. Okla 64.
See also *1657, 2856, 2596, 2600, 2880, 2883, 3319, 3321, 3328, 3334, 3337, 3341, 3410, 3575, 3577, 3582, 3584, 3586, 3593, 3602, 3603, 3605, 3959, 3963, 3968, 3972, 4008, 4107, 4145, 4232, 4261, 4294, 4298.*

WEST AND FRONTIER

4524 Baker, Hugh C. Reading Tastes in California, 1849-1959. Stanford 51.
4525 Choate, J. E., Jr. The Myth of the American Cowboy. Vanderbilt 54.
4526 Clifford, John. Social and Political Attitudes of Fiction of Ranch and Range. Iowa H 54.
4527 Culmsee, Carlton F. The Rise of the Concept of Hostile Nature in Novelists of the American Frontier. Iowa 40.

4528 Eyring, Rose. The Portrayal of the California Gold-Rush Period in Imaginative Literature from 1848 to 1875. UCB 44.
4529 Gaither, James M. A Return to the Village: A Study of Santa Fe and Taos, New Mexico, as Cultural Centers, 1900-1934. Minn 57.
4530 Haefner, John H. The West as Seen through Frontier Biography. Iowa H 42.
4531 Hendricks, George D. Western Wild Animals and Man. Tex 51.
4532 Hodgins, Francis E., Jr. The Literary Emancipation of a Region: The Changing Image of the American West in Fiction. Mich State 57.
4533 Jody, Marilyn. Alaskan Literature: Local Color on the Last Frontier. Ind.
4534 Longtin, Ray C. The Image of Paradise in Oregon. Columbia 56.
4535 Neubauer, Heinz. Amerikanische Goldgräberliteratur (Bret Harte, Mark Twain, Jack London). Greifswald 36 publ.
4536 Past, Raymond E. "Illustrated by the Author": A Study of Six Western-American Writer-Artists. Tex 50.
4537 Shrell, Darwin H. Concepts of the Frontier in the *North American Review, 1815-1850.* Tex 51.
4538 Smith, Henry Nash. American Emotional and Imaginative Attitudes toward the Great Plains and the Rocky Mountains, 1803-1850. Harvard A 40.
4539 Todd, Edgeley W. Literary Interest in the Fur Trade and Fur Trapper of the Trans-Mississippi West. Northwestern 52.
4540 Tweito, Thomas E. The Correspondent in the West, 1850-1860. Iowa H 39.
4541 Walterhouse, Roger R. Bret Harte, Joaquin Miller, and the Western Local-Color Story: A Study in the Origins of Popular Fiction. Chicago 37.
4542 West, Ray B. Rocky Mountain Reader, an Anthology of Contemporary Writing in the Rocky Mountain Region, Including a Critical Introduction and Summary. Iowa 45.
See also 2400, 2408, 2680, 2693, 2795, 2936, 2951, 3315, 3316, 3332, 3374, 3417, 3421, 3428, 3491, 3572, 3580, 3594, 3844, 3868, 3967, 3989, 4026, 4065, 4066, 4071, 4348, 4352.

RELIGION

4543 Brown, Jerry W. Conflict and Criticism: Biblical Studies in New England, 1800-60. Princeton R 64.
4544 Brumm, Ursula. Die religiöse Typologie im amerikanischen Denken: Ihre Bedeutung für die amerikanische Literatur-und Geistes-geschichte. Berlin (F) 63 publ.
4545 Chable, Eugene R. A Study of the Interpretation of the New Testament in New England Unitarianism. Columbia R 55.
4546 Cowan, Richard O. Mormonism in National Periodicals. Stanford 61.
4547 Dorough, C. Dwight. Religion in the Old South: A Pattern of Behavior and Thought. Tex 46.
4548 Drummond, Edward J. Catholic Criticism in America: Studies of Brownson, Azarias, and Egan, with an Essay for Catholic Critics. Iowa 42.
4549 Durick, Jeremiah K. Catholicism and the Literature of New England (1815-1865). Ottawa 43.
4550 Dusenberry, Robert B. Attitude toward Religion in Representative Novels of the American Frontier, 1820-1890. Wash 52.
4551 Flory, John S. Literary Activity of the German Baptist Brethren in the Eighteenth Century. Va 07.
4552 Gorman, Robert. Catholic Apologetical Literature in the United States (1784-1858). Catholic H 39.
4553 Hall, David D. The Congregational Clergy of New England Prior to the Great Awakening. Yale.
4554 Halprin, Lee S. Attempts to Break Out of the Edwards-Franklin Dialogue in the Nineteenth Century. Harvard.

4555   Hock, Cassie H.   The Mormons in Fiction.   Colo 41.
4556   Jensen, H. E.   American Religious Journalism to 1845:   Its Role with Organization of American Christianity.   Chicago Soc 20.
4557   Johnson, Jane.   Through Change and through Storm: A Study of Federalist-Unitarian Thought, 1800 to 1860.   Harvard A 58.
4558   Kenney, William H.   The Great Awakening in the Middle Colonies: A Cultural Analysis, 1720-1750.   Pa.
4559   Lodge, Martin E.   The Great Awakening in the Middle Colonies.   UCB H 64.
4560   McInnis, Mary A.   The Contribution of Catholic Women to Catholic Thought in the Catholic Literary Periodicals of the United States in the Nineteenth Century.   Boston College 39.
4561   Morais, Herbert M.   Deism in Eighteenth Century America.   Columbia H 34.
4562   Powers, Sister Mary L.   The Contribution of American Catholic Commercial Publishers 1930-42.   Chicago LS 46.
4563   Reeves, John K.   Religious Thought in Boston in the 1740's as Reflected in the Periodicals.   Harvard 38.
4564   Root, Robert W.   The Religious Ideas of Some Major Early Writers of America.   Syracuse 59.
4565   Rosenfeld, William.   The Divided Burden: Common Elements in the Search for a Religious Synthesis in the Works of Theodore Parker, Horace Bushnell, Nathaniel Hawthorne and Herman Melville.   Minn 61.
4566   Sager, Allan H.   The Fundamentalist-Modernist Controversy, 1918-1930, in the History of American Public Address.   Northwestern S 63.
4567   Smithline, Arnold.   Natural Religion and American Literature.   NYU 62.
4568   Stibitz, Edward E.   The Treatment of Quakerism in American Historical and Literary Writing.   Mich A 51.
4569   Stoeffler, F. Ernest.   Mysticism in the German Devotional Literature of Colonial Pennsylvania.   Temple R 48.
4570   Taylor, R. Jean.   The "Return to Religion" in America in the Post-World War II Decade as Evidenced in Literature, Press, Public Speeches and Public Acts.   Minn A.
4571   Thompson, J. Earl.   A Perilous Experiment: New England Clergymen and American Destiny,   1796-1826.   Princeton R 66.
4572   Tolles, Frederick B.   The Quaker Merchants of Colonial Philadelphia: A Study in Social and Cultural History.   Harvard A 47.
4573   Ulbrich, Armand.   Attitudes toward Religion in the Modern American Novel, 1925-1951.   Mich 52.
4574   White, James A.   The Era of Good Intentions: A Survey of American Catholics' Writing between the Years 1880 and 1915.   Notre Dame H 57.
4575   Williams, Ray S.   The American National Covenant.   Fla State 65.
See also 375, 860, 877, 886, 944, 977, 987, 989, 1132, 1326, 1637, 1679, 1735, 1749, 1761, 1823, 1831, 1834a, 1846, 1923, 1965, 1967, 1995, 1996, 2067, 2670, 2677, 2704, 2732, 2750, 3025, 3027, 3461, 3526, 3534, 4124, 4301, 4321, 4343, 4356.

SCIENCE AND TECHNOLOGY

4576   Brawley, Agnes B.   Attitudes toward Realism and Science in the *Atlantic Monthly,* 1880-1900.   Wis 54.
4577   Clareson, Thomas D.   The Emergence of American Science Fiction, 1880-1915:   A Study of the Impact of Science upon American Romanticism.   Pa 56.
4578   De Jong, John A.   American Attitudes toward Evolution before Darwin.   Iowa H 62.
4579   Gerber, Gerald E.   Science vs. Poetry: The Beginnings of the Ideological Significance of a Modern Literary Idea.   Northwestern 64.
4580   Hirsch, Walter.   American Science Fiction, 1926-1950.   A Content Analysis.   Northwestern Soc 57.

4581 Marx, Leo. Hawthorne and Emerson: Studies in the Impact of the Machine
Technology upon the American Writer. Harvard A 50.
4582 Pfeifer, Edward J. History of the Reception of Darwinism in America to 1880:
Brown H 58.
4583 Tilley, Winthrop. The Literature of Science in the American Colonies from the
Beginnings to 1765. Brown 32.
4584 Van Benschoten, Virginia. The Influence of Scientific and Socio-Scientific
Ideologies on Some Examples of the Modern American Popular Novel. Mich 60.
See also 344, 1326, 1383, 1856, 2528, 2650, 4231, 4358.

TRANSCENDENTALISM

4585 Albrecht, Robert C. The New England Transcendentalists' Response to the Civil
War. Minn 63.
4586 Brickett, Elsie F. Poets and Poetry of New England Transcendentalism. Yale 37.
4587 Christy, Arthur E. The Orient in American Transcendentalism: A Study of
Emerson, Thoreau, and Alcott. Columbia 32.
4588 Gawronski, Donald V. Transcendentalism: An Ideological Basis for Manifest
Destiny. St. Louis H 64.
4589 Goddard, H. C. Studies in New England Transcendentalism. Columbia 08.
4590 Gohdes, Clarence. The Periodicals of American Transcendentalism. Columbia 30.
4591 Groth, John H. German Backgrounds of American Transcendentalism: Prolegomena
to the Study of Influence. Wash 41.
4592 Ladu, Arthur I. Political Ideas of New England Transcendentalism as Represented
by Five Typical Transcendentalists. NC 32.
4593 Le, Van-Diem. Puritan Idealism and the Transcendental Movement. Minn H 60.
4594 Leighton, Walter L. French Philosophers and New England Transcendentalism. Va 08.
4595 Metzger, Charles R. The Transcendental Esthetics in America: Essays on Emerson,
Greenough, Thoreau, and Whitman. Wash 54.
4596 Porter, Lawrence C. New England Transcendentalism: A Self-Portrait. Mich 64.
4597 Vance, William S. Carlyle and the American Transcendentalists. Chicago 41.
4598 Vogel, Stanley M. The Influence of German Culture on the New England Transcendentalists from 1810-1840. Yale 49.
4599 Wells, Ronald V. Three Christian Transcendentalists, James Marsh, Cabel Sprague
Henry, Frederic Henry Hedge. Columbia P 44.
4600 Williams, Paul O. The Transcendental Movement in American Poetry. Pa 62.
4601 Wilson, John B. Activities of the New England Transcendentalists in the Dissemina-
tion of Culture. NC 41.
See also 50, 207, 472, 624, 1158, 1652, 1917, 2096, 2142, 2273, 2274, 2517.

TRAVEL

4602 Anderson, Emmett H., Jr. Appraisal of American Life by French Travelers, 1860-1914.
Va 54.
4603 Ashmead, John, Jr. The Idea of Japan, 1853-1895: Japan as Described by American
and Other Travellers from the West. Harvard 51.
4604 Berger, Max. The British Traveller in America, 1836-1860. Columbia H 44.
4605 Callahan, Sister M. Generosa. The Literature of Travel in Texas, 1803-1846: An
Analysis of Attitudes and Ideas. Tex 46.
4606 Cook, Will M. French Travellers in the United States, 1840-1870. Brown RL 36.
4607 Eckman, James R. The British Traveler in America, 1875-1920. Georgetown H 46.
4608 Farnham, E. Carrie. American Travellers in Spain. Columbia RL 21.
4609 Fleck, Byron Y. The West as Viewed by Foreign Travelers, 1783-1840. Iowa
H 50.

4610　Giddings, Thomas H.　Yankee Journalists in Europe, 1830-1848.　Columbia 56.
4611　Greer, Ann L.　Early Development in America, 1825-1850, of Travel Books as Literature.　So Cal 55.
4612　Henline, Ruth.　Travel Literature of Colonists in America, 1754-1783:　An Annotated Bibliography with an Introduction and an Author Index.　Northwestern 47.
4613　Hildreth, William H.　Travel Literature of the Ohio River Valley (1794-1832).　Ohio State 45.
4614　Hillman, Margaret E.　Reluctant Pilgrims:　A Study of the Reports on England of American Writers Who Visited Great Britain between 1806 and 1886, Considered in Relation to General American Attitudes towards England.　Toronto 50.
4615　Hubbard, Genevieve G.　French Travelers in America, 1775-1840:　A Study of Their Observations.　American H 36.
4616　Lemelin, Robert E.　Ante-Bellum Travel Guides and Gazetteers as Cultural Indexes.　Md.
4617　Masterson, James R.　Records of Travel in North America, 1700-1776.　Harvard 36.
4618　Mesick, Jane L.　The English Traveller in America, 1785-1835.　Columbia 21.
4619　Rodrigue, Elisabeth M.　Les Voyageurs français aux États-Unis pendant la première moitié du dixneuvième siècle.　Radcliffe H 46.
4620　Ryan, Lee W.　French Travelers in America between 1775 and 1800 with Special Reference to the Southern States.　Va RL 34.
4621　Scott, Robert C.　American Travellers in France, 1830-1860.　Yale H 40.
4622　Torrielli, Andrew J.　Italian Opinion of the United States as Revealed by Italian Travellers, 1850-1900.　Harvard RL 40.
See also 1358, 1524, 1866, 2498, 3625, 3626, 3749, 3834.

WRITERS AND WRITINGS

4623　Barnes, Warner J.　A Critical Survey of Authors Represented in Blanck's *Bibliography of American Literature.*　Tex 63.
4624　Charters, Ann.　Writers in a Landscape:　Seven Writers, 1816-1917.　Columbia 65.
4625　Clarke, Edwin L.　American Men of Letters:　Their Nature and Nurture.　Columbia 16.
4626　Cronkhite, George F.　Literature as a Livelihood:　The Attitude of Certain American Writers toward Literature as a Profession from 1820 to the Civil War.　Harvard 48.
4627　Hamilton, John B.　The American Physician as Novelist.　NC 51.
4628　Hart, Robert C.　Writers on Writing:　The Opinions of Six Modern American Novelists on the Craft of Fiction (S. Anderson, Dos Passos, Farrell, Fitzgerald, Hemingway, Wolfe).　Northwestern 54.
4629　McKenzie, Barbara.　Region and World:　The Achievement of American Women Writers of Fiction Since 1930.　Fla State 63.
4630　Mondale, Clarence C.　Gentlemen of Letters in a Democracy:　Phi Beta Kappa Orations, 1788-1865.　Minn 60.
4631　Weiss, Robert M.　The Shock of Experience:　A Group of Chicago's Writers Face the Twentieth Century.　Wis H 66.
See also 4120, 4121, 4372, 4376.

Guiguet, J. 476
Guilds, J. 2354
Guimond, J. K. 2769
Gulbenkian, V. R. 3521
Gullason, T. 489
Gunter, B. 688
Gupta, R. K. 1849
Gurcke, G. 3411
Gustafson, W. W. 3897
Guth, H. P. 2264
Gutheim, M. F. 1975
Guthrie, H. N. 2511
Gutscher, M. 1486
Guttmann, A. 3997
Gvale, G. H. 2305
Gwathmey, E. M. 1634

Haack, D. 490
Haas, J. 4433
Haas, P. 2400
Haave, E. M. 1850
Haberman, D. C. 2741a
Haberman, L. D. 3081
Hadley, E. J. 1981
Hadley, R. H. 3184
Haefner, G. 2898
Haefner, G. E. 47
Haefner, J. H. 4530
Hagan, R. L. 3106
Hagemann, E. R. 542
Haggerty, W. J. 210
Hahn, V. T. 2056
Haines, P. 999
Hakac, J. R. 3412
Hakutani, Y. 605
Halbeisen, E. K. 2385
Hale, N. 3772
Hall, B. M. 3720
Hall, D. D. 4553
Hall, E. J. 3478
Hall, E. M. 436
Hall, H. E. 2104
Hall, J. J. 1851
Hall, J. S. 3939
Hall, L. S. 1171
Hall, M. J. 560
Hall, W. H. 4500
Hall, W. F. 1487
Hallam, V. 953
Haller, C. D. 1259
Halliday, E. M. 1276
Halline, A. G. 3029
Halperen, M. 3688
Halperin, I. 2803
Halperin, M. 2228
Halpert, H. N. 3591

Halprin, L. S. 4554
Halsey, V. R. 3320
Hamalian, L. 689
Hamilton, F. W. 2512
Hamilton, J. B. 4627
Hamlin, W. C. 2417
Hamm, G. C. 112
Hammack, J. A. 3127
Hammond, M. S. 2418
Hanawalt, M. H. 1751
Hancock, W. J. 282
Hand, C. J. 2105
Handley, J. G. 4222
Hands, C. B. 1000
Handy, Y. 283
Haney, C. W. 1488
Hankamer, E. W. 639
Hansen, E. A. 88
Hanson, M. J. 4378
Harbert, E. 11
Harcourt, J. B. 4350
Harden, E. F. 3413
Harding, W. 2513
Hardman, M. P. 3358
Harling, F. F. 667
Harlow, A. V. 2119
Harnack, M. F. 3998
Harper, H. M. 3414
Harper, R. D. 3219
Harrington, C. S. 4501
Harrington, R. P. 4223
Harris, B. 1794
Harris, E. L. 1042
Harris, I. W. 3321
Harris, J. W. 4024
Harris, M. 158
Harris, M. 954
Harris, P. C. 2349
Harrison, F. C. 1093
Harrison, J. G. 3522
Harrison, M. C. 3322
Harrison, S. R. 931
Hart, A. W. 491
Hart, J. A. 4224
Hart, J. A. 4304
Hart, J. D. 526
Hart, J. S. 1489
Hart, L. E. 1728
Hart, M. J. 180
Hart, R. C. 4628
Hartin, J. S. 4502
Hartley, L. T. 1797
Hartman, J. G. 2999
Hartman, M. 2057
Hartung, G. W. 437
Harvey, L. 266

Harvey, R. D. 4379
Harvey, S. K. 2571
Harvey, S. W. 2579
Harwick, R. D. 869
Harwood, C. E. 2899
Haselton, S. J. 4156
Haskell, J. 2470
Hasler, J. 1490
Hasler, R. A. 2346
Hassold, E. C. 4025
Hastings, A. L. 764
Hastings, G. E. 1331
Hathaway, R. D. 1629
Hatlen, T. 1303
Hatley, B. E. 1765
Hatvary, G. E. 2576
Hauck, R. B. 4225
Haugen, R. H. 2975
Haugh, R. F. 3479
Hausdorff, D. M. 3851
Hausel, H. 980
Havens, C. B. 370
Havens, D. F. 3000
Havens, E. A. 1656
Hawes, D. S. 187
Hawkins, E. O. 870
Hawkins, J. D. 3940
Hayakawa, S. I. 1320
Hayford, H. M. 1172
Hayman, A. 1852
Hayne, B. S. 195
Hays, J. Q. 371
Hays, P. 3981
Haywood, C. 3592
Hazard, L. L. 4026
Hazard, P. D. 941
Hazelrigg, C. T. 1315
Heagarty, M. A. 3480
Healy, M. A. 12
Hecht, H. E. 2154
Hecht, W. 2868
Hecken, D. 3773
Hedges, E. R. 3359
Hedges, W. L. 1420
Heeney, St. A. 4055
Heffernan, M. M. 1699
Heflin, W. A. 3941
Heflin, W. L. 1853
Heidinger, M. M. 2900
Heil, J. A. 1752
Heilman, R. B. 2857
Heimert, A. 4381
Heinitz, K. L. 1172a
Heiser, M. 3852
Helmcke, H. 1854
Hemmer, J. M. 2615